Management for Professionals

The Springer series "Management for Professionals" comprises high-level business and management books for executives, MBA students, and practice-oriented business researchers. The topics cover all themes relevant to businesses and the business ecosystem. The authors are experienced business professionals and renowned professors who combine scientific backgrounds, best practices, and entrepreneurial vision to provide powerful insights into achieving business excellence.

The Series is SCOPUS-indexed.

Feifei Yang

AI and Consumer Interaction in Business

From Recommendation to Emotional Connection

Springer

Feifei Yang
Shanghai International School of Chief
Technology Officer, Asia Europe
Business School
East China Normal University
Shanghai, China

ISSN 2192-8096 ISSN 2192-810X (electronic)
Management for Professionals
ISBN 978-981-95-9429-0 ISBN 978-981-95-9430-6 (eBook)
https://doi.org/10.1007/978-981-95-9430-6

This work was supported by National Natural Science Foundation of China (72202067).

This Springer imprint is published by the registered company Springer Nature Singapore Pte Ltd.
The registered company address is: 152 Beach Road, #21-01/04 Gateway East, Singapore 189721, Singapore

Acknowledgements The research was funded by National Natural Science Foundation of China (Grant No. 72202067).

Competing Interests The author has no competing interests to declare that are relevant to the content of this manuscript.

Contents

Introduction 1

> *"Recent advances in AI development and the speed of AI integration and applications into the service delivery process by service companies suggest that the adoption of AI devices in the service context is not a fad, but a rising trend since AI devices have several advantages over human employees."*
> *(Gursoy et al., 2019, p. 157)*

> *"Transformative artificially intelligent tools, such as ChatGPT, designed to generate sophisticated text indistinguishable from that produced by a human, are applicable across a wide range of contexts. The technology presents opportunities as well as, often ethical and legal, challenges, and has the potential for both positive and negative impacts for organisations, society, and individuals."*
> *(Dwivedi & Kshetri, 2023, p. 1)*

1.1 Motivation

With the rapid advancement of artificial intelligence (AI) technologies, AI assistants have been widely adopted across various service industries, including retail, e-commerce, and hospitality. One prominent application of AI technologies is the online recommendation systems. Based on advanced data processing ability, AI-based online recommendation systems significantly reduce search costs, mitigate product choice uncertainty, and improve decision quality to improve customer experience (Marchand & Marx, 2020; Nguyen et al., 2024; Xu et al., 2020; Zhang et al., 2022). Particularly within e-commerce platforms, AI-driven recommendation mechanisms are now extensively deployed across various stages of the consumer purchase journey. For instance, e-commerce platforms including Amazon, Taobao,

F. Yang, *AI and Consumer Interaction in Business*, Management for Professionals,
https://doi.org/10.1007/978-981-95-9430-6_1

and JD.com have widely implemented AI-based recommendation technologies, achieving substantial increases in user satisfaction and platform revenue (Luo et al., 2019; Nguyen et al., 2024; Wien & Peluso, 2021; Yin et al., 2025). AI assistants, as an emerging brand communication method, have sparked significant academic and practical interest in its marketing performance.

AI agents not only possess vivid visual presentation and flexible human-computer dialogue capabilities (Cheng et al., 2023; De Cicco et al., 2024), and they also provide enterprises with opportunities to reduce labor costs, improve service efficiency and enhance consumer adaptability (Cheng et al., 2023; Verhagen et al., 2014). For instance, Alibaba's "Aliwen" and JD's "Xiaodong" have effectively improved the dialogue experience of customers by leveraging socialized expression and 24/7 instant response functions to handle user inquiries (Sands et al., 2021). These intelligent assistants have reshaped consumers' usage experiences and fundamentally changed the interaction patterns between consumers and brands (Blut et al., 2021). Existing studies have shown that AI agents can significantly enhance social presence, making users feel as realistic as interacting with real people, thereby promoting consumption behavior and generating positive effects (De Cicco et al., 2020).

By analyzing past browsing records and purchasing behaviors (Liao & Sundar, 2022; Weidig & Kuehnl, 2023; Yeomans et al., 2019), AI recommendations, as compared to their human counterparts, can more accurately provide products that meet individual consumer needs. However, some consumers exhibit "algorithm aversion" and skepticism toward the potential errors of AI service, which can cause them to feel anxiety or distrust with regard to AI and thereby negatively affect their attitudes toward brands associated with it (Hou et al., 2024; Lapointe & Rivard, 2005; Longoni et al., 2019). As such, it is interesting to examine how different sources of recommendation (AI versus human) affect customer experience. Despite the potential of AI recommendations in many scenarios, their performance faces limitations. For instance, when consumers believe AI cannot learn from mistakes like humans, they become more inclined to avoid adopting its advice (Reich et al., 2023). In distinguishing between true and false information, AI recommendations not only fail to enhance users' ability to identify misinformation but also weaken trust in and willingness to engage with truthful information (Ma et al., 2024). The differential impact of recommendation type (AI versus human) on purchase intention and consumer decisions remains complicated, influenced by numerous contextual and psychological factors requiring further investigation.

The communication styles of AI agents are also important touchpoints that shape the interaction between customers and brands. Task-oriented communication style centers on goals, has clear objectives, and focuses on task efficiency as well as minimizing costs, energy and time. In contrast, the social-oriented communication style places more emphasis on emotional elements, such as establishing emotional connections with consumers through daily greetings and casual chats (Bickmore & Cassell, 2001). From the customers' perspective, both of these approaches can meet actual needs by sharing product details and answering questions. However, adopting a more approachable communication style might meet the needs of social interaction. However, it could also consume additional time (Xu et al., 2022). Therefore, different communication styles (e. g. social-oriented versus task oriented) will affect customers' trust in AI agents and customers' attitudes toward brands. Therefore, it is interesting to examine how the communication style of AI agents can affect customer behavior and consequently their engagement with brands.

Compared to human employees, AI assistants offer distinct advantages such as high efficiency, rapid response times, and lower operational costs (Gursoy et al., 2019). However, current AI technologies are still imperfect—particularly when handling emotionally complex interactions or service failure scenarios. In such contexts, AI assistants often struggle to address customers' emotional needs or effectively repair trust after a failure. Crucially, emotional recovery and trust restoration following service failures are key factors influencing user continuance intention. Prior research has demonstrated that in service failure contexts, frontline employees' expressions of attitude, apology, and empathy significantly influence customer acceptance and satisfaction (Loureiro et al., 2024). However, as non-human agents, AI assistants are frequently perceived as lacking emotional warmth and social intelligence. In response, some scholars have begun incorporating humility into AI design (Liu et al., 2025). Humility, as a valued social trait, has been shown to support relationship repair during conflict (Bhattacharya et al., 2017), increase user acceptance and trust (Burr & Leslie, 2023), and evoke empathy and forgiveness (Sapmaz et al., 2016). These effects can improve the customer experience and enhance their willingness to continue using the assistant over time. Nevertheless, most existing studies focus on the general benefits of AI humility in everyday human-AI interactions, often overlooking its potential role in high-stakes service failure scenarios. To address this gap, this research aims to extend the investigation of AI assistant humility to failure contexts, exploring how it can help mitigate negative customer reactions and promote user continuance intention even after a poor service encounter.

A growing number of mainstream social media platforms have launched generative AI (GAI) bots that engage in user content interactions using lighthearted and witty language styles. By leveraging differentiated interaction forms, these bots attract widespread user attention and spontaneous discussions, serving as exemplary cases of emotional GAI applications. With the iterative optimization of machine learning algorithms and the deep penetration of cloud computing technology, GAI has evolved from a frontier exploration in the technological domain into an interactive medium, garnering extensive attention from both academia and industry (Dwivedi & Kshetri, 2023; Mariani & Dwivedi, 2024). GAI not only possesses functional advantages such as efficiently processing massive amounts of information and rapidly responding to user needs, but also transcends the boundaries of traditional tools through continuous interaction with users, becoming a significant medium capable of conveying emotions and evoking psychological resonance (Xu et al., 2024). Today, GAI applications extend beyond mere efficiency gains. The emotional value unlocked through human-like interaction design has become a critical variable shaping user experience perception (Shams et al., 2024; Sheehan et al., 2020).

Research suggests that integrating emotional design elements into GAI can effectively enhance pleasurable experiences during user interactions, thereby optimizing overall usability (Kanuck, 2019). In practical scenarios, GAI applications with emotional attributes like humorous expression are increasingly prevalent. By leveraging differentiated interaction forms, these bots attract widespread user attention and spontaneous discussions, serving as exemplary cases of emotional GAI applications (Kobel & Groeppel-Klein, 2021; Liu et al., 2023; Yang et al., 2022). Nevertheless, there is limited understanding on impact of GAI humor and user satisfaction.

To summarize, AI has penetrated into different platforms including e-commerce and social media. While the power of AI is undisputed, its persuasive power compared to a human counterpart remains unclear. Is AI recommendation more convincing than human counterpart? Understanding the differential impact of AI versus human recommendations on purchase intention is the foundational layer of this exploration. As AI-powered conversations become more and more prevalent for customer service, the conversational style of AI agents becomes paramount. This research explores how conversational AI—ranging from a purely task-oriented, problem-solving style to a social-oriented, relationship-building style—impacts the brand engagement of customers. In those high-stakes interactions such as service failure, the perceived "humanity" of an AI interface—its ability to express empathy, apologize sincerely, and demonstrate understanding—may be critical in whether a customer chooses to forgive and continue using the service. This research delves into this delicate arena, examining how the anthropomorphic qualities of AI can either de-escalate frustration or amplify it, directly influencing a customer's continuous use intention after a negative experience. Finally, the research investigates the frontier of AI interaction: the realm of social connection and entertainment. On social media platforms, brands are increasingly employing AI with personality, even humor. To explore the real-world implications of humorous AI, this book concludes by analyzing how AI-generated humor drives user engagement on social media. This analysis centrally considers the explanatory role of perceived warmth and how the relationship is contingent upon the user's pre-existing sense of humor. Collectively, these investigations chart a course from the AI's role as a simple recommender to its potential as an empathetic partner and an engaging social entity, providing a comprehensive guide to building the next generation of consumer-centric AI.

1.2 Research Questions

1.2.1 Research Question 1

Existing research has extensively explored the differential effectiveness of recommendation sources (AI versus human) across diverse consumption contexts, revealing that the varying effects of recommendation types on consumer responses are context-dependent (Longoni & Cian, 2022). For example, concerning product type, AI recommendations demonstrate greater effectiveness when it comes to utilitarian products, whereas human recommendations exhibit greater persuasiveness for hedonic products. Likewise, consumers tend to like human-provided recommendations more when facing to experiential products but place greater trust in AI recommendations for search products (Jin & Zhang, 2025). Recommender attributes are also crucial, anthropomorphized AI agents (e.g., enhanced perceived similarity, social perception) are able to upgrade product attitude and purchase intention Existing research has extensively ex (Ahn et al., 2021; Cheng et al., 2022). In specific social contexts, AI services demonstrate advantages, for instance, in service environments involving embarrassing consumption, AI recommenders are more readily accepted than human service providers (Holthöwer & Van Doorn, 2023). Furthermore, the gender of AI influences recommendation effectiveness, in particular, when it comes to utilitarian products. Specifically, male AI is viewed as more professional, whereas female AI is deemed better for hedonic product recommendations (Ahn et al., 2022). Compared to ordinary human or AI recommenders, AI agents assigned managerial titles are more likely to arise consumer trust, and perceptions of expertise (Jeon, 2022). Despite the benefits of AI recommendations in many scenarios, their performance is not always satisfactory. AI recommendations can also backfire; for products are framed to be vice (versus virtue), they can diminish perceived warmth and competence towards the recommender, thereby decreasing purchase intention (Yang et al., 2024). Therefore, there is still limited understanding regarding the mechanism through which the recommender type (AI versus human) affects purchase intention and the boundary conditions that shape the effects.

Within the online product recommendation context, beyond recommendation type, consumers' product attitude is also a critical factor influencing their decisions (Hung & Chang, 2024; Sun & Wang, 2020). Research indicates that consumers typically exhibit stronger purchase intention when holding a positive product attitude; conversely, a negative product attitude often weakens it (Cheah et al., 2021). Thus, product attitude may serve as a key moderator in the effect of recommendation source (AI versus human) on consumers' purchase intention. When consumers encounter the same type recommender (AI or human), variance in product attitudes may lead to differential responses to recommendation effectiveness, resulting in divergent purchase intention.

Therefore, current research focuses on the application of different recommendation types (AI versus human) on online platforms, investigating their differential impact on consumer purchase intention. Specifically, the research will examine whether human recommendations significantly enhance purchase intention compared to AI recommendations. Furthermore, this research seeks to uncover the underlying mechanism and boundary condition of the main effect. Specifically, the research will examine how the influence of recommendation type on purchase intention is mediated through perceived warmth, and how product attitude interacts with recommendation type to generate a differential influence on purchase intention. Therefore, this research aims to investigate:

Research Question 1 How does AI (versus human) recommendation affect consumers' purchase intention? How does product attitude affect the relationship between recommender type (AI versus human) and consumers' purchase intention?

1.2.2 Research Question 2

With the rapid development of AI technology, more and more brands are adopting AI chatbot to enhance user experience. AI technology is reshaping modern service interaction models at an unprecedented pace, significantly altering the communication between businesses and consumers. One notable outcome of this technological evolution is the gradual replacement of certain human roles by AI agents in direct consumer interactions, offering businesses opportunities to reduce labor costs while enhancing service efficiency and consumer adaptability (Garvey et al., 2023; Verhagen et al., 2014). For example, Facebook's virtual assistant "M" assists consumers in tasks such as shopping, booking hotels, and organizing trips.

Central to these interactions is the role of communication style, which has been shown to significantly shape consumers' responses. Studies highlight that linguistic elements such as pronouns, metaphorical expressions, and tone can influence users' attitudes toward the communicator (Kronrod et al., 2012; Sela et al., 2012). This becomes particularly relevant in AI-driven service scenarios, where agents have evolved from basic tools into sophisticated, conversational entities capable of simulating natural human dialogue (Go & Sundar, 2019; Schuetzler et al., 2020). Among these linguistic cues, communication styles of AI agents are typically categorized as task-oriented or social-oriented. Task-oriented styles emphasize efficiency and problem-solving, while social-oriented styles focus on warmth and connection, using informal and friendly expressions (Feine et al., 2019; Lee et al., 2020). These distinct approaches reflect divergent design philosophies, each eliciting unique consumer responses that influence acceptance and behavioral intentions.

Task-oriented communication style is goal orientated and purposeful. It emphasizes task efficiency and minimum cost, effort and time. By contrast, social-oriented communication style places greater emphasis on affective components, such as building emotional connections with consumers through customary greetings and small talk (Bickmore & Cassell, 2001). Both communication styles can fulfill practical needs by sharing product details and responding to queries. However, a friendlier, chat-based method might also address social interaction needs, though it could also waste extra time (Xu et al., 2022). Accordingly, different communication styles can affect consumers' trust and customers' attitude toward the brand. Most importantly, consumers at different age levels may also respond differently as their level of AI acceptance might be different.

In view of the above discussion, this research aims to explore the mechanism by which the communication style of AI agents affects consumers' brand engagement by analyzing its practical application in e-commerce platforms. At the same time, the research further analyzes the operational path behind this influence. That is, how the communication style of intelligent agents interacts with age, and clarify the moderating effect it plays in the entire mechanism. Therefore, this research aims to investigate:

Research Question 2 How does AI communication styles (task-oriented versus social oriented) affect consumers' brand engagement? How does age moderate the relationship between AI communication style and consumers' brand engagement?

1.2.3 Research Question 3

Current research has shown that in service failure scenarios, factors such as attitude, apology, and empathy have a significant impact on customer forgiveness and satisfaction (Loureiro et al., 2024). These interpersonal elements repair the relational breach caused by the failure. However, the increasing deployment of AI assistants as front-line service agents presents a unique challenge, as they are fundamentally perceived as "non-human actors" often lacking the innate warmth and sociability of human employees. To bridge this perceived emotional gap, researchers have begun exploring the intentional design of human-like social cues in AI, with recent studies introducing the concept of humility into AI design (Liu et al., 2025). Preliminary findings suggest that humble AI can improve relationship repair (Bhattacharya et al., 2017), increase acceptance and trust (Burr & Leslie, 2023), and foster empathy and tolerance (Sapmaz et al., 2016), thereby potentially improving the overall customer experience.

Despite these promising general findings, a significant research gap persists. Existing studies have predominantly examined the positive effects of AI humility within routine, low-stakes human-AI interaction scenarios. The specific mechanism through which AI assistant humility operates in the high-risk, emotionally charged context of service failure remains largely neglected. This oversight is critical, as the stakes for effective recovery are dramatically higher following a failure, and customer perceptions of an AI's authenticity are put to the ultimate test. Therefore, it is both timely and valuable to extend the investigation of AI humility into this volatile context. The present research aims to address this gap by exploring how humble communication from an AI assistant can function as a critical recovery tool, specifically examining the pathways through which it mitigates negative emotions, rebuilds trust, and ultimately improves the customer satisfaction experience after a service failure. This investigation seeks to translate a human-centric virtue into an effective algorithmic design principle for high-stakes service recovery. Therefore, it is worthwhile to extend the study of AI assistant humility to service failure scenarios and explore how it can improve customer satisfaction experience after service failure. To take the research opportunities, the research aims to address:

Research Question 3 In service failure context, how does AI humanity affect user continuous use intention? How does users' characteristics such as frequency of communication with AI assistants moderate the relationship between AI humanity and user continuous use intention?

1.2.4 Research Question 4

From a social cognitive theory perspective, humor, as a quintessential contextual stimulus can rapidly activate users' emotional responses within the open, interactive environment of social media. This delivers a relaxed, pleasurable psychological experience, thereby fulfilling users' emotional needs (Bil-Jaruzelska & Monzer, 2022; Chang et al., 2015; Lehmann-Willenbrock & Allen, 2014). According to social response theory, when GAI exhibits behavioral traits aligned with human social habits (e.g., humorous expressions, personalized responses), users unconsciously project psychological attributes onto the GAI, attributing human social characteristics to it. This tendency makes users more willing to establish deep interactive relationships with socially-attributed GAI (Holzwarth et al., 2006). Socially endowed GAI can reduce users' psychological distance, thereby diminishing feelings of alienation and rejection toward technological tools (Li & Sung, 2021). Furthermore, existing research indicates that among factors influencing user satisfaction, emotional appeals significantly outperform rational content appeals (Kim et al., 2013). Particularly in social media contexts, data reveals that 64% of users' time spent is allocated to entertainment-related activities (Grover & Kar, 2020). This characteristic makes the fulfillment of emotional needs far more impactful on user experience than functional demands (Bil-Jaruzelska & Monzer, 2022). According to the theory of violation of expectations, the reason humorous expressions in GAI elicit strong emotional responses from users lies in their disruption of users' preconceived notions of GAI as "functional tools." By employing interaction forms that exceed expectations, they stimulate positive psychological reactions in users (Shin et al., 2022; Um et al., 2022). Simultaneously, integrating humor into GAI-user interactions fosters a more natural, warm-toned conversational atmosphere. This ambiance directly influences users' perceived warmth—the psychological sense of being cared for and understood during interactions (Fiske et al., 2007, Fiske et al., 2002; Kull et al., 2021). As a crucial emotional dimension, perceived warmth is closely correlated with users' positive evaluations of services or products. Consequently, investigating the mechanism through which GAI humor impacts user satisfaction in social media contexts not only enriches theoretical research on emotional AI interactions but also provides practical guidance for enhancing user experience and strengthening user loyalty, holding significant academic and applied value.

According to the attribution theory, individuals' responses and evaluations of external stimuli are influenced not only by contextual factors but also closely related to their intrinsic traits. The user's perceived humor ability, which means the capacity to recognize, understand, and appreciate humorous information, emerges as a key intrinsic trait variable exhibiting a moderating effect distinct from conventional cognition (Yang et al., 2022). Lower individual perceived humor ability paradoxically amplifies GAI humor's positive impact on perceived warmth, thereby enhancing its promotional effect on user satisfaction. This moderation logic can be explained through two mechanisms: "differences in expectation thresholds" (Kopalle & Lehmann, 2001) and "emotional compensation needs" (Chuangxin et al., 2024). On one hand, users with strong humor perception abilities encounter richer humorous content daily and possess higher aesthetic thresholds for humor. Consequently, GAI's humorous expressions are more likely to be categorized as "conventional humor," failing to generate unexpected emotional impact and thus having a relatively limited effect on enhancing perceived warmth. For users with lower humor perception abilities, their frequency and efficiency in receiving and understanding humorous information are lower, and their expected threshold for humor remains at a low level. The humorous interactions initiated by GAI break their preconceived notion that "AI lacks emotion," creating a stronger sense of psychological surprise. This surprise further translates into a warm perception of GAI's "proactive care," significantly enhancing overall interaction satisfaction. On the other hand, users with lower humor perception abilities may experience fewer joyful moments from humor in daily social interactions, creating a certain emotional compensation need. GAI's humorous expressions precisely fill this gap, allowing them to gain emotional fulfillment of "being valued and understood" during interactions. This sense of fulfillment amplifies the positive effect of perceived warmth on user satisfaction. For users with strong humor perception abilities, who can already access humorous experiences through multiple channels, GAI's humor expressions struggle to generate additional emotional compensation value. Consequently, their reinforcing effect on perceived warmth and user satisfaction is weaker. While existing research has examined the influence of individual cognitive traits on perceptions of AI emotional design (Chi et al., 2023), it has yet to reveal the "reverse moderation" mechanism of humor perception ability. Building upon existing research, this research extends the focus to the unique moderating role of individual sense of humor. Therefore, the research aims to address:

Research Question 4 How does the GAI humor affect user satisfaction? How does user's own sense of humor moderate the relationship between GAI humor and user satisfaction?

1.3 Theoretical and Practical Contributions

1.3.1 Theoretical Contributions

The study offers theoretical contributions to the current literature in multiple ways. First, it extends existing research on how recommendation type (AI versus human) influences consumer purchase decisions. Prior work has primarily examined differences in persuasion efficacy such as information adoption (Ahn et al., 2022), consumer preferences toward AI recommendations (Jeon, 2022), and comparative effectiveness across product categories including utilitarian versus hedonic or search versus experiential products (Jin & Zhang, 2025; Longoni & Cian, 2022). However, few studies have examined the impact of recommendation type

(AI versus human) on purchase intention and incorporated consumers' product attitudes into their consideration. Our research advances this stream of research by adding product attitude as a critical psychological boundary condition. By introducing product attitude as a moderator that interacts with recommendation type to shape purchase intention, the research presents the boundary conditions that influence how effective recommendations are. This research also contributes to social cognition theory by extending the stereotype content model to human-AI interaction contexts. The study identifies and empirically validates perceived warmth as a mediating mechanism that explains how recommendation type influences purchase intention. This finding not only clarifies the psychological process underlying consumer responses to different recommenders but further broadens social cognition theory, shifting its scope from human-human interactions to human-AI communication. The effectiveness of a recommendation source is mediated through perceived warmth, a key social attribute. This mechanism explains why human recommendations, generally perceived as warmer, more strongly shape consumer purchase intentions than AI recommendations (Choi et al., 2024; Kim et al., 2022). Moreover, the study establishes that a consumer's pre-existing product attitude is a critical moderator of recommendation source effectiveness. The findings contribute to the theory by specifying the contextual conditions under which the social attributes of a human recommender exert their greatest influence on downstream behavioral intentions.

Second, this study addresses a significant gap in the extant literature concerning the impact of AI communication styles on consumer attitudes. While extensive research has explored how communication styles influence consumer attitude in traditional service environments (Berger et al., 2020; Tsai et al., 2021), limited attention has been paid to the mechanisms by which AI communication styles affect consumer intentions through emotional and cognitive pathways in AI-integrated service contexts (Luo et al., 2019). This study systematically analyzes the differentiated effects of two typical interaction styles—task-oriented and social-oriented—on customer resistance and purchase intention, offering a novel perspective for theoretical advancements in AI agent and consumer attitude research. Furthermore, this study introduces customers' trust as a mediating variable, thereby unveiling the mechanism through which interaction styles influence consumer attitudes and intentions. Furthermore, the study explores the moderating effect of consumer age on customer emotions and intentions under various interaction styles. This approach not only broadens the theoretical applicability of AI agent interaction styles research but also deepens our understanding of its impacts on brand engagement.

Third, this study contributes to the theoretical advancement of service marketing by examining the emerging concept of humility within the context of service failure. Specifically, it extends current understanding by exploring how the humility of AI assistants influences user continuance intention, a relatively underexplored area in the literature—with existing work only recently beginning to link humble AI to consumer responses (Liu et al., 2025). Furthermore, by introducing AI acceptance as a mediating variable, this research develops a more comprehensive explanatory mechanism, offering deeper insight into the cognitive and emotional processes that shape user responses during human-AI interactions; this aligns with frameworks identifying humility as a key social cue that shapes perceptions of AI agents (Feine et al., 2019). In addition, the inclusion of communication frequency with AI assistants as moderating variables helps uncover how users with different backgrounds respond differently to humility expressed by AI, building on work that highlights user heterogeneity in reactions to AI's interpersonal traits (Schuetzler et al., 2020). This adds nuance to the theoretical discourse on individual differences in AI service encounters and contributes to a more granular understanding of user heterogeneity in AI-enabled service settings. From a practical standpoint, as AI assistants become increasingly embedded in customer service, occasional service failures are inevitable. This study demonstrates that AI assistants exhibiting humility can better facilitate customer relationship repair and enhance post-failure satisfaction, offering valuable contributions for service-oriented organizations. Firms can apply these insights to optimize assistant communication scripts, strengthen affective computing capabilities, and refine response mechanisms—especially in recovery situations.

Fourth, this study also focuses on GAI humor as a social trait and explores its impact on user satisfaction in social media and the mediating mechanism of perceived warmth, thereby enriching research in the field of GAI characteristics and user emotional responses—an area where prior work has begun to highlight humor as a critical conversational cue for AI agents (Liu et al., 2023). Meanwhile, addressing the research gap in GAI applications in social media scenarios, this study clarifies the effect of GAI humor in promoting user satisfaction through perceived warmth, providing new empirical evidence for research on user satisfaction in the context of generative artificial intelligence; this builds on existing findings that AI humor can significantly shape consumer evaluations of service interactions (Shin et al., 2022). Furthermore, this research contributes theoretically to enrich the application scenarios of social response theory and attribution theory in human-AI interaction, shedding light on how emotional cues such as humor drive social responses toward GAI, which is consistent with frameworks that identify humor as a key driver of engagement in AI service encounters (Kobel & Groeppel-Klein, 2021). Building upon existing research, this research extends the focus to the unique moderating role of individual sense of humor. It aims to validate the "low-ability enhancement effect" of individual sense of humor, complementing recent work that emphasizes the contextual dependency of AI humor's effectiveness (Shams et al., 2024). This approach seeks to more precisely and comprehensively reveal the boundary condition of how GAI humor impacts user satisfaction.

1.3.2 Practical Contributions

First, this research yields practical contributions that guide the strategic deployment and design of recommendation systems. Overall, our findings suggest that compared to AI recommendations, the purchase intention of consumers is higher with human recommendations. Critically, the findings caution against a one-size-fits-all automation strategy. For products where consumer attitude is neutral or negative—such as new market entries, complex services, or items requiring a reputation recovery—firms should prioritize human recommenders. The warmth they generate is essential to overcoming skepticism and building trust, directly driving purchase intention where AI would likely fail. Conversely, for established products with strong positive attitudes, AI can be leveraged efficiently without a significant persuasion penalty. To enhance AI's effectiveness more broadly, however, designers must intentionally engineer perceived warmth into interfaces using empathetic language, anthropomorphic cues, and communications that signal genuine care, thereby mitigating its inherent coldness.

Second, the practical contributions of this research are crucial for brands integrating AI agents into customer service and marketing touchpoints. The findings provide a clear directive for AI design: to maximize brand engagement, developers must prioritize a social-oriented communication style—one that employs empathy, informal language, and relational cues—over a purely efficient, task-focused approach. This style builds trust, the critical psychological bridge between interaction and engagement, making customers more receptive to the brand. Moreover, the moderating role of age advises against a uniform implementation. Brands targeting younger demographics should invest heavily in making their AI agents socially sophisticated and personable, as this cohort responds more strongly to such cues. For services aimed at older audiences, while a social style is still beneficial, the relative advantage may be smaller, allowing for a slightly greater emphasis on clarity and task efficiency without a significant loss in engagement. Ultimately, this research argues that AI should be programmed not merely as a transactional tool, but as a brand ambassador capable of fostering warmth and trust, with its communication strategy finely tuned to the relational expectations of its target demographic.

Third, this research yields crucial practical contributions for designing AI assistants to foster loyalty, especially after service failures. The findings advocate for a paradigm shift from infallible AI to humility-driven AI, where systems are programmed to acknowledge errors, express limitations, and avoid defensive explanations. This design cue is not merely polite but strategically builds AI acceptance, the key mediator that converts a negative experience into sustained usage. For broader applications, incorporating scalable humility cues (e.g., "I'm still learning, but based on available information ...") can universally enhance trust. For AI developers and designers, this means architecting systems with scalable, context-aware "humility cues"—such as transparent error acknowledgment, competence-calibrated limitations, and forward-learning offers—that are strategically engineered to build AI acceptance, the key mediator that converts negative experiences into sustained usage. Ultimately, this research positions humility not as a superficial trait but as a critical reliability-repair mechanism and a foundational standard for responsible AI, advising that an AI's response to failure is more important for long-term engagement than its ability to avoid errors altogether.

Fourth, social media platforms should simultaneously emphasize both the functional roles of GAI and the emotional value it can deliver. Given that 64% of users' time on social media is spent on entertainment (Grover & Kar, 2020), platforms should leverage this by endowing GAI with humorous traits—such as adopting human-like humor styles and incorporating emojis (Liu et al., 2023)—to enhance users' perceived warmth during interactions. Humorous responses from GAI can strengthen emotional connections, thereby boosting user satisfaction and platform engagement, ultimately driving greater benefits for the platform. Moreover, social media service providers need to optimize GAI's expressions to enhance perceived anthropomorphism. Recognizing that over half of social media users prioritize the platform for entertainment and socialization (Grover & Kar, 2020), integrating elements that foster perceived anthropomorphism across interaction touchpoints (e.g., conversational tone, response timing) will effectively elevate user satisfaction. This study also highlights the need for tailored GAI humor strategies based on users' sense of humor. Given that the positive impact of GAI humor on user satisfaction is stronger for users with lower sense of humor, platforms should segment their user base. Specifically, for users with lower sense of humor, GAI should employ more explicit humorous cues (e.g., straightforward jokes, playful emojis) to compensate for their reduced internal humor processing; for those with higher sense of humor, context-aware humor can maintain engagement without overwhelming them. Additionally, platforms can cultivate users' receptivity to humor through targeted content (e.g., humorous posts, interactive challenges), thereby amplifying the effectiveness of GAI humor across broader user groups. Since improving user satisfaction remains a significant challenge (Shams et al., 2024), these strategies offer actionable pathways to enhance platform performance and user loyalty.

1.4 Organization of the Book

This book consists of 7 chapters. The next chapter (Chap. 2) provides a literature review that addresses the four major literature streams investigated by this research: AI versus human recommendation literature, AI communication styles literature, AI agent humanity literature, and GAI humor literature. This is followed by a theory and hypothesis development chapter (Chap. 3) in which theorized relationships were developed for the four models regarding AI versus human recommendation (addressing Research Question 1), AI communication style (addressing Research Question 2), AI agent humanity (addressing Research Question 3), and GAI humor (addressing Research Question 4). Chapter 4 presents practical insights from interviews, providing real-world context and insights from practitioners talking about the topics of this research. Chapter 5 details the methodology, covering the experiments, pretests, main tests, and surveys from which empirical evidence was collected. Chapter 6 presents the analysis and empirical results, showing the data assessment and hypothesis tests for each model, including a series of robustness checks. Chap. 7 discusses the theoretical and practical implications of the research in more depth, presents the limitations and future research directions, and summarizes and concludes the book. Additional supporting documents are presented in the appendices.

References

Ahn, J., Kim, J., & Sung, Y. (2021). AI-powered recommendations: The roles of perceived similarity and psychological distance on persuasion. *International Journal of Advertising, 40*(8), 1366–1384.

Ahn, J., Kim, J., & Sung, Y. (2022). The effect of gender stereotypes on artificial intelligence recommendations. *Journal of Business Research, 141*, 50–59.

Berger, J., Humphreys, A., Ludwig, S., Moe, W. W., Netzer, O., & Schweidel, D. A. (2020). Uniting the tribes: Using text for marketing insight. *Journal of Marketing, 84*(1), 1–25.

Bhattacharya, O., Chatterjee, A., & Basu, J. (2017). Humility: An emerging construct in moral psychology. *Psychological Studies, 62*(1), 1–11.

Bickmore, T., & Cassell, J. (2001). *Relational agents: A model and implementation of building user trust*. Proceedings of the SIGCHI Conference on Human Factors in Computing Systems.

Bil-Jaruzelska, A., & Monzer, C. (2022). All about feelings? Emotional appeals as drivers of user engagement with facebook posts. *Politics and Governance, 10*(1), 172–184.

Blut, M., Wang, C., Wünderlich, N., & Brock, C. (2021). Understanding anthropomorphism in service provision: A meta-analysis of physical robots, chatbots, and other AI. *Journal of the Academy of Marketing Science, 49*(4), 632–658.

Burr, C., & Leslie, D. (2023). Ethical assurance: A practical approach to the responsible design, development, and deployment of data-driven technologies. *AI and Ethics, 3*(1), 73–98.

Chang, Y. T., Yu, H., & Lu, H. P. (2015). Persuasive messages, popularity cohesion, and message diffusion in social media marketing. *Journal of Business Research, 68*(4), 777–782.

Cheah, I., Teah, M., Lee, S., & Davies, Z. (2021). Straight eye for the queer ad: Attitudes, skepticism, inferences of manipulative intent and willingness to buy. *Asia Pacific Journal of Marketing and Logistics, 33*(5), 1220–1238.

Cheng, X., Qiao, L., Yang, B., & Li, Z. (2023). An investigation on the influencing factors of elderly people's intention to use financial AI customer service. *Internet Research, 34*(3), 690–717.

Cheng, X., Zhang, X., Cohen, J., & Mou, J. (2022). Human versus AI: Understanding the impact of anthropomorphism on consumer response to chatbots from the perspective of trust and relationship norms. *Information Processing & Management, 59*(3), 102940.

Chi, O. H., Chi, C. G., Gursoy, D., & Nunkoo, R. (2023). Customers' acceptance of artificially intelligent service robots: The influence of trust and culture. *International Journal of Information Management, 70*, 102623.

Choi, S., Yi, Y., & Zhao, X. (2024). The human touch versus AI efficiency: How perceived status, effort, and loyalty shape consumer satisfaction with preferential treatment. *Journal of Retailing and Consumer Services, 81*, 103969.

Chuangxin, L., Meng, L., & Dongxue, H. (2024). Mental dilemmas and escape compensation: A study on the formation pathways of "Special Forces-style Tourism" behavior. *Journal of Chinese Ecotourism, 14*(5), 1027–1041.

De Cicco, R., Iacobucci, S., Cannito, L., Onesti, G., Ceccato, I., & Palumbo, R. (2024). Virtual versus human influencer: Effects on users' perceptions and brand outcomes. *Technology in Society, 77*, 102488.

De Cicco, R., Silva, S., & Alparone, F. (2020). Millennials' attitude toward chatbots: An experimental study in a social relationship perspective. *International Journal of Retail & Distribution Management, 48*(11), 1213–1233.

Dwivedi, Y. K., & Kshetri, N. (2023). Opinion paper: "So what if ChatGPT wrote it?" Multidisciplinary perspectives on opportunities, challenges and implications of generative conversational AI for research, practice and policy. *International Journal of Information Management, 71*, 102642.

Feine, J., Gnewuch, U., Morana, S., & Maedche, A. (2019). A taxonomy of social cues for conversational agents. *International Journal of Human-Computer Studies, 132*, 138–161.

Fiske, S. T., Cuddy, A. J., Glick, P., & Xu, J. (2002). A model of (often mixed) stereotype content: Competence and warmth respectively follow from perceived status and competition. *Journal of Personality and Social Psychology, 82*(6), 878–902.

Fiske, S. T., Cuddy, A. J. C., & Glick, P. (2007). Universal dimensions of social cognition: Warmth and competence. *Trends in Cognitive Sciences, 11*(2), 77–83.

Garvey, A. M., Kim, T., & Duhachek, A. (2023). Bad news? Send an AI. Good news? Send a human. *Journal of Marketing, 87*(1), 10–25.

Go, E., & Sundar, S. S. (2019). Humanizing chatbots: The effects of visual, identity and conversational cues on humanness perceptions. *Computers in Human Behavior, 97*, 304–316.

Grover, P., & Kar, A. K. (2020). User engagement for mobile payment service providers – Introducing the social media engagement model. *Journal of Retailing and Consumer Services, 53*, 101718.

Gursoy, D., Chi, O. H., Lu, L., & Nunkoo, R. (2019). Consumers acceptance of artificially intelligent (AI) device use in service delivery. *International Journal of Information Management, 49*, 157–169.

Holthöwer, J., & Van Doorn, J. (2023). Robots do not judge: Service robots can alleviate embarrassment in service encounters. *Journal of the Academy of Marketing Science, 51*(4), 767–784.

Holzwarth, M., Janiszewski, C., & Neumann, M. M. (2006). The influence of avatars on online consumer shopping behavior. *Journal of Marketing, 70*(4), 19–36.

Hou, T. Y., Tseng, Y. C., & Yuan, C. W. (2024). Is this AI sexist? The effects of a biased AI's anthropomorphic appearance and explainability on users' bias perceptions and trust. *International Journal of Information Management, 76*, 102775.

Hung, C. Z., & Chang, T. W. (2024). Have I purchased the right product? Consumer behavior under corporate greenwash behavior. *Journal of Consumer Behaviour, 23*(3), 1102–1113.

Jeon, Y. A. (2022). Let me transfer you to our AI-based manager: Impact of manager-level job titles assigned to AI-based agents on marketing outcomes. *Journal of Business Research, 145*, 892–904.

Jin, F., & Zhang, X. (2025). Artificial intelligence or human: When and why consumers prefer AI recommendations. *Information Technology & People, 38*(1), 279–303.

Kanuck, S. (2019). Humor, ethics, and dignity: Being human in the age of artificial intelligence. *Ethics & International Affairs, 33*(1), 3–12.

Kim, T. W., Jiang, L., Duhachek, A., Lee, H., & Garvey, A. (2022). Do you mind if I ask you a personal question? How AI service agents alter consumer self-disclosure. *Journal of Service Research, 25*(4), 649–666.

Kim, Y. H., Kim, D. J., & Wachter, K. (2013). A study of mobile user engagement (MoEN): Engagement motivations, perceived value, satisfaction, and continued engagement intention. *Decision Support Systems, 56*, 361–370.

Kobel, S., & Groeppel-Klein, A. (2021). No laughing matter, or a secret weapon? Exploring the effect of humor in service failure situations. *Journal of Business Research, 132*, 260–269.

Kopalle, P., & Lehmann, D. (2001). Strategic management of expectations: The role of disconfirmation sensitivity and perfectionism. *Journal of Marketing Research, 38*(3), 386–394.

Kronrod, A., Grinstein, A., & Wathieu, L. (2012). Go green! Should environmental messages be so assertive? *Journal of Marketing, 76*(1), 95–102.

Kull, A. J., Romero, M., & Monahan, L. (2021). How may I help you? Driving brand engagement through the warmth of an initial chatbot message. *Journal of Business Research, 135*, 840–850.

Lapointe, L., & Rivard, S. (2005). A multilevel model of resistance to information technology implementation. *MIS Quarterly*, *3*, 461–491.
Lee, S., Lee, N., & Sah, Y. J. (2020). Perceiving a mind in a chatbot: Effect of mind perception and social cues on co-presence, closeness, and intention to use. *International Journal of Human–Computer Interaction*, *36*(10), 930–940.
Lehmann-Willenbrock, N., & Allen, J. A. (2014). How fun are your meetings? Investigating the relationship between humor patterns in team interactions and team performance. *Journal of Applied Psychology*, *99*(6), 1278–1287.
Li, X., & Sung, Y. (2021). Anthropomorphism brings us closer: The mediating role of psychological distance in User–AI assistant interactions. *Computers in Human Behavior*, *118*, 106680.
Liao, M. Q., & Sundar, S. S. (2022). When e-commerce personalization systems show and tell: Investigating the relative persuasive appeal of content-based versus collaborative filtering. *Journal of Advertising*, *51*(2), 256–267.
Liu, D., Lv, Y., & Huang, W. (2023). How do consumers react to chatbots' humorous emojis in service failures. *Technology in Society*, *73*, 102244.
Liu, J., Hsu, F. C., Yu, J., Cao, J., & Mai, H. (2025). When humble AI meets narcissistic customers: A terror management perspective. *International Journal of Information Management*, *83*, 102904.
Longoni, C., Bonezzi, A., & Morewedge, C. K. (2019). Resistance to medical artificial intelligence. *Journal of Consumer Research*, *46*(4), 629–650.
Longoni, C., & Cian, L. (2022). Artificial intelligence in utilitarian versus hedonic contexts: The "word-of-machine" effect. *Journal of Marketing*, *86*(1), 91–108.
Loureiro, S. M. C., Jiménez-Barreto, J., Bilro, R. G., & Romero, J. (2024). Me and my AI: Exploring the effects of consumer self-construal and AI-based experience on avoiding similarity and willingness to pay. *Psychology & Marketing*, *41*(1), 151–167.
Luo, X., Tong, S., Fang, Z., & Qu, Z. (2019). Frontiers: Machines versus humans: The impact of artificial intelligence chatbot disclosure on customer purchases. *Marketing Science*, *38*(6), 937–947.
Ma, H., Huang, W., & Dennis, A. R. (2024). Unintended consequences of disclosing recommendations by artificial intelligence versus humans on true and fake news believability and engagement. *Journal of Management Information Systems*, *41*(3), 616–644.
Marchand, A., & Marx, P. (2020). Automated product recommendations with preference-based explanations. *Journal of Retailing*, *96*(3), 328–343.
Mariani, M., & Dwivedi, Y. K. (2024). Generative artificial intelligence in innovation management: A preview of future research developments. *Journal of Business Research*, *175*, 114542.
Nguyen, D. N., Nguyen, V. H., Trinh, T., Ho, T., & Le, H. S. (2024). A personalized product recommendation model in e-commerce based on retrieval strategy. *Journal of Open Innovation: Technology, Market, and Complexity*, *10*(2), 100303.
Reich, T., Kaju, A., & Maglio, S. J. (2023). How to overcome algorithm aversion: Learning from mistakes. *Journal of Consumer Psychology*, *33*(2), 285–302.
Sands, S., Ferraro, C., Campbell, C., & Tsao, H. Y. (2021). Managing the human–chatbot divide: How service scripts influence service experience. *Journal of Service Management*, *32*(2), 246–264.
Sapmaz, F., Yıldırım, M., Topcuoğlu, P., Nalbant, D., & Sızır, U. (2016). Gratitude, forgiveness and humility as predictors of subjective well-being among university students. *International Online Journal of Educational Sciences*, *8*(1), 38–47.
Schuetzler, R. M., Grimes, G. M., & Scott Giboney, J. (2020). The impact of chatbot conversational skill on engagement and perceived humanness. *Journal of Management Information Systems*, *37*(3), 875–900.
Sela, A., Wheeler, S. C., & Sarial-Abi, G. (2012). We are not the same as you and I: Causal effects of minor language variations on consumers' attitudes toward brands. *Journal of Consumer Research*, *39*(3), 644–661.

Shams, G., Kim, K. K., & Kim, K. (2024). Enhancing service recovery satisfaction with chatbots: The role of humor and informal language. *International Journal of Hospitality Management, 120*, 103782.

Sheehan, B., Jin, H. S., & Gottlieb, U. (2020). Customer service chatbots: Anthropomorphism and adoption. *Journal of Business Research, 115*, 14–24.

Shin, H., Bunosso, I., & Levine, L. R. (2022). The influence of chatbot humor on consumer evaluations of services. *International Journal of Consumer Studies, 47*(2), 545–562.

Sun, Y., & Wang, S. (2020). Understanding consumers' intentions to purchase green products in the social media marketing context. *Asia Pacific Journal of Marketing and Logistics, 32*(4), 860–878.

Tsai, W. H. S., Liu, Y., & Chuan, C. H. (2021). How chatbots' social presence communication enhances consumer engagement: The mediating role of parasocial interaction and dialogue. *Journal of Research in Interactive Marketing, 15*(3), 460–482.

Um, C. T., Guo, S. L., Lumineau, F., Shi, W., & Song, R. (2022). The downside of CFO function-based language incongruity. *Academy of Management Journal, 65*(6), 1984–2013.

Verhagen, T., Van Nes, J., Feldberg, F., & Van Dolen, W. (2014). Virtual customer service agents: Using social presence and personalization to shape online service encounters. *Journal of Computer-Mediated Communication, 19*(3), 529–545.

Weidig, J., & Kuehnl, C. (2023). Improving the effectiveness of personalized recommendations through attributional cues. *Psychology & Marketing, 40*(12), 2559–2575.

Wien, A. H., & Peluso, A. M. (2021). Influence of human versus AI recommenders: The roles of product type and cognitive processes. *Journal of Business Research, 137*, 13–27.

Xu, J., Benbasat, I., & Cenfetelli, R. T. (2020). The relative effect of the convergence of product recommendations from various online sources. *Journal of Management Information Systems, 37*(3), 788–819.

Xu, M., Du, H., Niyato, D., Kang, J., Xiong, Z., Mao, S., Han, Z., Jamalipour, A., Kim, D. I., Shen, X., Leung, V. C. M., & Poor, H. V. (2024). Unleashing the power of edge-cloud generative AI in mobile networks: A survey of AIGC services. *IEEE Communications Surveys & Tutorials, 26*(2), 1127–1170.

Xu, Y., Zhang, J., & Deng, G. (2022). Enhancing customer satisfaction with chatbots: The influence of communication styles and consumer attachment anxiety. *Frontiers in Psychology, 13*, 902782.

Yang, H., Xu, H., Zhang, Y., Liang, Y., & Lyu, T. (2022). Exploring the effect of humor in robot failure. *Annals of Tourism Research, 95*, 103425.

Yang, Y., Zheng, J., Yu, Y., Qiu, Y., & Wang, L. (2024). The role of recommendation sources and attribute framing in online product recommendations. *Journal of Business Research, 174*, 114498.

Yeomans, M., Shah, A., Mullainathan, S., & Kleinberg, J. (2019). Making sense of recommendations. *Journal of Behavioral Decision Making, 32*(4), 403–414.

Yin, J., Qiu, X., & Wang, Y. (2025). The impact of AI-Personalized recommendations on clicking intentions: Evidence from Chinese E-Commerce. *Journal of Theoretical and Applied Electronic Commerce Research, 20*(1), 21.

Zhang, J., Balaji, M. S., Luo, J., & Jha, S. (2022). Effectiveness of product recommendation framing on online retail platforms. *Journal of Business Research, 153*, 185–197.

Literature Review

2

This chapter presents a comprehensive literature review on key themes in user-AI interactions: AI vs. human recommendations, AI communication styles, AI humanity, and GAI humor. The review synthesizes foundational theoretical frameworks and integrates recent research findings to summarize established knowledge and identify research opportunities. To provide structural clarity and facilitate scholarly comparison, each thematic section will be supported by a dedicated table summarizing prior major research findings.

2.1 AI vs. Human Recommendation

AI recommendation is an information system for customer decision support (Grenci & Todd, 2002), which consists of inputs, processes, and outputs. It can be based on an automated software system of computer programs and algorithms to give recommendations based on an individual's interests or preferences (Xiao & Benbasat, 2007). The emergence of AI recommendations relies on developing technologies such as machine learning, deep learning, and natural language processing. This information system collects structured or unstructured data from human input (e.g., consumers' historical consumption of product prices, browsing behaviors), and through algorithms that mimic the neural network of the human brain. It automatically learns the intrinsic rules of the collected data and processes the reasoning to ultimately send the reasoned recommendation content back to the human recipients to support the consumer's decision-making (Dehnert & Mongeau, 2022). AI recommendations can be categorized into non-interactive recommendation agents and interactive recommendation agents, contingent upon their modes of interaction (Chang & Park, 2024; Ebrahimi et al., 2022; Xiao & Benbasat, 2007). Further differentiation within conversational AI recommendations can be made based on the presence or absence of non-verbal communication

F. Yang, *AI and Consumer Interaction in Business*, Management for Professionals,
https://doi.org/10.1007/978-981-95-9430-6_2

cues, distinguishing physical agents from non-physical agents (Araujo, 2018; Von der Pütten et al., 2010). This research focuses on interactive and non-physical conversation AI agents. Human recommendations, on the other hand, refer to "other human subjects" who provide consumers with recommendations, including experts, such as doctors, counselors, and salespeople, and other ordinary consumers, such as key opinion leaders on the Internet, family members, relatives, and friends (Senecal & Nantel, 2004; Wien & Peluso, 2021).

In the comparative study of the effectiveness of AI vs. human recommendations on consumer behavior, there are two different views in the literature. Some scholars believe that AI recommendations are more accurate than human recommendations (Yeomans et al., 2019). However, more attention should be directed to explain how AI recommendations can be easily understood (Jeon, 2022; Yeomans et al., 2019). In contrast, other scholars support that human recommendations are more effective than AI recommendations (Chen et al., 2023; Longoni & Cian, 2022; Kim & Duhachek, 2020; Wien & Peluso, 2021). Even if AI can process and

Table 2.1 Existing research on AI versus human recommendations

Sources	Major findings
Yeomans et al. (2019)	AI recommenders outperform humans (including close friends/family) in joke recommendation (61% vs. 57% accuracy); however, people exhibit distinct algorithm aversion, partly due to the subjective perception that human recommendation processes are more understandable than machine-driven ones
Jeon (2022)	Consumers perceive the AI manager more positively in terms of likeability, knowledgeability, and trustworthiness than the AI representative and the human manager
Kim and Duhachek (2020)	People would interpret artificial agent's actions at lower level construals as a default compared with the same action performed by humans. Low-construal messages (vs. high-construal messages) are more effective when the message is delivered by artificial agents (vs. human agents)
Ruan and Mezei (2022)	The impact of service agents on customer satisfaction varies by product attribute type: human frontline employees perform better for experiential products, while AI chatbots excel for functional products, with these differences explained by perceived information quality, waiting time, and positive emotions
Jin and Zhang (2025)	People consider AI recommendations to be more competent for material products, while they perceive human recommendations to be more competent for experiential products
Longoni and Cian (2022)	AI recommenders are more competent than human recommenders in the utilitarian realm and less competent than human recommenders in the hedonic realm
Yang et al. (2024)	When products are framed as vice, AI recommendations (vs. human recommendation) are more likely to reduce consumers' perceptions of warmth and competence of the recommendation source, leading to negative effects on purchase intention and related outcomes

compute big data, consumers still have "algorism aversion" (Kim & Kankanhalli, 2009). In addition, data privacy and security, consumer resistance, and distrust of algorithms can also cause consumer concerns about AI recommendations (Baek & Morimoto, 2012; Segijn et al., 2021). While human recommendations may have high training costs and limited work efficiency, they usually possess direct product experience (Longoni & Cian, 2022), enabling a better understanding of consumers' personalized needs unique requirements (Yeomans et al., 2019). At the same time, human recommendations are more likely to establish emotional connections and trust with consumers, which enhances the consumer experience and promotes the formation of positive brand impressions.

Notably, there are theoretical boundaries to the effectiveness of human recommendations versus AI recommendations, which are influenced by factors such as type of information, type of product, type of job, and brand image (Castelo et al., 2019; Longoni & Cian, 2022; Wien & Peluso, 2021). Studies have shown that AI is better suited than humans to recommend material products, while humans are better suited than AI to recommend experiential products (Jin & Zhang, 2025). In addition, AI recommendations are more capable than human recommendations in the utilitarian domain, while AI recommendations are more capable than human recommendations in the hedonistic domain (Longoni & Cian, 2022). Table 2.1 presents existing studies conducted in AI vs. human recommendations.

2.2 AI Communication Styles

Language use plays a crucial role in service interactions (Holmqvist et al., 2017). Scholars have examined the impact of changes in the way of information delivery on consumer responses in online communication, such as the use of different pronouns, metaphors, or direct language shape consumer attitude and intention (Kronrod et al., 2012; Sela et al., 2012; Wu et al., 2017). At the beginning, chatbots were often perceived as mechanized entities lack personal emotion and trustworthiness (Luo et al., 2019). However, with the rapid development of AI technologies, have enabled chatbots to mimic human conversations, thereby facilitating more seamless and natural communication (Go & Sundar, 2019; Schuetzler et al., 2020). This advancement has led to a significant enhancement in customers' perception of chatbots as humanized. Given the technological feasibility of this development, scholars have begun to focus on and explore which factors can further enhance customers' humanized perception of chatbots. Specifically, the role of verbal cues in chatbot communication has received significant attention (Araujo, 2018; Go & Sundar, 2019; Lee et al., 2020). Feine et al. (2019) further proposes the key linguistic cue of style, defined as the linguistic variants employed in a message that can elicit a socialization response in a chatbot's interaction with a customer.

Style exerts a substantial influence on the formation of the customer's impression of the communication and is a controllable design element during chatbot development (Thomas et al., 2018). The employment of a humanized style in communication has been shown to positively influence customer perception (Kelleher, 2009). Task-oriented and social-oriented styles are two common interaction styles, each having a significant impact on different communication goals. Task-oriented styles are characterized by a focus on the execution of a particular task, with the employment of clear and efficient language serving to enhance communication (Chattaraman et al., 2019). However, overly direct and functional expressions may ignore the emotional needs of the customer, which in turn triggers indifference or resistance to the chatbot (Kull et al., 2021; Roy & Naidoo, 2021). This phenomenon can be explained by the stereotype content model, which posits that a communication style that emphasizes "competence" over "warmth" may reduce customers' emotional identification and engagement (Kelleher, 2009).

From a functional perspective, task-oriented styles demonstrate better performance in scenarios that require quick problem solving or conveying specific information (Chen et al., 2021) while social-oriented styles have significant advantages in situations that enhance emotional support or promote long-term relationship building (De Cicco et al., 2020). Furthermore, studies have demonstrated that styles that are social-oriented can enhance customers' experience and brand loyalty in scenarios such as food delivery and online shopping (Xu et al., 2022). In contrast, social-oriented style builds emotional interactions with "common, informal, familiar, casual" language features (McArthur et al., 2018). This approach aims to convey a sense of humanity and intimacy by creating a warm and intimate communication atmosphere (Lee et al., 2020; Xu et al., 2022). This engaging and natural communication style has been shown to effectively reduce the perception of unnaturalness or lack of personalization of chatbots, thereby enhancing brand attitude and customer satisfaction (Kelleher, 2009; Li & Wang, 2023).

Communication style plays a crucial role in AI-human interactions, which has been shown to significantly shape consumers' cognitive and emotional responses. Studies highlight that linguistic features, including pronouns, metaphors, and tone, can shape users' perceptions of the communicator (Kronrod et al., 2012; Sela et al., 2012). Previous researches have shown that the communication style of offline customer service can affect customer trust (Crosby et al., 1990). The same applies to online customer service. Research has also found that the communication style of online customer service has great impact on the relationship between customers and online customer service (Verhagen et al., 2014). Generally speaking, the communication style of intelligent chatbot can be divided into two categories: social-oriented and task-oriented. The social-oriented communication style aims to establish interpersonal relationships with customers, while task-oriented communication style aims to improve task efficiency, achieve task objectives, and minimize communication costs (Verhagen et al., 2014). Researches have noted that social-oriented communication style can better enhance the positive effects of anthropomorphism and alleviate customers' aversion (Verhagen et al., 2014). Table 2.2 presents a summary of existing research on communication styles in general marketing and AI communication styles in specific.

Table 2.2 Existing research on communication styles in marketing and AI communication styles

Sources	Main finding
Crosby et al. (1990)	In complex service selling, communication style is pivotal to relationship quality. Key relational communication behaviors including contact intensity, mutual disclosure, and cooperative intentions strongly enhance relationship quality by building trust and satisfaction
Verhagen et al. (2014)	Virtual Customer Service Agents' (VCSA) communication style shapes online service encounters. VCSAs perceived as friendly and knowledgeable strongly enhance customers' feelings of social presence and personalization, which in turn boost service satisfaction. A socially-oriented communication style (vs. task-oriented) further strengthens these positive effects, making interactions feel more human and personalized
Wang et al. (2025)	Social-oriented chatbots generate higher service recovery satisfaction than task-oriented ones. This effect is mediated by both cognition-based and affect-based trust. Task complexity moderates cognition-based trust, but relationship orientation shows no significant moderating effect
Bickmore and Cassell (2001)	An Embodied Conversational Agent (REA) using social dialogue can build user trust, but its effectiveness depends on user personality. Small talk significantly increased perceived trust, credibility, and interaction quality for extroverts, while introverts preferred the task-only agent. This highlights the importance of relational strategies in human-agent interaction
Feine et al. (2019)	This paper develops a taxonomy to classify social cues of conversational agents (CAs) into four main categories (verbal, visual, auditory, and invisible) and ten subcategories. Derived via literature review and evaluated through card sorting, this framework helps researchers systematically organize knowledge and assists practitioners in designing more effective, socially aware CAs
Chattaraman et al. (2019)	AI assistants' interaction style should match older adults' Internet competency: social-oriented style boosts trust and interactivity for high-competency users, while task-oriented style reduces cognitive load and enhances self-efficacy for low-competency users during online shopping
Kelleher (2009)	An organization's use of a conversational human voice and communicated relational commitment in interactive online communication (like blogs) positively correlates with key public relations outcomes: trust, satisfaction, commitment, and control mutuality. Frequent exposure to such communication strengthens these relational benefits
Chen et al. (2021)	When customers interact with chatbots, they will perceive higher cognitive fit if the chatbots provide them with suggestive guidance and communicate in a friendly style especially when they perform a searching task. Task-oriented styles demonstrate better performance in scenarios that require quick problem solving or conveying specific information

(continued)

Table 2.2 (continued)

Sources	Main finding
De Cicco et al. (2020)	For millennials, a social-oriented chatbot interaction style (using informal language, emojis, and exclamations) significantly increases social presence, which in turn boosts perceived enjoyment and trust, leading to a more positive attitude. Avatar presence, however, had no significant effect on social presence
Li and Wang (2023)	Chatbots using informal (vs. formal) language increase customers' continuance usage intention and brand attitude, mediated by para-social interaction. However, this positive effect weakens for non-customers, highlighting brand affiliation as a key moderator
Xu et al. (2023)	Using a social-oriented communication style boosts customer satisfaction. Warmth perception of the chatbot mediates this effect, while chatbot's anthropomorphized role (servant versus partner) moderates this effect
Jakic et al. (2017)	Brands adapting their language style to match customers' in social media (convergence) indirectly increase brand trust through perceived relationship investments (effort, benevolence, interaction quality). While the direct effect is negative, the overall indirect effect is positive. An informal style enhances this effect, but purchase involvement and content valence show no significant impact
Gretry et al. (2017)	Using an informal communication style on social media increases brand trust for familiar brands but decreases it for unfamiliar ones. The effect is mediated by perceived appropriateness, as consumers expect brands to follow social norms based on their familiarity level

2.3 AI Humanity

2.3.1 Service Failure and Service Recovery

Service failure refers to any actual form of accident or customer-perceived accident or error that occurs during the customer experience phase (Palmer et al., 2000), where the process provides a service that deviates from the expected functionality and does not meet the real needs of the customer. The current research on service failure in AI focuses on the failure of service robots in the retail, e-commerce, tourism, and hospitality industries. Among them, robots in the retail and hotel industries are mainly used for delivery and robots in the tourism industry can make reservations for various types of transportation and plan travel routes. In the above fields, the main manifestations of service failure include encountering obstacles during operation, taking wrong actions, not producing any actions, producing inappropriate language, and repeating expressions (Honig & Oron-Gilad, 2018). In addition to this, there are some studies focusing on chatbots in industries such as e-commerce. For this type of chatbots, their algorithms can accurately and quickly deal with objective and procedural questions with a certain level of intelligence.

However, limited by technology, this type of robots lacks the ability comparable to human beings as well as the way of thinking. As such, these robots are not good at dealing with the uniqueness of the user's problems and can only deal with numerous repetitive and simple tasks (Xing et al., 2022).

At the same time, timely service recovery is needed to alleviate customers' negative emotions after a service failure (Kuo & Wu, 2012). Service recovery was initially defined as a service provider's response to address customer complaints and dissatisfied behaviors after a service failure has occurred (Gronroos, 1988). In this regard, scholars have conducted a large number of studies on service recovery, which can be divided into two paths: utilitarian recovery through the provision of material resources, and symbolic recovery through the provision of psychological or social resources, in order to compensate for, apologize for, and ultimately alleviate the customer's negative emotions by rescuing the customer's economic and emotional losses caused by the service failure (Zhang et al., 2023). Compared with utilitarian recovery, symbolic recovery has become the preferred measure of service recovery due to its cost-effective characteristics (Zhang et al., 2023). Current research also suggests that service recovery subject types can be accomplished by both humans and AIs. More research has focused on the process of service recovery done by humans, mainly emphasizing that companies or brands can use both physical and mental recovery to make up for customer losses. A small amount of research centres on the process of service recovery by AIs, which can apologize, explain, and even empathize with failures (Choi et al., 2020).

2.3.2 Humility and AI Assistant

Humility, as a positive force of character, originates from the ethical traditions of different cultures, and is both an individual trait and a social virtue that emphasizes an individual's awareness of self-limitations, respect for others, and a continuous learning attitude. In Western culture, humility is regarded as an important embodiment of self-awareness (Wimbush, 2014), whereas in Eastern culture, humility is regarded as an inner cultivation of cultivating one's own body and family, especially under the influence of Confucianism, which emphasizes the reflection and learning attitude of "Seeing the virtuous and learning from the wise," attitude of reflection and learning (Li, 2016).

Previous research has found that humility significantly enhances individuals' well-being and relationship quality (Davis et al., 2010). Humility not only helps individuals perceive self-limitations and reduce self-centeredness, but also encourages openness, acceptance, and error acknowledgement, which promotes social cohesion and psychological well-being (Bhattacharya et al., 2017; Sapmaz et al., 2016). Research in social and organizational psychology positions humility as a pivotal trait for navigating interpersonal conflict. Its function in relational repair is mediated through reduced defensiveness and an increased propensity for concession-making. Concurrently, humility enhances other-oriented perspective-taking, a core component of empathy, which allows for more accurate attribution of intent and mitigates negative affect. The cumulative effect of these processes—repair and empathy—is the restoration of perceived integrity and benevolence, the two key facets of interpersonal trust. Consequently, humility operates as a multifaceted construct that addresses the cognitive, affective, and behavioral barriers to reconciliation.

In AI assistant scenarios, researchers have begun to introduce the trait of humility into AI design, proposing it as an important ethical trait for AI anthropomorphization (Liu et al., 2025), and that AI assistants with the trait of humility are more capable of demonstrating ethical self-awareness, higher transparency and adaptability, and easier to be accepted and trusted by customers (Burr & Leslie, 2023). The humility of AI assistants is often reflected in behaviors such as admitting mistakes, requesting feedback, and expressing willingness to learn, which is a "self-limiting" expression that can help repair customer relationships and inspire customer empathy and tolerance in high-risk situations such as service failure (Sapmaz et al., 2016).

However, existing humility studies mostly focus on human subjects. Studies on AI assistant humility traits mainly focus on the positive effects in general human-AI interaction scenarios, generally ignoring the role of AI assistant humility in the high-risk scenario of service failure. Crucially, there is a lack of in-depth understanding of how—and to what extent—an AI's expression of humility influences critical outcome variables like customer satisfaction following a failure. Based on this, this study investigates the impact of different degree of AI assistant humility on customer satisfaction in service failure scenarios. Table 2.3 presents a summary of research findings on humanity in general and AI humanity in specific.

Table 2.3 Existing research on humanity and the AI humanity

Sources	Main Finding
Bell and Fincham (2017)	Humility is related to relationship satisfaction in emerging adult females. Specifically, humility contributes to self-forgiveness, which in turn leads to partner-forgiveness, ultimately enhancing relationship satisfaction
Bhattacharya et al. (2017)	Humility has an important role in contributing to personal and social well-being. It highlights the need for further research to clarify the definition, measurement, and implications of humility within both scientific and traditional contexts
Bollinger (2017)	Research on humility and forgiveness is evolving from studies primarily using university student samples to more diverse adult populations. Humility may enhance the capacity for forgiveness and vice versa

(continued)

Table 2.3 (continued)

Sources	Main Finding
Chancellor and Lyubomirsky (2013)	Two promising strategies are identified for studying humility: using personality judgments and conducting "stress tests" to observe humility-relevant behavior in various contexts. And five hallmarks of humility distinguished from related concepts like narcissism and low self-esteem are identified, which include a secure identity, freedom from distortion, openness to new information, other-focus, and egalitarian beliefs
Choi et al. (2020)	Consumers react more negatively to service failures caused by humanoid robots compared to nonhumanoid robots. Humanoid robots can effectively recover from service failures through apologies and explanations. Human intervention can enhance recovery efforts when nonhumanoid robots fail
Davis et al. (2010)	The article critiques existing various measurement strategies for humility and introduces the concept of relational humility, defining it as a relationship-specific personality judgment influenced by interpersonal factors and the observer's experiences with the target person
Li (2016)	Humility is more highly valued and prevalent in Confucian-heritage cultures (CHCs), where it is deeply integrated into social and educational practices. Humility can develop into a virtue in children within CHCs through the multiple promoting effects of the family, teachers and cultural narratives
Liu et al. (2025)	Humble AI assistants can enhance customer satisfaction through improved para-social interactions, especially among customers with low to moderate narcissism when perceived AI threat is low. Under high AI threat, the effectiveness of humble AI may diminish for customers with lower narcissism, while highly narcissistic individuals may still benefit from interactions with humble AI
Owens et al. (2013)	Expressed humility positively influences various organizational outcomes, including individual performance, team contributions, job satisfaction, and employee engagement. Humility can compensate for lower general mental ability. Leader-expressed humility fosters a supportive team environment, leading to increased learning orientation and lower turnover rates among employees
Sapmaz et al. (2016)	Gratitude significantly predicts subjective well-being among university students. Among the sub-dimensions of forgiveness, only "forgiveness of situation" was found to significantly predict happiness. "Forgiveness of self" and "forgiveness of others" did not show a significant predictive relationship with subjective well-being. The sub-dimensions of humility, particularly "openness" and "modest self-assessment," were found to significantly contribute to subjective well-being. However, "self-forgetfulness" and "focus on others" did not predict happiness
Zabel et al. (2025)	Lower scores in honesty-humility are associated with a more favorable attitude towards AI. Honesty-humility has a stronger predictive power regarding attitudes towards AI than other personality traits

2.4 AI Humor

In recent years, generative artificial intelligence (GAI) has transcended the confines of computer science as a singular field of study, emerging as a research hotspot across multiple disciplines including sociology, psychology, and business management, and attracting widespread attention from scholars across various fields (Dwivedi & Kshetri, 2023; Mariani & Dwivedi, 2024). From a disciplinary perspective, artificial intelligence is closely related to the field of computer science, with its core research direction being "simulating human intelligent behavior through computer systems" or "endowing machines with the ability to mimic human behavior" (Ji, 2024; Li & Sung, 2021). GAI, as an advanced form of AI, can precisely analyze the semantic connotations and emotional tendencies within human language inputs, generating feedback in ways that align with human cognitive habits. It can automatically produce diverse content types, including text, images, and speech in a short timeframe. Current mainstream systems such as ChatGPT, Deepseek, Doubao, Tongyi Qianwen, and Wenxin Yiyan all fall into this category (Kshetri et al., 2024).

Today, GAI transcends mere functional utility to serve as a core enabler for optimizing commercial activities. Specifically, it delivers customized business solutions for individuals and organizations and helps brands boost productivity and reduce operational costs, leading to widespread adoption across diverse scenarios (Mariani & Dwivedi, 2024). At this stage, GAI has become one of the fastest-growing branches in the AI field due to its rapid technological iteration and strong adaptability to various scenarios. Its applications are increasingly mature in areas such as customer service and social media interaction. By engaging in real-time interactions with users, GAI can directly handle inquiries, feedback, and emotional companionship needs. While improving service response efficiency and reducing corporate costs, it is gradually evolving from a "functional service provider" to an "emotional interactor" (Riemer & Peter, 2024). As user expectations for AI interactions evolve from "efficient problem-solving" to "high-quality emotional experiences," the design of GAI's emotional characteristics has become a focal point in both research and practice. Humor, serving as a vital vehicle for conveying emotions and bridging social gaps in human interactions, naturally emerges as a key direction for GAI's emotional enhancement.

Existing research has thoroughly demonstrated that variations in GAI traits exert differentiated influences on consumer behavior. Academic studies on GAI traits predominantly revolve around two core dimensions: "warmth" and "competence" (Fiske et al., 2007). This dimensional framework originates from fundamental principles of interpersonal judgment: when forming impressions of others or situations, "warmth" and "competence" encompass nearly all critical evaluation criteria, fully explaining individuals' cognitive and evaluative logic toward interaction partners (Fiske et al., 2007, 2002). The assessment of "warmth traits" centers on the motivation and emotional communication effectiveness of the interaction partner

(Kull et al., 2021). This manifests as friendly attitudes, approachable interaction styles, willingness to assist proactively, sincere expressions, positive emotional feedback, and traits that reduce psychological distance through humor. These characteristics directly determine the strength of emotional connection during user interactions, with emotional bonding serving as the critical prerequisite influencing users' perception of warmth and satisfaction (Brender-Ilan & Reizer, 2021; Kim et al., 2013; Xie et al., 2024). In contrast, "capability traits" focus on the functional performance of GAI, such as information processing speed, knowledge base scale, task execution precision, and skill adaptability, with the core being the assessment of GAI's level of completing predetermined tasks (Fiske et al., 2002). Based on this, to achieve deep emotional interaction with users and enhance satisfaction, GAI algorithm design typically optimizes across the dual dimensions of "warmth" and "competence". Strengthening warmth traits, such as integrating humor elements, has become a key direction (Kobel & Groeppel-Klein, 2021; Xie et al., 2024).

Conceptually, humor is defined as "a form of stimulation that elicits laughter, provides entertainment, or conveys amusement" (Warren et al., 2018). Existing research on humor primarily focuses on human contexts. GAI humor, however, refers to the integration of mechanisms that mimic human humor logic into GAI algorithm design, enabling the generation of humorous content during human-AI interactions. Research indicates humor acts as a "lubricant" in interpersonal relationships, reducing tension and conflict by fostering connections (Kobel & Groeppel-Klein, 2021; Lehmann-Willenbrock & Allen, 2014). It also significantly enhances attention levels and positive emotional experiences (Martin et al., 2003). In commercial settings, service robots with humorous traits have been proven to enhance consumers' positive evaluations of e-commerce platforms, including service satisfaction, willingness to revisit the platform, and willingness to recommend it (Yang et al., 2023). In AI-human interaction research, humorous AI is regarded as a core quality. It makes interactions more engaging, appealing, and credible while endowing chatbots with distinctive personalized traits (Xie et al., 2024; Yang et al., 2022; Zhang et al., 2025).

It is worth noting that the current application of GAI on social media platforms remains limited, with most implementations concentrated in intelligent customer service scenarios for Q&A services, while applications of humorous GAI remain relatively scarce (Ghanem et al., 2024). In 2023, Sina Weibo introduced an interactive social media GAI that broke this pattern, becoming the first platform to integrate humor elements into its GAI algorithm. Its GAI externalization entity was named "Comment Robert". By learning the logical structures and contextual cues of human humor, this GAI proactively engages with user-generated content (UGC) in comment sections, generating replies that incorporate humorous text and emojis. Specifically, when users post UGC (such as lifestyle shares or opinion pieces), Comment Robert automatically responds in the comment section, incorporating humorous elements to enhance emotional resonance.

2.4.1 Social Response Theory and User Satisfaction

In the field of social media consumer behavior research, user satisfaction serves as a core metric for evaluating platform service quality, interaction effectiveness, and user experience. Conceptually, Oliver (1980) expectancy-confirmation theory provides a foundational framework for understanding user satisfaction, which is defined as "the positive emotional state and subjective approval arising from comparing actual experiences with preformed expectations after receiving a service or using a product" (Mou & Xu, 2017). This research further expands the dimensions of this concept, positing that user satisfaction encompasses not only emotional pleasure but also cognitive value recognition—specifically, users' subjective assessment of how well a service or platform fulfills their core needs, such as entertainment, social interaction, and emotional fulfillment (Campbell et al., 2001; Pennington & Hall, 2014). This extension aligns the concept of user satisfaction more closely with the diverse needs of social media users.

Regarding platform characteristics, content quality serves as the core driver of user satisfaction. Research indicates that the information accessibility, entertainment value, relaxation potential, social attributes, and informational consistency of social media content directly influence users' perceived satisfaction with the platform (Agnihotri et al., 2022). Users' pursuit of enjoyment constitutes a core need; when platform content fulfills these needs, user satisfaction levels significantly increase (McQuail, 1987). Regarding interaction characteristics, GAI's emotional expression emerges as a key influencing variable. Research confirms that the personalization and naturalness of GAI interactions indirectly foster positive satisfaction evaluations by enhancing users' emotional experiences (Hussain et al., 2024). In social media contexts, emotional feedback from GAI—such as humor and positive emotional expressions—effectively reduces users' technological alienation and diminishes resistance toward AI, thereby enhancing overall satisfaction with platform services (Sörensen et al., 2023). User satisfaction plays a decisive role in the survival and development of social media platforms, serving not only as a core prerequisite for user retention and repeat visits but also as a vital safeguard for platform profitability. Research indicates that highly satisfied users are more likely to develop loyalty toward the platform, leading to positive word-of-mouth dissemination and proactive recommendations (O'Brien & Toms, 2014; Santos et al., 2022). These behaviors directly impact the platform's user scale and commercial value. Indeed, social media platforms' monetization models—such as advertising and content monetization—heavily depend on user stickiness and activity levels, with long-term stable satisfaction perceptions being the core driver of user stickiness (Agnihotri et al., 2022; Chang et al., 2015). Currently, as GAI expands its application in social media contexts, exploring the influence mechanisms of GAI traits (particularly humor) on user satisfaction represents a critical direction for filling gaps in research on emotional interaction in social media GAI. Previous studies have predominantly focused on the application of GAI humor in service failure scenarios on e-commerce platforms (Kobel & Groeppel-Klein,

2021; Yang et al., 2022), with limited research examining the relationship between GAI humor and user satisfaction in social media settings. Furthermore, social reaction theory provides crucial support for understanding the pathways through which GAI humor influences user satisfaction. This theory posits that humans unconsciously apply interpersonal social rules and responses when interacting with AI, even when explicitly aware that the entity is not a real human (Mou & Xu, 2017). People unconsciously respond to GAI's socialized traits—such as humor—through social norms like emotional resonance and trust-building (Waytz et al., 2014). When GAI conveys "friendliness" and "approachability" through humorous expressions, users experience warmth akin to interpersonal interactions. This reduces psychological distance and diminishes technological resistance (Li & Sung, 2021), creating the positive psychological state essential for user satisfaction. Thus, GAI humor can activate users' automatic social responses, transforming warm feelings into positive evaluations. This logic provides a theoretical foundation for subsequent exploration of the mechanisms through which GAI humor influences user satisfaction.

2.4.2 Perceived Warmth

In the field of human-AI interaction and consumer behavior research, perceived warmth serves as a core psychological variable for measuring the strength of an individual's emotional connection to an interactive entity. Its study has progressively become a significant branch within AI affective interaction research, exhibiting close associations with social traits of GAI, such as humor. Conceptually, Fiske et al. (2002) positioned "warmth" alongside "competence" as two core dimensions in the stereotype content model for human perception of others or non-human entities (Fiske et al., 2002). Perceived warmth is defined as "an individual's subjective judgment regarding whether an interaction partner exhibits emotional dispositions such as friendliness, care, or empathy." This definition emphasizes perceived warmth's emotional attributes and social orientation (Chi et al., 2021). Subsequent research extended this concept to AI interaction scenarios, specifying that perceived warmth in GAI refers to "users' psychological perception of whether GAI conveys caring intentions and can evoke emotional resonance, based on its behavioral expressions (e.g., humorous remarks, empathetic responses) during interactions" (Prebensen & Rosengren, 2016). Unlike anthropomorphism perception, which focuses on "whether AI possesses human characteristics," perceived warmth emphasizes "whether AI behaviors evoke emotional closeness and a sense of being valued." This distinction positions it as a key mediating variable explaining the impact of GAI's emotional design on user satisfaction.

Theoretically, social reaction theory provides support for the relationship between GAI humor and perceived warmth. This theory posits that humans unconsciously apply interpersonal social rules when interacting with technology

(Mou & Xu, 2017). Humor, as a quintessential human social behavior conveying friendliness and bridging distances, activates users' "automatic social responses" when mimicked and applied by GAI in interactions. Users interpret GAI's humorous expressions as human-like "proactive overtures," fostering the psychological cognition that GAI attends to their emotional needs. This cognition serves as the core prerequisite for perceived warmth (Heider, 2013; Waytz et al., 2014). For instance, studies have found that when chatbots employed lighthearted humor during interactions, users perceived significantly greater warmth compared to bots using mechanical language. This stems from humor subverting the entrenched belief that AI lacks emotion, fostering a more human-like conversational atmosphere. Furthermore, the theory of violation of expectations offers complementary insights into this relationship. Users typically expect GAI to provide only functional responses, whereas humorous expressions from GAI constitute positive behaviors exceeding expectations. Such behaviors trigger surprise in users, and this sense of surprise further reinforces the warm perception of GAI's proactive care (Shin et al., 2022; Um et al., 2022).

From a practical perspective, existing research consistently confirms that perceived warmth plays a crucial mediating role between GAI interactions and positive user responses (such as satisfaction, trust, and willingness to use). In e-commerce service scenarios, Zhang et al. (2021) found that GAI customer service agents exhibiting warmth traits (e.g., conveying care through humorous expressions) significantly enhance users' perceived warmth (Zhu et al., 2022). This perception further reduces users' technological alienation, ultimately driving the formation of positive satisfaction evaluations (Dhiman et al., 2023). In social media contexts, Li and Wang (2023) empirically demonstrated that humorous GAI responses correlate positively with perceived warmth, with perceived warmth fully mediating the positive impact of GAI humor on user platform loyalty (Liu et al., 2023). This occurs because perceived warmth fulfills users' emotional needs in social interactions, fostering a positive psychological state of being understood and cared for (Rhee & Choi, 2020). Furthermore, the influence of perceived warmth on user decisions and attitudes extends to trust-building: when users experience higher perceived warmth toward GAI, they are more willing to share personal information with it and place greater trust in its recommendations (Olafsson et al., 2020). This trust relationship further enhances user satisfaction with GAI-related services (Xu et al., 2023). While perceived warmth has garnered attention in AI interaction studies, empirical research on how GAI humor influences user satisfaction through perceived warmth in social media contexts remains unexplored. Past studies have primarily focused on warm expressions by GAI in e-commerce service failure scenarios (Kobel & Groeppel-Klein, 2021; Yang et al., 2022) or examined the impact of GAI's warm traits on user trust in isolation (Xu et al., 2023), without integrating the specific social trait of humor with perceived warmth, and user satisfaction into a unified research framework. Furthermore, existing studies often measure perceived warmth using single dimensions, failing to fully capture its multidimensional characteristics in GAI humor interactions (e.g., emotional resonance, psychological closeness). Based on this, this study focuses on social media scenarios to explore the mechanism through which GAI humor influences user satisfaction via perceived warmth.

2.4.3 Attribution Theory and Sense of Humor

In the field of human cognition and social interaction research, individual sense of humor serves as a core trait variable reflecting an individual's ability to perceive, understand, and appreciate humor. Individual differences in this trait significantly influence psychological responses and behavioral tendencies toward humorous stimuli, playing a key moderating role in the relationship chain linking GAI humor with users' perceptions of warmth and satisfaction. Conceptually, Thorson and Powell (1993a, 1993b) defined personal sense of humor as "a stable psychological trait enabling individuals to recognize punchlines, experience pleasure, and provide positive feedback after receiving humorous information". This definition emphasizes the capability attribute and stability of personal sense of humor. Subsequent research further refined its dimensions, identifying three sub-dimensions: humor recognition ability (the capacity to swiftly grasp the core logic of humorous messages), humor appreciation level (acceptance and preference for different humor types), and humor feedback tendency (willingness to actively respond to or share humor after receiving it) (Yang et al., 2022). These inherent differences in processing humor directly determine user interpretation of GAI humor and emotional responses, making them key variables in regulating GAI humor's mechanisms of action.

From a theoretical perspective, attribution theory provides a core analytical framework for examining the interaction between individual humor sensitivity and GAI humor. Attribution theory posits that when individuals encounter external stimuli (such as GAI humor), they interpret the impact of these stimuli through both internal attribution (personal traits) and external attribution (the stimulus itself), thereby generating distinct cognitive and emotional responses (Folkes, 1984; Heider, 2013). In GAI humor interaction scenarios, GAI humor constitutes the external stimulus, while personal humor sensitivity represents the internal trait. When users receive GAI humor messages, they first assess whether they can understand this humor based on their humor sensitivity level. They then further attribute the quality of the humor effect to either GAI design or their own ability, ultimately influencing the formation of perceived warmth and satisfaction. For instance, Martin and Ford (2006) found that individuals with higher personal humor sensitivity were more likely to attribute positive outcomes to the high-quality humor design of external stimuli when exposed to humorous stimuli. Conversely, those with lower humor sensitivity who failed to understand the humor tended to attribute negative experiences to their own lack of ability or the external stimulus being meaningless (Cann & Calhoun, 2001). This attribution difference directly leads to divergent effects of GAI humor on users with varying humor sensibilities.

Individual differences in humor sensibility significantly moderate the impact of GAI humor on user satisfaction, exhibiting an inverse moderation effect (i.e., lower humor sensibility yields stronger positive effects from GAI humor). Specifically, for users with higher personal humor sensitivity: their daily exposure to humorous content is more frequent, and they possess stronger aesthetic thresholds and comprehension abilities for humor. GAI humor is easily categorized as conventional humor, making it difficult to generate emotional impact beyond expectations (Shin et al., 2022). In this context, users perceive GAI humor more as functional entertainment rather than warmth signals of active care, limiting its enhancement of perceived warmth and consequently weakening its promotion of user satisfaction. For users with lower personal humor sensitivity, they have fewer opportunities to receive and comprehend humorous content in daily life, maintaining a low threshold for humor expectations. When GAI initiates humorous interactions, it disrupts their preconceived notion that AI lacks emotion and only provides functional services (Um et al., 2022), generating a strong psychological sense of surprise. This surprise leads users to interpret GAI humor as a signal that GAI actively cares about their emotional needs, significantly enhancing their perception of warmth. Users with lower humor sensitivity reported significantly higher levels of sense of care and emotional closeness after receiving GAI humor compared to those with higher humor sensitivity (Evans et al., 2019). This heightened perception of warmth ultimately translates more effectively into user satisfaction.

Existing research on individual humor perception primarily focuses on interpersonal social contexts (e.g., the role of humor in intimate relationships and team collaboration) (Campbell et al., 2001; Cooper et al., 2018; Linge, 2009), with relatively limited application in AI interaction scenarios. A small number of related studies have only examined the direct impact of personal humor sense on AI service acceptance (e.g., users with higher humor sense are more willing to try AI humor features) (Kobel & Groeppel-Klein, 2021). Empirical testing in social media contexts is particularly lacking. Furthermore, past studies have predominantly measured personal humor sense using single dimensions (e.g., "liking humor") (Cann & Matson, 2014; Yam et al., 2018), failing to adequately capture its multidimensional variations in GAI interactions. Therefore, this study combines attribution theory and violation-of-expectations theory to systematically explore the moderating role of individual humor sense in the influence of GAI humor on user satisfaction. This not only fills a gap in existing research but also provides a theoretical basis for the precise design of GAI humor (e.g., adjusting humor styles for users with different humor senses). Table 2.4 presents the summary of the findings regarding AI humor.

Table 2.4 Existing research on the AI humor

Sources	Main findings
Bower and Steyvers (2021)	When joke source is unknown, participants rate jokes guessed as human created funnier than those guessed as AI created. However, when sources are explicitly labeled, there's no difference in ratings for human created jokes framed as human or AI. Actual human created jokes are rated funnier than AI created ones
Cao et al. (2025)	GPT-4o outperforms humans in sentence-based humor and humor coping in negative contexts. Self-enhancing humor is rated most effective by both humans and GPT-4o. AI-assisted humor improves conflict resolution feedback from senders and recipients
Christ et al. (2025)	For spontaneous humor, video features perform best in humor recognition and sentiment prediction. Text features are best for humor direction prediction. The proposed VFMM multimodal model achieves the highest humor recognition
Frank et al. (2025)	Combining anthropomorphism and satire in scientists' Twitter posts about AI elicits the highest mirth. Mirth mediates the effect of humor types on scientists' perceived likability and the legitimacy of the content as a science information source
Johanson et al. (2020)	A healthcare robot using humor in flu vaccination scenarios increases perceived likeability, safety, empathy and sociability. More participants laugh during interactions with the humorous robot than the neutral one
Yang et al. (2023)	AI's self-deprecating humor responses improve customers' service recovery satisfaction, mediated by perceived sincerity and perceived intelligence. High sense of power strengthens the effect via perceived sincerity; process failure (vs outcome failure) enhances the effect via perceived intelligence
Zhai and Wibowo (2022)	Cross-cultural, empathetic and humorous dimensions of chatbots positively impact learning outcomes. Chatbots with cross-cultural awareness reduce anxiety; empathetic features support emotional needs; humorous responses boost engagement
Smakman et al. (2022)	Most primary school students trust social robots in first interactions, regardless of tested features (intonation, voice gender, humor). Adding humor to robots' dialogue negatively impacts trust, especially for girls and children without prior robot experience. Both robot interaction and classical music reduce children's stress (though not significantly), with similar effectiveness
Xie, Liang, Zhou, Zhu, et al. (2024)	Chatbot-expressed humor (comic wit) significantly boosts online customer service satisfaction. This effect is mediated by perceived competence, entertainment, and social presence. Chatbot identity disclosure negatively moderates the links between humor and both service satisfaction and competence
Ushijima et al. (2024)	A machine learning-based humor effectiveness predictor (considering situation and discomfort) helps select optimal humorous phrases for security robots to stop line-cutting. Humorous phrases selected by this system are more effective at discouraging line-cutting than typical non-humorous phrases in video experiments

(*continued*)

Table 2.4 (continued)

Sources	Main findings
Zhang et al. (2021)	Humanlike robot appearance increases performance expectancy, mascot-like appearance boosts positive emotions, and machine-like appearance raises effort expectancy. Sense of humor moderates acceptance for humanlike and mascot-like robots but not for machine-like robots
Liu and Xu (2023)	In hedonic-dominant service contexts, both self-deprecating and self-enhancing humor increase AI continuous usage intention; in utilitarian-dominant contexts, only self-deprecating humor works. Positive emotion and inferred negative motives mediate this effect, and higher AI anthropomorphism strengthens the interaction between humor type and service context
Shan et al. (2024)	Service robots with warm social perception using humorous responses in service recovery led to better service evaluations; those with competent social perception using rational responses perform better. Perceived relief mediates the effect of warm and humor robots, while perceived sincerity mediates competent robots rationality. Locus of responsibility moderates the humor works for all robots when customers cause failures
Niculescu et al. (2013)	Higher voice pitch of social robot receptionists significantly improves overall interaction quality, robot appeal, and user enjoyment. Humor enhances users' perception of task enjoyment, robot personality, and speaking style. Empathy improves evaluation of robot's receptive behavior and interaction ease
Yang et al. (2022)	In low-severity robot failure, humorous responses increase humor appreciation and positive customer evaluations. In high-severity failure, humorous responses raise perceived insincerity and negative evaluations. High robot anthropomorphism strengthens the interaction between humor and failure severity on customer evaluations
Tay et al. (2016)	Participants perceive non-disparaging jokes as more humorous when performed by human actors than robot actors. For disparaging jokes, participants show less disgusted facial expressions when the jokes are performed by robots than humans, though subjective ratings of humor and offense do not differ by actor type. Additionally, higher perceived humor of robot-performed jokes correlates with greater perceived social presence of the robot, and male participants rate the jokes as more humorous than female participants
Xie et al. (2025)	AI agents expressing humor enhance customer forgiveness in service failures, with self-defeating humor being most effective. Both humor types boost customers' positive emotion and relief. The positive effect of AI humor persists in low severity failures but disappears in medium and high severity failures. Customer forgiveness also increases service satisfaction and reduces negative word-of-mouth

(*continued*)

Table 2.4 (continued)

Sources	Main findings
Xu and Liu (2022)	AI agents' humorous responses positively improve customer tolerance of service failures. Perceived warmth and perceived competence mediate this effect. Customer inoculation strengthens the positive impact of humor on warmth, competence, and tolerance; high time pressure reverses humor's positive effect, while low time pressure enhances it
Xie et al. (2023)	For smart home assistants, emotional cues (humor) and auditory cues directly boost interaction satisfaction and further improve it via enhancing intimacy. Visual cues improve satisfaction only through intimacy
Schanke et al. (2021)	Adding anthropomorphic features (social presence, communication delays, humor) to customer service chatbots increases transaction conversion. Receiving all three features makes customers more offer-sensitive. The conversion benefit partly comes from customers' greater willingness to disclose personal information needed for transactions

References

Agnihotri, A., Bhattacharya, S., Yannopoulou, N., & Liu, M. J. (2022). Examining social media engagement through health-related message framing in different cultures. *Journal of Business Research*, *152*, 349–360.

Araujo, T. (2018). Living up to the chatbot hype: The influence of anthropomorphic design cues and communicative agency framing on conversational agent and company perceptions. *Computers in Human Behavior*, *85*, 183–189.

Baek, T. H., & Morimoto, M. (2012). Stay away from me. *Journal of Advertising*, *41*(1), 59–76.

Bell, C. A., & Fincham, F. D. (2017). Humility, forgiveness, and emerging adult female romantic relationships. *Journal of Marital and Family Therapy*, *45*(1), 149–160.

Bhattacharya, O., Chatterjee, A., & Basu, J. (2017). Humility: An emerging construct in moral psychology. *Psychological Studies*, *62*(1), 1–11.

Bickmore, T., & Cassell, J. (2001). *Relational agents: A model and implementation of building user trust*. Proceedings of the SIGCHI conference on human factors in computing systems.

Bollinger, R. A. (2017). Reflections on and future directions in humility and forgiveness research. *Research in Human Development*, *15*(1), 88–93.

Bower, A. H., & Steyvers, M. (2021). Perceptions of AI engaging in human expression. *Scientific Reports*, *11*(1), 21181.

Brender-Ilan, Y., & Reizer, A. (2021). How do we perceive a humorous manager? Manager humor, impression management, and employee willingness to work with the manager. *Frontiers in Psychology*, *12*, 628350.

Burr, C., & Leslie, D. (2023). Ethical assurance: A practical approach to the responsible design, development, and deployment of data-driven technologies. *AI and Ethics*, *3*(1), 73–98.

Campbell, K. L., Martin, M. M., & Wanzer, M. B. (2001). Employee perceptions of manager humor orientation, assertiveness, responsiveness, approach/avoidance strategies, and satisfaction. *Communication Research Reports*, *18*(1), 67–74.

Cann, A., & Calhoun, L. G. (2001). Perceived personality associations with differences in sense of humor: Stereotypes of hypothetical others with high or low senses of humor. *Humor*, *14*(2), 117–130.

Cann, A., & Matson, C. (2014). Sense of humor and social desirability: Understanding how humor styles are perceived. *Personality and Individual Differences, 66*, 176–180.
Cao, Y., Cao, J., Hou, Y., & Ji, L. J. (2025). How humorous is AI? Exploring ChatGPT's role in humor generation and human-AI interaction. *Computers in Human Behavior Reports, 20*, 100807.
Castelo, N., Bos, M. W., & Lehmann, D. R. (2019). Task-dependent algorithm aversion. *Journal of Marketing Research, 56*(5), 809–825.
Chancellor, J., & Lyubomirsky, S. (2013). Humble beginnings: Current trends, state perspectives, and hallmarks of humility. *Social and Personality Psychology Compass, 7*(11), 819–833.
Chang, W., & Park, J. (2024). A comparative study on the effect of ChatGPT recommendation and AI recommender systems on the formation of a consideration set. *Journal of Retailing and Consumer Services, 78*, 103743.
Chang, Y. T., Yu, H., & Lu, H. P. (2015). Persuasive messages, popularity cohesion, and message diffusion in social media marketing. *Journal of Business Research, 68*(4), 777–782.
Chattaraman, V., Kwon, W. S., Gilbert, J. E., & Ross, K. (2019). Should AI-Based, conversational digital assistants employ social-or task-oriented interaction style? A task-competency and reciprocity perspective for older adults. *Computers in Human Behavior, 90*, 315–330.
Chen, J. V., Thi Le, H., & Tran, S. T. T. (2021). Understanding automated conversational agent as a decision aid: Matching agent's conversation with customer's shopping task. *Internet Research, 31*(4), 1376–1404.
Chen, S., Li, X., Liu, K., & Wang, X. (2023). Chatbot or human? The impact of online customer service on consumers' purchase intentions. *Psychology and Marketing, 40*(11), 2186–2200.
Chi, O. H., Jia, S., Li, Y., & Gursoy, D. (2021). Developing a formative scale to measure consumers' trust toward interaction with artificially intelligent (AI) social robots in service delivery. *Computers in Human Behavior, 118*, 106700.
Choi, S., Mattila, A. S., & Bolton, L. E. (2020). To err is human(-oid): How do consumers react to robot service failure and recovery? *Journal of Service Research, 24*(3), 354–371.
Christ, L., Amiriparian, S., Kathan, A., Müller, N., König, A., & Schuller, B. W. (2025). Towards multimodal prediction of spontaneous humor: A novel dataset and first results. *IEEE Transactions on Affective Computing, 16*(2), 844–860.
Cooper, C. D., Kong, D. T., & Crossley, C. D. (2018). Leader humor as an interpersonal resource: Integrating three theoretical perspectives. *Academy of Management Journal, 61*(2), 769–796.
Crosby, L. A., Evans, K. R., & Cowles, D. (1990). Relationship quality in services selling: An interpersonal influence perspective. *Journal of Marketing, 54*(3), 68–81.
Davis, D. E., Worthington Jr, E. L., & Hook, J. N. (2010). Humility: Review of measurement strategies and conceptualization as personality judgment. *The Journal of Positive Psychology, 5*(4), 243–252.
De Cicco, R., Silva, S. C., & Alparone, F. R. (2020). Millennials' attitude toward chatbots: An experimental study in a social relationship perspective. *International Journal of Retail and Distribution Management, 48*(11), 1213–1233.
Dehnert, M., & Mongeau, P. A. (2022). Persuasion in the age of artificial intelligence (AI): Theories and complications of AI-based persuasion. *Human Communication Research, 48*(3), 386–403.
Dhiman, N., Jamwal, M., & Kumar, A. (2023). Enhancing value in customer journey by considering the (ad)option of artificial intelligence tools. *Journal of Business Research, 167*, 114142.
Dwivedi, Y. K., & Kshetri, N. (2023). Opinion paper: "So what if ChatGPT wrote it?" Multidisciplinary perspectives on opportunities, challenges and implications of generative conversational AI for research, practice and policy. *International Journal of Information Management, 71*, 102642.
Ebrahimi, S., Ghasemaghaei, M., & Benbasat, I. (2022). The impact of trust and recommendation quality on adopting interactive and non-interactive recommendation agents: A meta-analysis. *Journal of Management Information Systems, 39*(3), 733–764.

Evans, J. B., Slaughter, J. E., Ellis, A. P. J., & Rivin, J. M. (2019). Gender and the evaluation of humor at work. *Journal of Applied Psychology, 104*(8), 1077–1087.

Feine, J., Gnewuch, U., Morana, S., & Maedche, A. (2019). A taxonomy of social cues for conversational agents. *International Journal of Human-computer Studies, 132*, 138–161.

Fiske, S. T., Cuddy, A. J., Glick, P., & Xu, J. (2002). A model of (often mixed) stereotype content: Competence and warmth respectively follow from perceived status and competition. *Journal of Personality and Social Psychology, 82*(6), 878–902.

Fiske, S. T., Cuddy, A. J. C., & Glick, P. (2007). Universal dimensions of social cognition: Warmth and competence. *Trends in Cognitive Sciences, 11*(2), 77–83.

Folkes, V. S. (1984). Consumer reactions to product failure: An attributional approach. *Journal of Consumer Research, 10*(4), 398–409.

Frank, A., Cacciatore, M., Yeo, S., & Su, L. (2025). Wit meets wisdom: The relationship between satire and anthropomorphic humor on scientists' likability and legitimacy. *Journal of Science Communication, 24*(1). Article 0204.

Ghanem, Y. K., Rouhi, A. D., Al-Houssan, A., Saleh, Z., Moccia, M. C., Joshi, H., Dumon, K. R., Hong, Y., Spitz, F., Joshi, A. R., & Kwiatt, M. (2024). Dr. Google to Dr. ChatGPT: Assessing the content and quality of artificial intelligence-generated medical information on appendicitis. *Surgical Endoscopy, 38*(5), 2887–2893.

Go, E., & Sundar, S. S. (2019). Humanizing chatbots: The effects of visual, identity and conversational cues on humanness perceptions. *Computers in Human Behavior, 97*, 304–316.

Grenci, R. T., & Todd, P. A. (2002). Solutions-driven marketing. *Communications of the Association for Computing Machinery, 45*(3), 64–71.

Gretry, A., Horváth, C., Belei, N., & van Riel, A. C. (2017). "Don't pretend to be my friend!" When an informal brand communication style backfires on social media. *Journal of Business Research, 74*, 77–89.

Gronroos, C. (1988). Service quality: The six criteria of good perceived service. *Review of Business, 9*(3), 10.

Heider, F. (2013). *The Psychology of Interpersonal Relations*. Psychology Press.

Holmqvist, J., Van Vaerenbergh, Y., & Grönroos, C. (2017). Language use in services: Recent advances and directions for future research. *Journal of Business Research, 72*, 114–118.

Honig, S., & Oron-Gilad, T. (2018). Understanding and resolving failures in human-robot interaction: Literature review and model development. *Frontiers in Psychology, 9*, 861.

Hussain, K., Khan, M. L., & Malik, A. (2024). Exploring audience engagement with ChatGPT-related content on YouTube: Implications for content creators and AI tool developers. *Digital Business, 4*(1), 100071.

Jakic, A., Wagner, M. O., & Meyer, A. (2017). The impact of language style accommodation during social media interactions on brand trust. *Journal of Service Management, 28*(3), 418–441.

Jeon, Y. A. (2022). Let me transfer you to our AI-based manager: Impact of manager-level job titles assigned to AI-based agents on marketing outcomes. *Journal of Business Research, 145*, 892–904.

Ji, J. J. (2024). Demystify ChatGPT: Anthropomorphism around generative AI. *GRACE: Global Review of AI Community Ethics, 2*(1), 1–11.

Jin, F., & Zhang, X. (2025). Artificial intelligence or human: When and why consumers prefer AI recommendations. *Information Technology and People, 38*(1), 279–303.

Johanson, D., Ahn, H., Lim, J., Lee, C., Sebaratnam, G., Macdonald, B., & Broadbent, E. (2020). Use of humor by a healthcare robot positively affects user perceptions and behavior. *Technology, Mind, and Behavior, 1*(2).

Kelleher, T. (2009). Conversational voice, communicated commitment, and public relations outcomes in interactive online communication. *Journal of Communication, 59*(1), 172–188.

Kim, H. W., & Kankanhalli, A. (2009). Investigating user resistance to information systems implementation: A status quo bias perspective. *MIS Quarterly: Management Information Systems*, 567–582.

Kim, T. W., & Duhachek, A. (2020). Artificial intelligence and persuasion: A construal-level account. *Psychological Science, 31*(4), 363–380.
Kim, Y. H., Kim, D. J., & Wachter, K. (2013). A study of mobile user engagement (MoEN): Engagement motivations, perceived value, satisfaction, and continued engagement intention. *Decision Support Systems, 56*, 361–370.
Kobel, S., & Groeppel-Klein, A. (2021). No laughing matter, or a secret weapon? Exploring the effect of humor in service failure situations. *Journal of Business Research, 132*, 260–269.
Kronrod, A., Grinstein, A., & Wathieu, L. (2012). Enjoy! Hedonic consumption and compliance with assertive messages. *Journal of Consumer Research, 39*(1), 51–61.
Kshetri, N., Dwivedi, Y. K., Davenport, T. H., & Panteli, N. (2024). Generative artificial intelligence in marketing: Applications, opportunities, challenges, and research agenda. *International Journal of Information Management, 75*, 102716.
Kull, A. J., Romero, M., & Monahan, L. (2021). How may I help you? Driving brand engagement through the warmth of an initial chatbot message. *Journal of Business Research, 135*, 840–850.
Kuo, Y. F., & Wu, C. M. (2012). Satisfaction and post-purchase intentions with service recovery of online shopping websites: Perspectives on perceived justice and emotions. *International Journal of Information Management, 32*(2), 127–138.
Lee, S., Lee, N., & Sah, Y. J. (2020). Perceiving a mind in a chatbot: Effect of mind perception and social cues on co-presence, closeness, and intention to use. *International Journal of Human-Computer Interaction, 36*(10), 930–940.
Lehmann-Willenbrock, N., & Allen, J. A. (2014). How fun are your meetings? Investigating the relationship between humor patterns in team interactions and team performance. *Journal of Applied Psychology, 99*(6), 1278–1287.
Li, J. (2016). Humility in learning: A Confucian perspective. *Journal of Moral Education, 45*(2), 147–165.
Li, M., & Wang, R. (2023). Chatbots in e-commerce: The effect of chatbot language style on customers' continuance usage intention and attitude toward brand. *Journal of Retailing and Consumer Services, 71*, 103209.
Li, X., & Sung, Y. (2021). Anthropomorphism brings us closer: The mediating role of psychological distance in User–AI assistant interactions. *Computers in Human Behavior, 118*, 106680.
Linge, L. (2009). The function of humor in relation to affects: A longitudinal case study. *International Journal of Qualitative Studies on Health and Well-being, 1*(3), 167–177.
Liu, D., Lv, Y., & Huang, W. (2023). How do consumers react to chatbots' humorous emojis in service failures. *Technology in Society, 73*, 102244.
Liu, J., Hsu, F. C., Yu, J., Cao, J., & Mai, H. (2025). When humble AI meets narcissistic customers: A terror management perspective. *International Journal of Information Management, 83*, 102904.
Liu, J., & Xu, X. A. (2023). Humor type and service context shape AI service recovery. *Annals of Tourism Research, 103*, 103668.
Longoni, C., & Cian, L. (2022). Artificial intelligence in utilitarian vs. hedonic contexts: The "word-of-machine" effect. *Journal of Marketing, 86*(1), 91–108.
Luo, X., Tong, S., Fang, Z., & Qu, Z. (2019). Frontiers: Machines vs. humans: The impact of artificial intelligence chatbot disclosure on customer purchases. *Marketing Science, 38*(6), 937–947.
Mariani, M., & Dwivedi, Y. K. (2024). Generative artificial intelligence in innovation management: A preview of future research developments. *Journal of Business Research, 175*, 114542.
Martin, R. A., & Ford, T. (2006). The psychology of humor. In *Burlington* (pp. 2). *Elsevier*.
Martin, R. A., Puhlik-Doris, P., Larsen, G., Gray, J., & Weir, K. (2003). Individual differences in uses of humor and their relation to psychological well-being: Development of the humor styles questionnaire. *Journal of Research in Personality, 37*(1), 48–75.

McArthur, T., Lam-mcarthur, J., & Fontaine, L. (2018). *Oxford companion to the english language*. Oxford University Press.

McQuail, D. (1987). *Mass communication theory: An introduction*. Sage Publications, Inc.

Mou, Y., & Xu, K. (2017). The media inequality: Comparing the initial human-human and human-AI social interactions. *Computers in Human Behavior*, *72*, 432–440.

Niculescu, A., van Dijk, B., Nijholt, A., Li, H., & See, S. L. (2013). Making social robots more attractive: The effects of voice pitch, humor and empathy. *International Journal of Social Robotics*, *5*(2), 171–191.

O'Brien, H. L., & Toms, E. G. (2014). The development and evaluation of a survey to measure user engagement. *Journal of the Association for Information Science and Technology*, *61*(1), 50–69.

Olafsson, S., O'Leary, T. K., & Bickmore, T. W. (2020). *Motivating health behavior change with humorous virtual agents*. Proceedings of the 20th ACM International Conference on Intelligent Virtual Agents.

Oliver, R. L. (1980). A cognitive model of the antecedents and consequences of satisfaction decisions. *Journal of Marketing Research*, *17*(4), 460–469.

Owens, B. P., Johnson, M. D., & Mitchell, T. R. (2013). Expressed humility in organizations: Implications for performance, teams, and leadership. *Organization Science*, *24*(5), 1517–1538.

Palmer, A., Beggs, R., & Keown-mcmullan, C. (2000). Equity and repurchase intention following service failure. *Journal of Services Marketing*, *14*(6), 513–528.

Pennington, N., & Hall, J. A. (2014). An analysis of humor orientation on Facebook: A lens model approach. *Humor*, *27*(1), 1–21.

Prebensen, N. K., & Rosengren, S. (2016). Experience value as a function of hedonic and utilitarian dominant services. *International Journal of Contemporary Hospitality Management*, *28*(1), 113–135.

Rhee, C. E., & Choi, J. (2020). Effects of personalization and social role in voice shopping: An experimental study on product recommendation by a conversational voice agent. *Computers in Human Behavior*, *109*, 106359.

Riemer, K., & Peter, S. (2024). Conceptualizing generative AI as style engines: Application archetypes and implications. *International Journal of Information Management*, *79*, 102824.

Roy, R., & Naidoo, V. (2021). Enhancing chatbot effectiveness: The role of anthropomorphic conversational styles and time orientation. *Journal of Business Research*, *126*, 23–34.

Ruan, Y., & Mezei, J. (2022). When do AI chatbots lead to higher customer satisfaction than human frontline employees in online shopping assistance? Considering product attribute type. *Journal of Retailing and Consumer Services*, *68*.

Santos, Z. R., Cheung, C. M. K., Coelho, P. S., & Rita, P. (2022). Consumer engagement in social media brand communities: A literature review. *International Journal of Information Management*, *63*, 102457.

Sapmaz, F., Yıldırım, M., Topcuoğlu, P., Nalbant, D., & Sızır, U. (2016). Gratitude, forgiveness and humility as predictors of subjective well-being among university students. *International Online Journal of Educational Sciences*, *8*(1), 38–47.

Schanke, S., Burtch, G., & Ray, G. (2021). Estimating the impact of "Humanizing" customer service chatbots. *Information Systems Research*, *32*(3), 736–751.

Schuetzler, R. M., Grimes, G. M., & Scott Giboney, J. (2020). The impact of chatbot conversational skill on engagement and perceived humanness. *Journal of Management Information Systems*, *37*(3), 875–900.

Segijn, C. M., Voorveld, H. A., & Vakeel, K. A. (2021). The role of ad sequence and privacy concerns in personalized advertising: An eye-tracking study into synced advertising effects. *Journal of Advertising*, *50*(3), 320–329.

Sela, A., Wheeler, S. C., & Sarial-Abi, G. (2012). We are not the same as you and I: Causal effects of minor language variations on consumers' attitudes toward brands. *Journal of Consumer Research*, *39*(3), 644–661.

Senecal, S., & Nantel, J. (2004). The influence of online product recommendations on consumers' online choices. *Journal of Retailing*, *80*(2), 159–169.

Shan, M., Zhu, Z., Chen, H., & Sun, S. (2024). Service robot's responses in service recovery and service evaluation: The moderating role of robots' social perception. *Journal of Hospitality Marketing and Management*, *33*(2), 145–168.

Shin, H., Bunosso, I., & Levine, L. R. (2022). The influence of chatbot humour on consumer evaluations of services. *International Journal of Consumer Studies*, *47*(2), 545–562.

Smakman, M. H. J., Vanegas, D. F. P., Smit, K., Leewis, S., Okkerse, Y., Obbes, J., Uffing, T., Soliman, M., van der Krogt, T., & Tönjes, L. (2022). A trustworthy robot buddy for primary school children. *Multimodal Technologies and Interaction*, *6*(4), 29.

Sörensen, I., Vogler, D., Fürst, S., & Schäfer, M. S. (2023). Platforms matter: Analyzing user engagement with social media content of Swiss higher education institutions. *Journal of Marketing for Higher Education*, 1–20.

Tay, B. T. C., Low, S. C., Ko, K. H., & Park, T. (2016). Types of humor that robots can play. *Computers in Human Behavior*, *60*, 19–28.

Thomas, P., Czerwinski, M., McDuff, D., Craswell, N., & Mark, G. (2018). *Style and alignment in information-seeking conversation*. Proceedings of the 2018 Conference on Human Information Interaction & Retrieval.

Thorson, J. A., & Powell, F. C. (1993a). Development and validation of a multidimensional sense of humor scale. *Journal of Clinical Psychology*, *49*(1), 13–23.

Thorson, J. A., & Powell, F. C. (1993b). Relationships of death anxiety and sense of humor. *Psychological Reports*, *72*(3), 1364–1366.

Um, C. T., Guo, S. L., Lumineau, F., Shi, W., & Song, R. (2022). The downside of CFO function-based language incongruity. *Academy of Management Journal*, *65*(6), 1984–2013.

Ushijima, Y., Satake, S., & Kanda, T. (2024). Predicting humor effectiveness of robots for human line cutting. *Frontiers in Robotics and AI*, *11*, 1407095.

Verhagen, T., Van Nes, J., Feldberg, F., & Van Dolen, W. (2014). Virtual customer service agents: Using social presence and personalization to shape online service encounters. *Journal of Computer-Mediated Communication*, *19*(3), 529–545.

Von der Pütten, A. M., Krämer, N. C., Gratch, J., & Kang, S. H. (2010). "It doesn't matter what you are!" Explaining social effects of agents and avatars. *Computers in Human Behavior*, *26*(6), 1641–1650.

Wang, S., Yan, Q., & Wang, L. (2025). Task-oriented vs. social-oriented: Chatbot communication styles in electronic commerce service recovery. *Electronic Commerce Research*, *25*(3), 1793–1825.

Warren, C., Barsky, A., McGraw, A. P., Morwitz, V., & MacInnis, D. (2018). Humor, comedy, and consumer behavior. *Journal of Consumer Research*, *45*(3), 529–552.

Waytz, A., Heafner, J., & Epley, N. (2014). The mind in the machine: Anthropomorphism increases trust in an autonomous vehicle. *Journal of Experimental Social Psychology*, *52*, 113–117.

Wien, A. H., & Peluso, A. M. (2021). Influence of human versus AI recommenders: The roles of product type and cognitive processes. *Journal of Business Research*, *137*, 13–27.

Wimbush, A. (2014). Humility, self-awareness, and religious ambivalence: Another look at beckett's 'Humanistic Quietism'. *Journal of Beckett Studies*, *23*(2), 202–221.

Wu, L., Shen, H., Fan, A., & Mattila, A. S. (2017). The impact of language style on consumers' reactions to online reviews. *Tourism Management*, *59*, 590–596.

Xiao, B., & Benbasat, I. (2007). E-commerce product recommendation agents: Use, characteristics, and impact. *MIS Quarterly: Management Information Systems*, 137–209.

Xie, Y., Liang, C., Zhou, P., & Jiang, L. (2024). Exploring the influence mechanism of chatbot-expressed humor on service satisfaction in online customer service. *Journal of Retailing and Consumer Services*, *76*, 103599.

Xie, Y., Liang, C., Zhou, P., & Zhu, J. (2024). When should chatbots express humor? Exploring different influence mechanisms of humor on service satisfaction. *Computers in Human Behavior*, *156*, 108238.

Xie, Y., Zhou, P., Liang, C., Zhao, S., & Lu, W. (2025). Affiliative or self-defeating? Exploring the effect of humor types on customer forgiveness in the context of AI agents' service failure. *Journal of Business Research, 194*, 115381.

Xie, Y., Zhu, K., Zhou, P., & Liang, C. (2023). How does anthropomorphism improve human-AI interaction satisfaction: A dual-path model. *Computers in Human Behavior, 148*, 107878.

Xing, X., Song, M., Duan, Y., & Mou, J. (2022). Effects of different service failure types and recovery strategies on the consumer response mechanism of chatbots. *Technology in Society, 70*.

Xu, C., Zheng, X., & Yang, F. (2023). Examining the effects of negative emotions on review helpfulness: The moderating role of product price. *Computers in Human Behavior, 139*, 107501.

Xu, X. A., & Liu, J. (2022). Artificial intelligence humor in service recovery. *Annals of Tourism Research, 95*, 103439.

Xu, Y., Zhang, J., Chi, R., & Deng, G. (2023). Enhancing customer satisfaction with chatbots: The influence of anthropomorphic communication styles and anthropomorphized roles. *Nankai Business Review International, 14*(2), 249–271.

Xu, Y., Zhang, J., & Deng, G. (2022). Enhancing customer satisfaction with chatbots: The influence of communication styles and consumer attachment anxiety. *Frontiers in Psychology, 13*, 902782.

Yam, K. C., Christian, M. S., Wei, W., Liao, Z., & Nai, J. (2018). The mixed blessing of leader sense of humor: Examining costs and benefits. *Academy of Management Journal, 61*(1), 348–369.

Yang, B., Sun, Y., & Shen, X. L. (2023). Understanding AI-based customer service resistance: A perspective of defective AI features and tri-dimensional distrusting beliefs. *Information Processing and Management, 60*(3), 103257.

Yang, H., Xu, H., Zhang, Y., Liang, Y., & Lyu, T. (2022). Exploring the effect of humor in robot failure. *Annals of Tourism Research, 95*, 103425.

Yang, Y. K., Zheng, J. H., Yu, Y. N., Qiu, Y. L., & Wang, L. (2024). The role of recommendation sources and attribute framing in online product recommendations. *Journal of Business Research, 174*, 114498.

Yang, Z., Zhou, J., & Yang, H. (2023). The impact of AI's response method on service recovery satisfaction in the context of service failure. *Sustainability, 15*(4), 3294.

Yeomans, M., Shah, A., Mullainathan, S., & Kleinberg, J. (2019). Making sense of recommendations. *Journal of Behavioral Decision Making, 32*(4), 403–414.

Zabel, S., Pensini, P., & Otto, S. (2025). Unveiling the role of honesty-humility in shaping attitudes towards artificial intelligence. *Personality and Individual Differences, 238*, 113072.

Zhai, C., & Wibowo, S. (2022). A systematic review on cross-culture, humor and empathy dimensions in conversational chatbots: The case of second language acquisition. *Heliyon, 8*(12).

Zhang, J., Jain, L., Guo, Y., Chen, J., Zhou, K., Suresh, S., Wagenmaker, A., Sievert, S., Rogers, T. T., & Jamieson, K. G. (2025). Humor in AI: Massive scale crowd-sourced preferences and benchmarks for cartoon captioning. *Advances in Neural Information Processing Systems, 37*, 125264–125286.

Zhang, J., Zhu, Y., Wu, J., & Yu-Buck, G. F. (2023). A natural apology is sincere: Understanding chatbots' performance in symbolic recovery. *International Journal of Hospitality Management, 108*, 103387.

Zhang, M., Gursoy, D., Zhu, Z., & Shi, S. (2021). Impact of anthropomorphic features of artificially intelligent service robots on consumer acceptance: Moderating role of sense of humor. *International Journal of Contemporary Hospitality Management, 33*(11), 3883–3905.

Zhu, Y., Zhang, J., Wu, J., & Liu, Y. (2022). AI is better when I'm sure: The influence of certainty of needs on consumers' acceptance of AI chatbots. *Journal of Business Research, 150*, 642–652.

Research Model and Hypothesis Development

3

This chapter presents the research model and hypothesis development for examining user-AI interactions in online shopping and social media contexts. Drawing on theories such as the stereotype content model, social response theory, and attribution theory, the researcher proposes hypotheses on the effects of recommendation types (AI versus human), AI communication styles (task-oriented versus social-oriented), AI humility traits (low versus high humility), and GAI humor (low versus high humor) on customer intention and behaviors. The following sections will detail the theoretical foundations, hypotheses, and the integrated research framework.

3.1 AI vs. Human Recommendation

To visually illustrate the relationships between the core variables and the proposed theoretical logic of this study regarding recommendation type, the theoretical model is presented in Fig. 3.1. The model shows the effects of recommendation type (AI vs. human recommendation) on purchase intention, the mediating effects of perceived warmth and the moderating effects of product attitude.

3.1.1 Recommendation Type and Purchase Intention

AI recommendation is a personalized information system driven by algorithms, which processes user data to provide tailored suggestions aimed at aiding individual decision-making (Grenci & Todd, 2002). Therefore, AI recommendation has a remarkable advantage in processing efficiency, data driven precision and automation scalability for complex repetitive tasks (Baek & Morimoto, 2012; Kumar et al., 2024; Piao et al., 2023). Human recommendation refers to recommenders from experts who give tips from their experiences and emotions by suggesting

F. Yang, *AI and Consumer Interaction in Business*, Management for Professionals,
https://doi.org/10.1007/978-981-95-9430-6_3

certain products to others (Senecal & Nantel, 2004; Wien & Peluso, 2021). Human recommendation appears to be more empathic and context sensitive in interpersonal interactions and helps build emotional trust and social interactions, which improve user attitudes and purchase decision making (Longoni & Cian, 2022; Yeomans et al., 2019). Although human recommendation is less scalable, humans can provide warmer and context sensitive advices in ambiguous decision-making contexts or emotionally charged situations. Therefore, human recommendation still has irreplaceable advantages in trust establishment and authenticity interaction (Jin & Zhang, 2025; Yang et al., 2024).

Previous studies on recommendation type (AI vs. human) have examined their impacts in various contexts and product types. As for contextual factors, research findings suggest consumers' differential preferences for AI or human recommenders in terms of situational characteristics. In embarrassing service encounters, consumers prefer AI recommenders (e.g., robots) over humans due to reduced social judgment (Holthöwer & Van Doorn, 2023). In contrast, when ethical issues are attached to recommendations, AI recommendations decrease perceived warmth and competence, and weaken purchase intentions (Yang et al., 2024). Prior researches also focus on the attribute framing of products. For utilitarian or search products, consumers prefer AI over human recommenders because the former highlight product functionality (Jin & Zhang, 2025; Longoni & Cian, 2022). In contrast, for hedonic or experiential products, human recommenders perform better by highlighting the emotional connection and warmth (Cheng et al., 2022; Wien & Peluso, 2021). Interestingly, if anthropomorphism can be applied to recommend products, that is, recommend by human-like AI agents (e.g., warmth, managerial titles), the consumers will be more likely to trust and be persuaded (Ahn et al., 2021; Jeon, 2022).

This study extends the prior literature by examining the differential responses to different types of recommendations. Despite the advantages of AI recommendation systems, which can provide highly efficient and accurate product recommendations

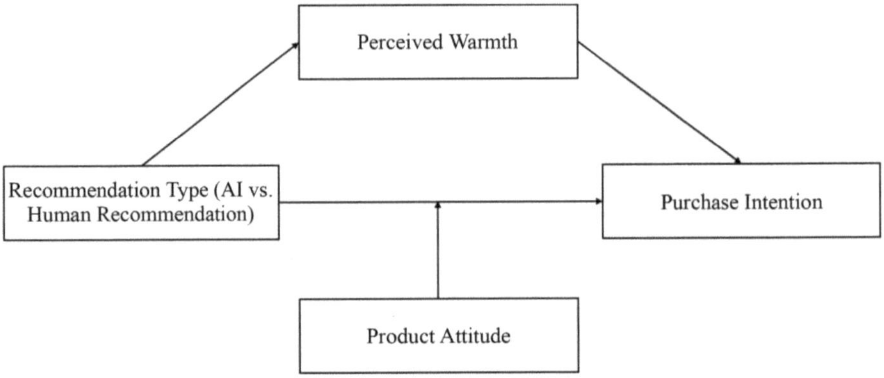

Fig. 3.1 Theoretical model of the effects of recommendation type on purchase intention

based on massive data processing and algorithm optimization, consumers do not necessarily accept such suggestions in an approving way (Kim & Duhachek, 2020; Sun et al., 2025). In addition, many consumers doubt whether the AI can comprehend the emotions of human beings or even their deeper psychological needs. They think that the AI lacks true learning and cannot be empathic enough, which makes it impossible for consumers to establish emotional connections or trust the recommender (Jin & Zhang, 2025; Sun et al., 2025; Trzebiński & Marciniak, 2022).

Conversely, human recommendations are based on the recommender's social identity, personality characteristics, and relational similarity to the recipient, which results in higher levels of communication and interpersonal warmth (Adamopoulos & Todri, 2024; Ahn et al., 2022; Peng et al., 2022). In close face-to-face or socially embedded interactions, humans can transmit emotional signals to the recipient through their language, tone, and facial expressions, which enable the recommender to resonate emotionally with the recipient and to have a deeper understanding of others' needs, leading to more positive evaluations of the recommender and greater receptivity to the recommendation (Concannon et al., 2023; Markovitch et al., 2024). Furthermore, as humans usually have firsthand experience with the product, they are more likely to provide personal usage experiences, product evaluations, and emotional interactions with the brand (Duprez et al., 2015). These firsthand experiences and stories make the information source more credible. In summary, when the recommender is a human, consumers tend to present positive evaluations and purchase intentions (Liang et al., 2024; Shen, 2014).

To summarize, this hypothesis is grounded in several interrelated psychological and sociological mechanisms that elevate the perceived value of human recommendation. Fundamentally, human recommendations carry an inherent weight of social proof and shared experience. That is, consumers trust that a human advisor has drawn upon a nuanced understanding of context, taste, and unspoken needs—elements they believe AI, as a statistical model, cannot genuinely comprehend. This trust is reinforced by attribution bias, where a human suggestion is perceived as originating from intentionality, empathy, and perhaps even altruism, whereas an AI's suggestion is attributed to impersonal data processing and commercial algorithms, raising skepticism about its true objectivity. Furthermore, the emotional and relational component is critical. Specifically, a recommendation from a person, even a stranger in a review, creates a para-social connection and a sense of validation that an AI cannot replicate. In contexts involving high-involvement, experiential, or identity-expressive products (e.g., fashion, luxury goods, complex services), the desire for curation and symbolic meaning makes human judgment appear more discerning and authentic. Consequently, the perceived lower risk and higher credibility associated with human-recommended choices lead to a stronger consumer commitment to act, manifesting as higher purchase intention compared to AI-generated alternatives. Thus, the following hypothesis is proposed:

Hypothesis 1 In comparison with AI recommendations, consumers' purchase intention is higher with human recommendations

3.1.2 The Mediating Role of Perceived Warmth

Social cognition theory was originally developed by Fiske et al. (2002) to account for people's evaluations of social groups, has recently been applied to people's evaluations of individuals, as well as to evaluations of organizations (Davvetas & Halkias, 2019; El Hedhli et al., 2023; Halkias & Diamantopoulos, 2020). According to the social cognition theory, social cognition is organized around only two dimensions, that is, warmth and competence, which are believed to have evolved to assist human navigation in social worlds (Fiske, 2018; Fiske et al., 2002; Oldmeadow, 2018). In general, the dimension of warmth includes attributes such as kindness, friendliness, trustworthiness, and also helpfulness, reflecting the intendedness of others. In contrast, competence reflects people's judgments about others' ability, including how intelligent, effective, skillful, and powerful others are (Fiske, 2018; Halkias & Diamantopoulos, 2020; Kervyn et al., 2013). In total, these two dimensions account for an almost complete inventory of how people form impressions about others (Halkias & Diamantopoulos, 2020; Swencionis et al., 2017).

As scholars start to study the emotional interaction with new artificial entities (Chen et al., 2022; Wang et al., 2016), increasing attention has been paid to the evaluation of AI agents, chatbots, and service robots based on the dimension of warmth. For instance, Ahn et al. (2022) examined the stereotypes in AI built on genders, and found that females are evaluated as higher in warmth in comparison with males, whereas males are perceived as more competent than females. And Lee and Li (2023) demonstrate that specific attributes of chatbot interface affordances (e.g., visibility, interactivity) can influence users' perceptions of brand warmth, which further leads to customer-brand identification and loyalty. Similarly, Li et al. (2023) discover that both perceived warmth and competence in friendship-oriented chatbots contribute to users' continued usage intention and usage and this effect is particularly strong for users with a high need to belong. When service failure occurs in a customer service recovery context, social-oriented chatbot communication styles greatly enhance perceptions of warmth, which in turn positively affect trust and satisfaction evaluations of the service system (Cai et al., 2024). Besides, Roy and Naidoo (2025) focus on warmth perceptions and show that materialistic consumers prefer a warm over a competent chatbot for emotionally expressive services. However, few studies have directly compared the differences in the perceptions of warmth between AI and human agents in a consumption context.

In contrast to AI recommenders, humans are more likely to be perceived as warm because they can convey expressive features, personalized communication, and social presence (Haas et al., 2015; Ringwald & Wright, 2021). Such socio-emotional attributes are hard for AI to match because consumers perceive the latter to be emotionally void, handling all cases in a generic and lifeless way (Liu-Thompkins et al., 2022; Zhang et al., 2025). Although an AI agent may be consistent and objective, this quality can also lead consumers to perceive it as cold and distant (Sun et al., 2025; Usman et al., 2024). In addition, recommenders are perceived to put forth personal effort and intention into providing recommendations, which in turn enhances the perceived sincerity and genuineness of the recommendation (Luo et al., 2019). Therefore, it is argued that human (vs. AI) recommendation sources are more likely to increase perceived warmth.

Previous research has shown that the perceived brand warmth makes consumers admire the products of the brand, which in turn leads to higher purchase intentions (Joo & Kim, 2021; Kolbl et al., 2020). Conversely, low sense of warmth is associated with avoidance, leading individuals to avoid being proximate to the source (Follmer & Jones, 2017; Grazzini et al., 2023; Kim & Read, 2021). For example, Luo et al. (2019) showed reductions in an agent's perceived warmth negatively impacted the length of customer's interaction with the agent and subsequent purchase behavior.

To summarize, the differential effect of recommendation source on purchase intention can be explained through the mediating role of perceived warmth encompassing traits such as friendliness, benevolence, and genuine intent, is a foundational dimension in social evaluation that is more readily attributed to human agents than to artificial systems. When a recommendation originates from a human source, consumers are more likely to infer a capacity for empathy, shared experience, and prosocial motivation. This attribution of warmth fosters a parasocial connection and enhances the perceived sincerity and trustworthiness of the recommendation. In turn, this affective-evaluative state reduces psychological resistance and perceived risk, making the endorsed product or service more acceptable. Thus, the positive influence of human recommendations on purchase intention is not merely a direct outcome of the source but is fundamentally channeled through the heightened perception of warmth that human sources evoke, whereas AI recommendations, typically perceived as instrumental and calculative, fail to elicit this critical relational response. Therefore, the following hypothesis is proposed:

Hypothesis 2 Perceived warmth mediates the effect of recommendation type (AI recommendation vs. human recommendation) on purchase intention. That is, consumers feel more warmth to human recommendations (vs. AI recommendations) and have higher (vs. weaker) purchase intention.

3.1.3 The Moderating Role of Product Attitude

According to Fishbein and Ajzen (2011), attitude denotes an individual's evaluative judgment, taking either a positive or negative form, with regard to a specific object or concept. Attitude is further conceptualized as encompassing two distinct forms: (1) attitudes toward specific behaviors, such as using social networking platforms for entertainment, and (2) attitudes toward entities, including organizations, social issues, or consumer products. Within this framework, product attitude acts a pivotal part in shaping both the purchase intention and the real buying behavior. Product attitude functions alongside other influencing factors—such as the opinions of significant others and the availability of resources—to determine the likelihood of purchase. When consumers not only desire a product but also have a positive attitude toward it, the consumers' intention to purchase is much stronger (Saleem et al., 2015). According to Mitchell and Olson (1981), product attitudes are mostly mediated by beliefs about product attributes. Batra and Ahtola (1991) extended this result by differentiating between hedonic or emotional and utilitarian or functional sources of product attitudes and demonstrating that different product types trigger different weightings of these two dimensions. Wei et al. (2024) demonstrated that the influence of message framing on emotional responses and attitude formation is moderated by product type. The effects of message framing also occur through willingness to pay, which mediates the relationship between pricing strategies and product attitudes (Ayadi & Lapeyre, 2016).

While prior research has primarily focused on how product type influences product attitude and how product attitude, in turn, affects purchase intention, this research observes how the combined effect of recommendation type and product attitude shapes consumers' purchase intentions. It is proposed that when product attitudes are positive, consumers are already inclined to purchase, and their attention is directed more toward product features and personal preferences than the recommender type. Under such conditions, the effect of recommendation type (AI vs. human) on purchase intention tends to diminish, as the decision is primarily driven by internal product evaluation rather than external persuasion. However, when consumers hold negative attitudes toward a product, the recommendation type becomes more influential. In these low-attitude scenarios, human recommenders may have an advantage over AI due to their ability to elicit stronger perceptions of warmth (Luo et al., 2019; Van Doorn et al., 2017). As the stereotype content model suggests, warmth perceptions—encompassing traits such as empathy, trustworthiness, and emotional understanding—are critical in forming favorable evaluations and motivating approach behaviors (Fiske et al., 2002). Unlike AI, which is often perceived as emotionally neutral or even cold (Longoni & Cian, 2022; Nass & Moon, 2000), human recommenders can convey emotional expressiveness and interpersonal sincerity, even in the context of an unfavorable product. This perceived warmth may serve to soften consumers' initial resistance, making them more receptive to the recommendation and ultimately increasing their purchase intention.

To summarize, the relationship between recommendation type and purchase intention is contingent upon the consumer's pre-existing product attitude. When a consumer holds a negative product attitude, the credibility and subjective validity of the recommendation source become paramount in overcoming inherent skepticism. In this context, a human recommendation is perceived to possess greater empathetic understanding and nuanced judgment, making its persuasive appeal more effective at countering negative preconceptions. Conversely, an AI recommendation may be discounted as merely algorithmic and lacking genuine comprehension of the consumer's specific concerns or contextual needs. Therefore, the following hypothesis is proposed:

Hypothesis 3 Product attitude moderates the effect of recommendation type (AI recommendation vs. human recommendation) on purchase intention. Specifically, when product attitude is negative, consumers have higher purchase intention for human recommendations than AI recommendations.

3.2 AI Communication Style

To clarify the theoretical relationships among the core variables proposed in this study regarding AI communication style, the theoretical model is presented in Fig. 3.2. The model shows the effects of AI agent communication style (social-oriented vs. task-oriented) on brand engagement, as well as the mediating role of trust and the moderating role of age.

3.2.1 AI Communication Style and Brand Engagement

Communication style plays a crucial role in human-computer interaction, which has been proven to influence consumers' cognitive and emotional responses significantly. Previous researches show that language features, including pronouns, metaphors and intonation, can influence users' perception of the communicator (Kronrod et al., 2012; Sela et al., 2012). The communication methods of offline customer service can affect customers' trust (Crosby et al., 1990), and the same is true for online customer service. The style differences in AI agents' communication influence consumers' brand engagement to varying degrees. In the early days, due to technological limitations, agents were regarded as mechanical beings lacking emotions and credibility (Luo et al., 2019). However, with the innovation of technologies such as natural language processing, AI agents can simulate human

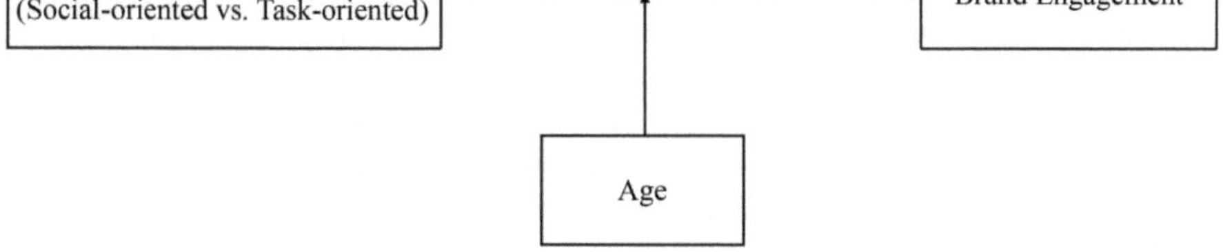

Fig. 3.2 Theoretical model of the effects of AI agent communication style (social-oriented vs. Task-oriented) on brand engagement

conversations, achieve natural and smooth communication, and enhance consumers' perception of its humanization prominently (Go & Sundar, 2019). Generally speaking, the communication styles of AI agents can be divided into two major categories: social and task-oriented. The social-oriented communication style aims to establish interpersonal relationships with clients, while the task-oriented communication style aims to enhance task efficiency, achieve task goals and minimize communication costs (Verhagen et al., 2014).

Task-oriented communication style takes the efficient completion of specific tasks as its primary goal. When transmitting information, the language expression strives to be concise and straightforward, getting to the core (Chattaraman et al., 2019). AI agents that adopt this style will provide the required information quickly and accurately, dedicated to resolving consumers' immediate problems and enhancing the efficiency of task processing promptly. However, this style emphasizes functionality and directness overly. Due to the lack of emotional elements, it may, to a certain extent, ignore consumers' emotional needs. A communication model that only emphasizes ability while neglecting warmth is prone to reducing consumers' emotional identification and participation enthusiasm (Kull et al., 2021; Roy & Naidoo, 2021), which in turn makes consumers feel alienated. Under this style, consumers' emotional needs are ignored, which may lead to a sense of alienation from the service process and thereby reduce their trust in the brand.

The social-oriented communication style focuses on establishing emotional connections with consumers and strives to create a warm and friendly communication atmosphere (Feine et al., 2019). AI agents that adopt this style are more personalized and social in interaction. They will use more emotional expressions and greetings, and at the same time pay attention to consumers' emotional states and give corresponding responses. Social style, through informal language interaction, makes it easier for consumers to AI agents as an existence with social attributes (De Cicco et al., 2020; Go & Sundar, 2019). Multiple marketing strategies, including building trust, enhancing engagement, improving fluency and promoting interactivity, have been identified as key factors influencing customers' brand engagement (Hollebeek, 2011). When AI agents participate in interactions in a partner-like manner, consumers' emotional needs are met, and their trust and satisfaction with the service process increase accordingly. Trust and satisfaction, as important leading variables of brand engagement (Hsieh & Lin, 2018), will further strengthen consumers' emotional connection and behavioral investment in the brand, thereby driving brand engagement positively.

To summarize, from a functional perspective, task-oriented style and social-oriented style have their own advantages respectively in different scenarios. Task-oriented style performs better in scenarios where problems need to be solved quickly or specific information needs to be conveyed (Chen et al., 2021). However, in situations that enhancing emotional support or promoting the establishment of long-term relationships is needed, the social-oriented style has significant advantages (De Cicco et al., 2020). The communication style of AI agents fundamentally shapes customer-brand interaction, establishing a key determinant of brand engagement. Specifically, a social-oriented communication style—which employs relational language, empathetic acknowledgment, and conversational rapport—proactively constructs a psychologically rich interactional space. This style fosters a sense of social presence and personal connection, making the brand feel more approachable, responsive, and invested in the customer's holistic experience rather than merely a transactional outcome. In contrast, a strictly task-oriented communication style, while efficient, restricts the interaction to a utilitarian exchange of information, often leaving the customer's affective and relational needs unmet. By simulating human-like warmth and demonstrating contextual understanding, the social-oriented style elevates the encounter beyond problem-solving, nurturing the emotional affinity and cognitive investment that compel customers to actively think about, feel connected to, and interact with the brand, thereby generating significantly higher levels of sustained engagement. Therefore, the following hypothesis is proposed:

Hypothesis 4 The communication style of AI agents generates a significant influence on customers' brand engagement. Specifically, social-oriented communication style enhances brand engagement more than task-oriented communication style.

3.2.2 The Mediating Role of Trust

Trust is an important cornerstone of human-computer interaction. It means that even in the face of potential uncertainties and loss risks, people are still willing to believe the intentions of the other party and rely on them (Söllner et al., 2016). In simple terms, trust is reflected in the expectation that trustees can bring about positive results. Specifically, trust in technology is usually regarded as a belief formed gradually through cognitive assessment (Colquitt & Rodell, 2011; McKnight & Chervany, 2002). In human-computer interaction, trust can affect consumers' willingness for human-computer interaction directly (Chi et al., 2021). The Technology Acceptance Model (TAM) emphasizes that consumers' trust in technology affects their motivation to use it (Marangunic & Granić, 2014). Numerous studies have confirmed that trust is a key factor determining what kind of behavior people take towards technology (Ha & Stoel, 2009; Van Pinxteren et al., 2019; Wu et al., 2011). This logic is also in line with the ternary interaction framework of "environment—cognition—behavior" in social cognitive theory. That is, individuals will be more deeply involved in those entities that are considered capable of effectively achieving their goals (Bandura, 2001). In the field of AI, a recent study defined trust in human-AI robot interaction as believing that interaction with AI social robots can lead to good service outcomes (Chi et al., 2021). Consumers' trust in human-computer interaction is a higher-order structure, formed by the combined effect of people's evaluations of multiple factors. The communication style of AI will affect brand engagement through the mediating mechanism of users' cognitive judgment of trust the communication style of intelligent customer service will enable users to form a perception of its trust, and this judgment of trust will further influence users' emotional tendencies and participation behaviors towards the brand.

Nowadays, more providers in the service industry have begun to introduce artificial intelligence agents and have them undertake front-line service work (Chi et al., 2020; Lin et al., 2020). With advanced anthropomorphic features and intelligent attributes, these service robots can demonstrate human-like social capabilities and interact directly with consumers (Rodriguez-Lizundia et al., 2015). When AI agents are regarded as having high capabilities, consumers' trust in agents will increase (Cheng et al., 2022). These factors have a positive impact on consumer behavior (Zogaj et al., 2020) and make consumers more loyal to brands (Belanche et al., 2021). AI agents can be considered as entities with social attributes rather than cold machines in service scenarios (Doorn et al., 2017). Therefore, consumers' evaluation of AI agents not only involves the performance of the robots themselves, but also covers considerations at the humanized level (Yu, 2020) and the social level (Gursoy et al., 2019). This means that the trust that consumers generate when interacting with artificial intelligence social agents is very likely to integrate the two traits of "people's trust in technology" and "people's trust in people". Based on this, they can use intelligent services more actively when users build trust in their interactions with such technologies.

AI agents that adopt a task-oriented communication style make consumers have difficulty sensing social cues, thereby their trust in intelligent customer service will be reduced. The social-oriented communication style will convey more warmth and friendliness. This emotional interaction method can alleviate the negative emotions of consumers caused by technological unfamiliarity and potential risks effectively (Chattaraman et al., 2019; Xu et al., 2022). When technology is rich in human-like characteristics, as consumers' demands are met, their evaluation of the practicality of technology will increase naturally (Toader et al., 2019), and the trust in intelligent technology has increased accordingly. Brand engagement can be enhanced eventually.

To summarize, the argument that trust mediates the relationship between an AI's communication style and customer brand engagement is rooted in the fundamental human need for relational connection in commercial interactions. When an AI adopts a social-oriented communication style—using empathetic language, pleasantries, and conversational cues—it mirrors human social exchange, which consumers interpret as warmth and relatability. This perceived social presence fosters greater trust, as customers feel the brand is more transparent, understanding, and invested in their well-being beyond a mere transaction. In contrast, a purely task-oriented style, while efficient, is perceived as impersonal and instrumental, limiting the development of emotional trust. Consequently, this enhanced trust becomes the critical psychological mechanism through which the social-oriented style translates into deeper brand engagement—manifesting as increased loyalty, advocacy, and proactive interaction—because consumers are more willing to invest themselves emotionally and behaviorally in a brand they believe is genuinely trustworthy and relationship-focused. Therefore, the following hypothesis is proposed:

Hypothesis 5 Trust mediates the relationship between communication style of AI and customers' brand engagement. Compared with the task-oriented communication style, consumers perceive higher trust in the social-oriented communication style and thus have a higher level of brand engagement.

3.2.3 The Moderating Role of Age

Young consumers attach more importance to immediate social connections, emotional resonance and experiential enjoyment (Lasane & Jones, 1999). Younger consumers, particularly digital natives from Generations Z and Millennials, have been socialized in digital environments where informal, relational, and socially-rich communication is the normative standard across social media, messaging apps, and interactive platforms. For this cohort, a social-oriented AI communication style—characterized by warmth, empathy, colloquial language, and relational cues—is not a novelty but an expected feature of any interactive interface. This style aligns seamlessly with their ingrained communication norms, thereby reducing psychological distance and fostering a sense of familiarity and connection with the brand. In contrast, older generations, who matured in an era where interactions with technology were predominantly transactional and functional, may perceive such social cues from a non-human agent as incongruent, superfluous, or even inauthentic. Their normative expectations for brand interactions may prioritize clarity, efficiency, and task completion over relational bonding. Consequently, the positive impact of a social-oriented style on brand engagement is hypothesized to be significantly amplified among younger users, for whom it fulfills a deeply ingrained expectation for digitally-mediated interaction. Prior studies suggest that the present-oriented group have a greater preference for warm agents and have a higher purchase intention for products with warm agents (Roy & Naidoo, 2021). As an important interactive tool for online services, the communication style of AI agents has a crucial impact on consumers' brand engagement. The social-oriented communication style, with its warm, natural and personified language traits, is more likely to attract the attention of the younger generation, as it meets both their present-focused tendencies.

To summarize, the effectiveness of an AI agent's communication style in fostering brand engagement is inherently shaped by the demographic characteristic of user age. Specifically, a social-oriented communication style—characterized by relational language, conversational cues, and empathetic acknowledgment—generates a stronger positive effect on brand engagement among younger consumers. This heightened receptivity stems from younger cohorts' developmental immersion in interactive digital media. For these users, an AI's use of warmth is not only familiar but also validates their preference for integrated social and transactional experiences, thereby deepening emotional connection and participatory involvement with the brand. In contrast, older consumers, whose formative experiences with technology often emphasize utility and explicit functionality, may derive less relational value from such stylistic cues and prioritize a clear, efficient task-oriented style. Consequently, the persuasive power of social-oriented communication diminishes as age increases, creating a continuum where youth amplifies its capacity to transform a digital service interaction into a meaningful engagement driver. Therefore, the following hypothesis is proposed:

Hypothesis 6 Age moderates the effect of the communication style of AI agents on brand engagement. Specifically, the younger the age, the stronger the positive effect of social-oriented communication style on brand engagement.

3.3 AI Humanity

To visualize the theoretical relationships among the core variables proposed in this study regarding AI humanity, the theoretical model is presented in Fig. 3.3. The model illustrates the influence of AI assistant humility (high vs. low) on user continuance intention, as well as the mediating role of AI acceptance and the moderating role of frequency of communication with AI assistants.

3.3.1 AI Humanity and User Continuance Use Intention

Humility, as a positive moral character trait, originates from diverse cultural and ethical traditions and is recognized as both a personal disposition and a social virtue. It reflects an individual's awareness of self-limitations, respect for others, and a commitment to continuous learning. In Western traditions, humility is often viewed as a key expression of self-awareness and personal growth (Wimbush, 2014). In contrast, Eastern philosophies, particularly Confucian thought, regard humility as an internal discipline tied to self-cultivation and relational harmony.

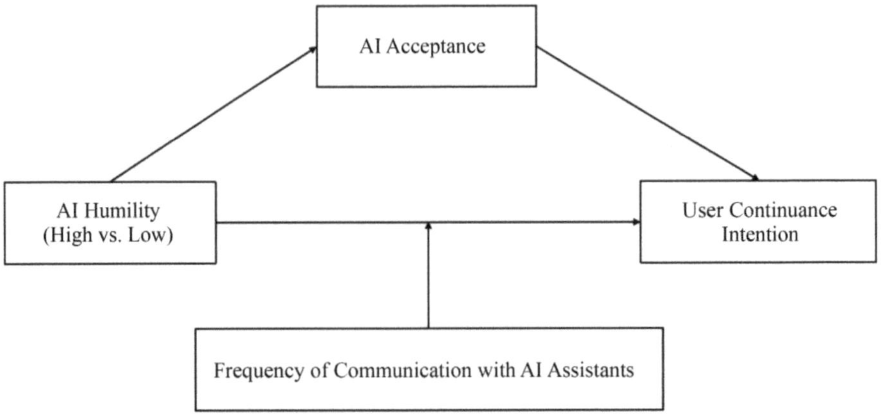

Fig. 3.3 Theoretical model of the effects of AI assistant humility on user continuance intention

Classical teachings such as "Seeing the virtuous and learning from them" and "Among any three people, one can be my teacher" emphasize humility as reflection and the willingness to learn from others (Li, 2016). Prior research has demonstrated that humility can significantly enhance individual well-being and the quality of interpersonal relationships (Davis et al., 2010). Humility fosters a reduction in self-centeredness by encouraging individuals to acknowledge limitations, accept feedback, and remain open to others. This, in turn, contributes to psychological well-being and strengthens social cohesion (Sapmaz et al., 2016). In interpersonal conflict contexts, humility has also been shown to promote empathy, build trust, and support relational repair (Bhattacharya et al., 2017).

Within the context of AI assistants, researchers have begun to incorporate humility as a desirable trait in AI design, proposing it as a crucial ethical dimension in the anthropomorphization of artificial agents (Liu et al., 2025). AI assistants that exhibit humility, through behaviors such as admitting errors, seeking feedback, or expressing a willingness to improve, can signal self-awareness and adaptability, thereby enhancing perceived transparency, trust, and customer acceptance (Burr & Leslie, 2023). In particular, such "self-limiting" behaviors serve as powerful relational cues in high-risk scenarios like service failure, helping to repair customer relationships and elicit empathy and forgiveness from users (Sapmaz et al., 2016).

However, existing research on humility largely centered on human agents. While some studies have explored the impact of AI assistant humility in general human-AI interaction settings, there is still a notable lack of investigation into its effects in service failure scenarios, where trust recovery and emotional sensitivity are especially critical. More importantly, few studies have systematically examined how AI assistant humility influences user continuance intention in such contexts. Addressing this gap, the present research explores how varying levels of AI assistant humility affect user continuance intention following service failure, thereby extending humility research into a more emotionally and relationally complex interaction domain.

User continuance intention refers to a user's sustained willingness to engage with a service or technology after initial adoption, and it is especially critical in high-stakes service scenarios where trust and emotional responses play a prominent role (Goyal et al., 2022; Zhao et al., 2013). Prior research identifies multiple psychological and functional drivers of user continuance intention, including perceived satisfaction, trust, perceived usefulness, and emotional gratification. For instance, perceived anthropomorphism and emotional support from AI chatbots have been shown to significantly increase continuance intention in AI-based banking services and customer support platforms (Lin & Lee, 2023). Similarly, warmth and competence, two key perceived traits linked to humility, enhance trust and engagement, thereby fostering ongoing usage (Li et al., 2023).

The service failure context introduces heightened user expectations for relational repair. Studies show that users are more likely to discontinue use of AI services following perceived failures unless there are mitigating relational behaviors, such as empathy, apology, and transparency (Sun et al., 2022). In these high-risk moments, AI assistants that display humility, acknowledge limitations, express willingness to improve, and see user feedback, signal social awareness and ethical self-regulation, which in turn foster trust and emotional reconciliation.

To summarize, in the context of service failure, AI assistant humility—characterized by transparent acknowledgment of limitations, apologies for errors, and the deferral to human expertise—serves to rebuild user trust and satisfaction by humanizing the interaction and mitigating the frustration of unmet expectations. This conduct directly reduces the perceived severity of the failure by validating the user's experience, thereby lowering negative emotional responses and preserving the user's sense of agency. Consequently, by demonstrating reliability through honesty, the AI fosters a more forgiving and collaborative relationship, which increases the user's perceived value of continued engagement and directly strengthens their intention to use the service again despite the initial setback. Therefore, the following hypothesis is proposed:

Hypothesis *7* AI assistant humility has a positive effect on user continuance intention in the context of service failure.

3.3.2 The Mediating Role of AI Acceptance

AI acceptance refers to the overall manifestation of customers' positive emotions and willingness to use AI in service interactions (Pelau et al., 2021). It originally stems from the traditional Technology Acceptance Model (TAM), which focuses on customers' attitudes toward and intentions to use new technologies (Venkatesh et al., 2012). However, in service scenarios, customers are not only concerned with whether the technology is "easy to use," but also whether it is "human-like," such as interaction quality, empathy, and psychological anthropomorphism characteristics, which significantly enhance customers' trust and acceptance of AI assistants (Lu et al., 2019). Based on this, Gursoy et al. (2019) drew on cognitive evaluation theory (Lazarus, 1991) and cognitive dissonance theory (Festinger, 1957) to propose the AI Device Use Acceptance (AIDUA) model, which divides the AI acceptance process into three stages: primary evaluation (e.g., social influence, pleasure motivation, anthropomorphic characteristics), secondary evaluation (e.g., performance expectations, effort expectations), and outcome evaluation, emphasizing that customer acceptance behavior is a dynamic decision-making process involving "emotion-cognition-behavior." Previous studies have also suggested that AI acceptance is not merely a static attitude but a dynamic social cognitive process. When customers feel respected and understood during interactions with AI assistants, their acceptance of AI assistants significantly increases; conversely, if AI customer service exhibits overly cold or mechanized responses, customers often reduce their acceptance (Gursoy et al., 2019).

To summarize, in the context of service failure, AI assistant humility—manifested through acknowledgment of error and limitations—directly shapes the user's perception of the technology's reliability and alignment with their expectations, thereby enhancing AI acceptance. Specifically, a high-humility response frames the AI as a cooperative and adaptable tool, reducing user frustration and increasing the perceived usefulness and ease of continued interaction. Conversely, low humility exacerbates negative perceptions of the AI as inflexible or incompetent, diminishing acceptance. Consequently, it is this elevated state of AI acceptance, fostered by humble conduct, that serves as the essential psychological pathway leading to a stronger user intention to continue using the service, as the user comes to view the AI not as a source of repeated failure but as a manageable and integrated component of their problem-solving process. Therefore, the following hypothesis is proposed:

Hypothesis 8 AI acceptance mediates the effect of AI assistant humility on user continuance intention in service failure contexts. Specifically, compared to AI assistant with low humility, AI assistant with high humility is more likely to enhance AI acceptance, thereby increasing user continuance intention.

3.3.3 The Moderating Role of Communication Frequency With AI Agent

Frequency of communication with AI assistants refers to the extent and regularity with which customers interact with such systems across their daily or service-related tasks. As customers accumulate more interactional experience with AI assistants, their familiarity and cognitive comfort with the technology often increase, influencing both their perception of the AI and their behavioral responses (Hsieh & Lee, 2021). Frequent interactions can lead to increased anthropomorphization and parasocial relationships, making users more likely to treat AI assistants as social partners rather than mechanical tools (Lee & Park, 2022). This heightened social connection can enhance the customer's sensitivity to the AI socio-emotional signals, including humility-related cues such as admitting faults or seeking feedback (Hsieh & Lee, 2024). Prior studies show that trust and acceptance of AI assistants grow with sustained usage, leading to higher continuance intention (Jo, 2022; Sun et al., 2022). Moreover, customers who engage with AI assistants frequently are more likely to appreciate social and emotional traits like humility, as they encounter a broader range of interaction contexts where such traits become salient (Chen & Park, 2021).

From a human-AI interaction perspective, the level of interaction frequency may determine the depth of relational bonding and the likelihood of trust formation, which in turn moderates the effectiveness of relational repair behaviors, such as humility, during service failures (Antona et al., 2023; Balakrishnan & Dwivedi, 2021). Usage frequency has also been found to significantly moderate the relationship between trust and continuance intention, especially when anthropomorphic features are present. Therefore, customers who frequently interact with AI assistants may be more attuned to and appreciative of humble behaviors in AI responses, thereby exhibiting stronger positive reactions (such as increased trust and continuance intention), compared to less frequent users. This aligns with findings in digital service contexts, where interaction frequency amplifies the impact of perceived service quality on user loyalty and ongoing engagement (Jo, 2022). Based on this, the following hypothesis is proposed:

Hypothesis 9 Frequency of communication with AI assistants moderates the relationship between AI assistant humility and user continuance intention. Specifically, the positive effect of AI assistant humility on continuance intention is stronger for customers with high frequency of communication with AI assistants than for those with low frequency.

3.4 AI Humor

To visualize the theoretical relationships among the core variables proposed in this study regarding AI humor, the theoretical model is presented in Fig. 3.4. The model illustrates the impact of GAI humor on user satisfaction, as well as the mediating role of perceived warmth and the moderating role of sense of humor.

3.4.1 AI Humor and User Satisfaction

Existing studies have confirmed that GAI not only has the ability to provide functional value but also can bring a sense of pleasure to users during interactions, thereby optimizing their overall emotional experience (Kanuck, 2019). From the perspective of the cognitive process influenced by social and situational stimuli, humorous expressions are highly likely to trigger users' emotional fluctuations on social media platforms (Bil-Jaruzelska & Monzer, 2022), delivering interesting and pleasant emotional value to users (Chang et al., 2015). According to the social response theory, people tend to establish connections with generative artificial

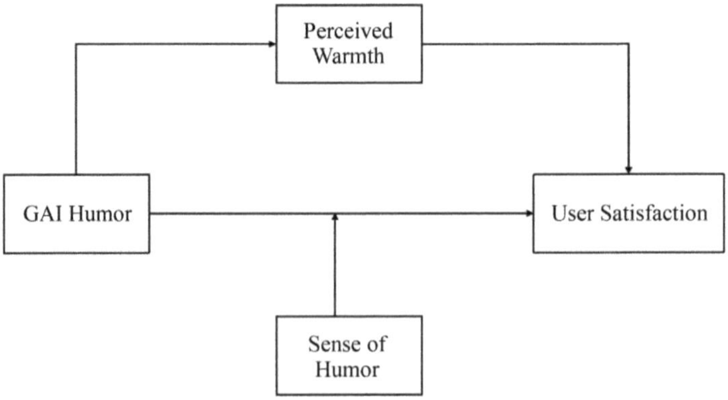

Fig. 3.4 Theoretical model of the effects of GAI humor on user satisfaction

intelligence that possess social attributes (Martin Holzwarth, Martin Holzwarth & Neumann, 2006), and such AI with social characteristics can reduce users' sense of rejection towards AI by narrowing the psychological distance with users (Martin Holzwarth & Neumann, 2006).

In addition, humor has always been considered as a unique social trait of humans (Campbell et al., 2001), which can improve the quality of interpersonal interactions and effectively alleviate tension and anxiety. Relevant studies have shown that the humorous traits of GAI can play a positive role even in situations where service failures occur, helping to enhance user satisfaction. In the context of social media, posts with humorous elements often gain higher user recognition, and content creators with a humorous style usually have more followers and fans (Barta et al., 2023; Pennington & Hall, 2014). The application of humor in creators' content on social media can not only encourage users to participate more actively in interactions (such as liking, collecting, commenting, forwarding, etc.) but also enhance the stickiness of fans to creators and even promote the growth of the number of fans. Thus, it can be seen that humor has potential effects on improving user satisfaction on social media.

In the operation of social media platforms, user satisfaction is a core indicator to measure their development effectiveness (Campbell et al., 2001; Fernandes & Moreira, 2019; Xiao & Yu, 2025). However, current research on the impact of GAI humor on user satisfaction in the field of social media is still insufficient. It is argued that GAI with the social trait of humor can trigger more positive emotional feedback from users, thereby having a positive impact on user satisfaction on social media. From the perspective of practical data, the success of GAI comment account "Robert" on Sina Weibo serves as a compelling case study, having garnered nearly 400,000 followers through its consistently humorous expressions and accumulating an impressive number of combined forwards, likes, and comments on its relevant content. This phenomenon directly illustrates how GAI-generated humor drives tangible user engagement by capturing attention, encouraging interaction, and fostering a sense of relatable entertainment. By creating shareable and amusing content that resonates with users, such AI-driven humor lowers barriers to participation, stimulates conversation threads, and enhances overall platform vitality. Consequently, this not only confirms the positive effect of GAI humor on users' attitudes but also underscores its significant role in boosting key metrics of social media engagement, from follower growth to active content dissemination and community interaction.

To summarize, within the dynamic environment of social media, where user attention is fragmented, and emotional resonance is paramount, the deployment of humorous GAI establishes a direct and positive pathway to user satisfaction. Unlike purely transactional contexts, social media interactions are fundamentally driven by entertainment, connection, and affective experience. GAI humor—when contextually appropriate, timely, and aligned with platform-specific norms—serves as a powerful relational tool that transforms a standard automated interaction into a memorable and enjoyable social moment. This use of wit or cleverness directly stimulates positive affective states, such as amusement and delight, which are core components of user satisfaction in this informal, leisure-oriented setting. Furthermore, it enhances the perceived social presence and likability of the AI agent, making the interaction feel less mechanistic and more aligned with the collaborative, community-driven ethos of social media platforms. By successfully navigating the nuanced social landscape to deliver humor, the GAI not only fulfills the user's instrumental need for information or service but also delivers unexpected value in the form of entertainment, thereby elevating the user's overall evaluation of the experience and strengthening their positive sentiment toward the interaction. Therefore, the following hypothesis is proposed:

Hypothesis 10 GAI humor is positively related to user satisfaction on social media.

3.4.2 The Mediating Role of Perceived Warmth

Humor, as a unique social trait of humans, has been deeply integrated into the emotional interaction design of artificial intelligence. Previous studies have extensively discussed the impact of GAI characteristics on two aspects: perceived ability and perceived warmth. This study focuses on in-depth exploration of perceived warmth. Nowadays, many enterprises incorporate humorous elements into the content generation of chatbots, aiming to make users' interactions with robots closer to the texture of interpersonal communication. Existing studies have confirmed that when chatbots exhibit humorous traits in communication with customers, customers will have a stronger perception of warmth towards them (Fiske et al., 2002). In the research literature on chatbots, it is also clearly indicated that the interaction style of artificial intelligence significantly affects consumers' perception of warmth towards it. Therefore, this study believes that GAI humor has a direct effect on users' perceived warmth.

Based on the social response theory, people tend to interact with computers in the same way as they interact with others (Martin Holzwarth & Neumann, 2006). Past studies have shown that when chatbots have clues that can trigger perceived warmth, people will consider them as interactive objects with emotional temperature and interact with them in an interpersonal social mode (Fiske et al., 2007). This kind of warm interaction can enhance user participation, which is also an important indicator to measure the success of social media platforms. In addition, literature in the field of social interaction points out that when consumers participate in artificial intelligence interactions, the impact of artificial intelligence's interaction style on consumers' service evaluation far exceeds other factors (such as service treatment, information quality, or task completion) (Liu et al., 2023). The influence of this interaction style will further extend to the emotional connection between service providers and consumers, for example, exhibiting a positive effect on purchase intention (Folkes, 1984). Thus, GAI humor can significantly enhance users' perceived warmth towards GAI, thereby affecting user participation on social media platforms.

To summarize, the impact of GAI humor on user satisfaction is fundamentally mediated by perceived warmth, as humor serves as a relational signal rather than merely a source of amusement. When GAI employs well-timed and contextually appropriate humor, it projects an impression of social awareness and benign intent, which users cognitively appraise as warmth—a sense of friendliness and supportive engagement. This perceived warmth transforms the interactional dynamic, making the experience feel more personal and less mechanistic, thereby fulfilling users' implicit expectations for socially intelligent interaction. Ultimately, it is this fostered sense of congenial connection, directly ignited by the humorous exchange, that elevates the user's overall emotional evaluation and leads to greater satisfaction with the AI and the interaction as a whole. Based on the above arguments, the following hypothesis is proposed:

Hypothesis 11 Perceived warmth mediates the impact of GAI humor on user satisfaction.

3.4.3 The Moderating Role of Sense of Humor

From the perspective of attribution theory examining the impact of social and environmental stimuli on cognition, the causes of individual behavior can usually be attributed to the combined effect of internal traits and external factors (Xiao & Yu, 2025). Within this framework, GAI humor, as an external content stimulus, exerts an influence on the user's behavior; while the user's own sense of humor, as an internal psychological trait, is also a key factor driving their participation in social media platform interactions (Cann & Calhoun, 2001; Cann & Matson, 2014). Internal traits and external stimuli shape the user's cognitive state through interaction, and further affect their behavior.

There are significant differences in individuals' sense of humor (Xiao & Yu, 2025) and these differences lead to variations in their interpretation and feedback effects of GAI humor. Given the inherently high correlation between sense of humor and the core characteristic of "humor", it is argued that individual sense of humor plays an important role in the transmission effect of GAI humor (Svebak, 1996). Especially in the social media context, studies have shown that 64% of users' time on social media is spent on entertainment activities (Grover & Kar, 2020), which means that the user group generally has a high demand for humorous content. Therefore, exploring the interaction effect between sense of humor and GAI humor has important theoretical and practical value for understanding social media user behavior.

It is argued that an individual's trait sense of humor functions as a critical moderator by fundamentally shaping the impact of GAI humor on user satisfaction. Specifically, for users with a higher sense of humor, they come into contact with more humorous content in their daily lives and have a higher aesthetic and cognitive standard for humor. Therefore, they tend to consider the humor generated by GAI as conventional expression, which is difficult to trigger an emotional experience beyond expectations. They tend to classify it as functional entertainment, and its effect on improving satisfaction is limited.

In contrast, users with a lower sense of humor have fewer opportunities to come into contact with humor in their daily lives and have a lower benchmark of expectations for it. When GAI shows humor, this expression breaks their fixed perception that AI lacks emotion and is only a tool, bringing a strong sense of psychological surprise. Users will interpret this as GAI exceeding their own expectations and proactively addressing their emotional needs, thereby significantly enhancing satisfaction. Furthermore, from a social-connective perspective, these individuals experience GAI's humorous output as a form of zero-risk social validation and a powerful trigger for anthropomorphism, transforming a transactional interaction into a perceived companionable exchange that mitigates machine coldness, which significantly enhances relational satisfaction. Based on the above arguments, the following hypothesis is proposed:

Hypothesis 12 Sense of humor moderates the impact of GAI humor on user satisfaction. Specifically, As the sense of humor decreases, GAI humor has a stronger positive impact on user satisfaction.

References

Adamopoulos, P., & Todri, V. (2024). Consumer social connectedness and persuasiveness of collaborative-filtering recommender systems: Evidence from an online-to-offline recommendation app. *Production and Operations Management*, *34*(12), 4015–4038.

Ahn, J., Kim, J., & Sung, Y. (2021). AI-powered recommendations: The roles of perceived similarity and psychological distance on persuasion. *International Journal of Advertising*, *40*(8), 1366–1384.

Ahn, J., Kim, J., & Sung, Y. (2022). The effect of gender stereotypes on artificial intelligence recommendations. *Journal of Business Research*, *141*, 50–59.

Antona, M., Margetis, G., Ntoa, S., & Degen, H. (2023). Special Issue on AI in HCI. *International Journal of Human–Computer Interaction*, *39*(9), 1723–1726.

Ayadi, N., & Lapeyre, A. (2016). Consumer purchase intentions for green products: Mediating role of WTP and moderating effects of framing. *Journal of Marketing Communications*, *22*(4), 367–384.

Baek, T. H., & Morimoto, M. (2012). Stay away from me. *Journal of Advertising*, *41*(1), 59–76.

Balakrishnan, J., & Dwivedi, Y. K. (2021). Role of cognitive absorption in building user trust and experience. *Psychology & Marketing*, *38*(4), 643–668.

Bandura, A. (2001). Social cognitive theory: An agentic perspective. *Annual Review of Psychology*, *52*, 1–26.

Barta, S., Belanche, D., Fernández, A., & Flavián, M. (2023). Influencer marketing on TikTok: The effectiveness of humor and followers' hedonic experience. *Journal of Retailing and Consumer Services*, *70*, 103149.

Batra, R., & Ahtola, O. T. (1991). Measuring the hedonic and utilitarian sources of consumer attitudes. *Marketing Letters*, *2*(2), 159–170.

Belanche, D., Casaló, L. V., Schepers, J., & Flavián, C. (2021). Examining the effects of robots' physical appearance, warmth, and competence in frontline services: The Humanness-Value-Loyalty model. *Psychology & Marketing*, *38*(12), 2357–2376.

Bhattacharya, O., Chatterjee, A., & Basu, J. (2017). Humility: An emerging construct in moral psychology. *Psychological Studies*, *62*(1), 1–11.

Bil-Jaruzelska, A., & Monzer, C. (2022). All about feelings? Emotional appeals as drivers of user engagement with facebook posts. *Politics and Governance, 10*(1), 172–184.

Burr, C., & Leslie, D. (2023). Ethical assurance: A practical approach to the responsible design, development, and deployment of data-driven technologies. *AI and Ethics, 3*(1), 73–98.

Cai, N., Gao, S., & Yan, J. (2024). How the communication style of chatbots influences consumers' satisfaction, trust, and engagement in the context of service failure. *Humanities and Social Sciences Communications, 11*(1), 1–11.

Campbell, K. L., Martin, M. M., & Wanzer, M. B. (2001). Employee perceptions of manager humor orientation, assertiveness, responsiveness, approach/avoidance strategies, and satisfaction. *Communication Research Reports, 18*(1), 67–74.

Cann, A., & Calhoun, L. G. (2001). Perceived personality associations with differences in sense of humor: Stereotypes of hypothetical others with high or low senses of humor. *Humor, 14*(2), 117–130.

Cann, A., & Matson, C. (2014). Sense of humor and social desirability: Understanding how humor styles are perceived. *Personality and Individual Differences, 66*, 176–180.

Chang, Y. T., Yu, H., & Lu, H. P. (2015). Persuasive messages, popularity cohesion, and message diffusion in social media marketing. *Journal of Business Research, 68*(4), 777–782.

Chattaraman, V., Kwon, W. S., Gilbert, J. E., & Ross, K. (2019). Should AI-Based, conversational digital assistants employ social-or task-oriented interaction style? A task-competency and reciprocity perspective for older adults. *Computers in Human Behavior, 90*, 315–330.

Chen, H., Chan Olmsted, S., Kim, J., & Mayor Sanabria, I. (2022). Consumers' perception on artificial intelligence applications in marketing communication. *Qualitative Market Research: An International Journal, 25*(1), 125–142.

Chen, J. V., Thi Le, H., & Tran, S. T. T. (2021). Understanding automated conversational agent as a decision aid: Matching agent's conversation with customer's shopping task. *Internet Research, 31*(4), 1376–1404.

Chen, Q. Q., & Park, H. J. (2021). How anthropomorphism affects trust in intelligent personal assistants. *Industrial Management & Data Systems, 121*(12), 2722–2737.

Cheng, X., Zhang, X., Cohen, J., & Mou, J. (2022). Human vs. AI: Understanding the impact of anthropomorphism on consumer response to chatbots from the perspective of trust and relationship norms. *Information Processing & Management, 59*(3), 102940.

Chi, O. H., Denton, G., & Gursoy, D. (2020). Artificially intelligent device use in service delivery: A systematic review, synthesis, and research agenda. *Journal of Hospitality Marketing & Management, 29*(7), 757–786.

Chi, O. H., Jia, S., Li, Y., & Gursoy, D. (2021). Developing a formative scale to measure consumers' trust toward interaction with artificially intelligent (AI) social robots in service delivery. *Computers in Human Behavior, 118*, 106700.

Colquitt, J. A., & Rodell, J. B. (2011). Justice, trust, and trustworthiness: A longitudinal analysis integrating three theoretical perspectives. *Academy of Management Journal, 54*(6), 1183–1206.

Concannon, S., Roberts, I., & Tomalin, M. (2023). An interactional account of empathy in human-machine communication. *Human-Machine Communication, 6*(1), 87–116.

Crosby, L. A., Evans, K. R., & Cowles, D. (1990). Relationship quality in services selling: An interpersonal influence perspective. *Journal of Marketing, 54*(3), 68–81.

Davis, D. E., Worthington Jr, E. L., & Hook, J. N. (2010). Humility: Review of measurement strategies and conceptualization as personality judgment. *The Journal of Positive Psychology, 5*(4), 243–252.

Davvetas, V., & Halkias, G. (2019). Global and local brand stereotypes: Formation, content transfer, and impact. *International Marketing Review, 36*(5), 675–701.

De Cicco, R., Silva, S., & Alparone, F. (2020). Millennials' attitude toward chatbots: An experimental study in a social relationship perspective. *International Journal of Retail & Distribution Management, 48*(11), 1213–1233.

Doorn, J. V., Mende, M., Noble, S. M., Hulland, J., & Petersen, J. A. (2017). Domo arigato Mr. Roboto: Emergence of automated social presence in organizational frontlines and customers' service experiences. *Journal of Service Research, 20*(1), 43–58.

Duprez, C., Christophe, V., Rimé, B., Congard, A., & Antoine, P. (2015). Motives for the social sharing of an emotional experience. *Journal of Social and Personal Relationships, 32*(6), 757–787.

El Hedhli, K., Zourrig, H., Al Khateeb, A., & Alnawas, I. (2023). Stereotyping human-like virtual influencers in retailing: Does warmth prevail over competence? *Journal of Retailing and Consumer Services, 75*, 103459.

Feine, J., Gnewuch, U., Morana, S., & Maedche, A. (2019). A taxonomy of social cues for conversational agents. *International Journal of Human-Computer Studies, 132*, 138–161.

Fernandes, T., & Moreira, M. (2019). Consumer brand engagement, satisfaction and brand loyalty: A comparative study between functional and emotional brand relationships. *Journal of Product & Brand Management, 28*(2), 274–286.

Festinger, L. (1957). *A theory of cognitive dissonance*. Stanford University Press.

Fishbein, M., & Ajzen, I. (2011). *Predicting and changing behavior: The reasoned action approach*. Psychology press.

Fiske, S. T. (2018). Stereotype content: Warmth and competence endure. *Current Directions in Psychological Science, 27*(2), 67–73.

Fiske, S. T., Cuddy, A. J., Glick, P., & Xu, J. (2002). A model of (often mixed) stereotype content: Competence and warmth respectively follow from perceived status and competition. *Journal of Personality and Social Psychology, 82*(6), 878–902.

Fiske, S. T., Cuddy, A. J. C., & Glick, P. (2007). Universal dimensions of social cognition: Warmth and competence. *Trends in Cognitive Sciences, 11*(2), 77–83.

Folkes, V. S. (1984). Consumer reactions to product failure: An attributional approach. *Journal of Consumer Research, 10*(4), 398–409.

Follmer, K. B., & Jones, K. S. (2017). Stereotype content and social distancing from employees with mental illness: The moderating roles of gender and social dominance orientation. *Journal of Applied Social Psychology, 47*(9), 492–504.

Go, E., & Sundar, S. S. (2019). Humanizing chatbots: The effects of visual, identity and conversational cues on humanness perceptions. *Computers in Human Behavior, 97*, 304–316.

Goyal, S., Venkatesh, V., & Shi, X. (2022). Role of users' status quo on continuance intentions. *Information & Management, 59*(8), 103686.

Grazzini, L., Viglia, G., & Nunan, D. (2023). Dashed expectations in service experiences. Effects of robots human-likeness on customers' responses. *European Journal of Marketing, 57*(4), 957–986.

Grenci, R. T., & Todd, P. A. (2002). Solutions-driven marketing. *Communications of the ACM, 45* (3), 64–71.

Grover, P., & Kar, A. K. (2020). User engagement for mobile payment service providers – Introducing the social media engagement model. *Journal of Retailing and Consumer Services, 53*, 101718.

Gursoy, D., Chi, O. H., Lu, L., & Nunkoo, R. (2019). Consumers acceptance of artificially intelligent (AI) device use in service delivery. *International Journal of Information Management, 49*, 157–169.

Ha, S., & Stoel, L. (2009). Consumer e-shopping acceptance: Antecedents in a technology acceptance model. *Journal of Business Research, 62*(5), 565–571.

Haas, B. W., Brook, M., Remillard, L., Ishak, A., Anderson, I. W., & Filkowski, M. M. (2015). I know how you feel: The warm-altruistic personality profile and the empathic brain. *PloS One, 10*(3), e0120639.

Halkias, G., & Diamantopoulos, A. (2020). Universal dimensions of individuals' perception: Revisiting the operationalization of warmth and competence with a mixed-method approach. *International Journal of Research in Marketing, 37*(4), 714–736.

Hollebeek, L. (2011). Demystifying customer brand engagement: Exploring the loyalty nexus. *Journal of Marketing Management*, *27*, 785–807.

Holthöwer, J., & Van Doorn, J. (2023). Robots do not judge: Service robots can alleviate embarrassment in service encounters. *Journal of the Academy of Marketing Science*, *51*(4), 767–784.

Hsieh, P. J., & Lin, W. S. (2018). Explaining resistance to system usage in the PharmaCloud: A view of the dual-factor model. *Information & Management*, *55*(1), 51–63.

Hsieh, S. H., & Lee, C. T. (2021). Hey Alexa: Examining the effect of perceived socialness in usage intentions of AI assistant-enabled smart speaker. *Journal of Research in Interactive Marketing*, *15*(2), 267–294.

Hsieh, S. H., & Lee, C. T. (2024). The AI humanness: How perceived personality builds trust and continuous usage intention. *Journal of Product & Brand Management*, *33*(5), 618–632.

Jeon, Y. A. (2022). Let me transfer you to our AI-based manager: Impact of manager-level job titles assigned to AI-based agents on marketing outcomes. *Journal of Business Research*, *145*, 892–904.

Jin, F., & Zhang, X. (2025). Artificial intelligence or human: When and why consumers prefer AI recommendations. *Information Technology & People*, *38*(1), 279–303.

Jo, H. (2022). Continuance intention to use artificial intelligence personal assistant: Type, gender, and use experience. *Heliyon*, *8*(9).

Joo, B. R., & Kim, H. Y. (2021). Repositioning luxury fashion brands as intentional agents: The roles of consumer envy and admiration. *Journal of Fashion Marketing and Management: An International Journal*, *25*(4), 606–624.

Kanuck, S. (2019). Humor, ethics, and dignity: Being human in the age of artificial intelligence. *Ethics & International Affairs*, *33*(1), 3–12.

Kervyn, N., Fiske, S. T., & Yzerbyt, V. Y. (2013). Integrating the stereotype content model (warmth and competence) and the Osgood semantic differential (evaluation, potency, and activity). *European Journal of Social Psychology*, *43*(7), 673–681.

Kim, T., & Read, G. L. (2021). Free smiles are worth a lot for social media influencers: The mediating roles of warmth, competence, and admiration. *Cyberpsychology, Behavior, and Social Networking*, *24*(2), 135–140.

Kim, T. W., & Duhachek, A. (2020). Artificial intelligence and persuasion: A construal-level account. *Psychological Science*, *31*(4), 363–380.

Kolbl, Ž., Diamantopoulos, A., Arslanagic-Kalajdzic, M., & Zabkar, V. (2020). Do brand warmth and brand competence add value to consumers? A stereotyping perspective. *Journal of Business Research*, *118*, 346–362.

Kronrod, A., Grinstein, A., & Wathieu, L. (2012). Enjoy! Hedonic consumption and compliance with assertive messages. *Journal of Consumer Research*, *39*, 51–61.

Kull, A. J., Romero, M., & Monahan, L. (2021). How may I help you? Driving brand engagement through the warmth of an initial chatbot message. *Journal of Business Research*, *135*, 840–850.

Kumar, V., Ashraf, A. R., & Nadeem, W. (2024). AI-powered marketing: What, where, and how? *International Journal of Information Management*, *77*, 102783.

Lasane, T. P., & Jones, J. M. (1999). Temporal orientation and academic goal-setting: The mediating properties of a motivational self. *Journal of Social Behavior & Personality*, *14*(1), 31–44.

Lazarus, R. S. (1991). Cognition and motivation in emotion. *American Psychologist*, *46*(4), 352.

Lee, K. W., & Li, C. Y. (2023). It is not merely a chat: Transforming chatbot affordances into dual identification and loyalty. *Journal of Retailing and Consumer Services*, *74*, 103447.

Lee, M., & Park, J. S. (2022). Do para-social relationships and the quality of communication with AI shopping chatbots determine middle-aged women consumers' continuance usage intentions? *Journal of Consumer Behaviour*, *21*(4), 842–854.

Li, B., Yao, R., & Nan, Y. (2023). How do friendship artificial intelligence chatbots (FAIC) benefit the continuance using intention and customer engagement? *Journal of Consumer Behaviour*, *22*(6), 1376–1398.

Li, J. (2016). Humility in learning: A Confucian perspective. *Journal of Moral Education*, *45*(2), 147–165.

Liang, K. H., Shi, W., Oh, Y. J., Wang, H. C., Zhang, J., & Yu, Z. (2024). Dialoging resonance in human-chatbot conversation: How users perceive and reciprocate recommendation chatbot's self-disclosure strategy. *Proceedings of the ACM on Human-Computer Interaction*, *8* (CSCW1), 1–28.

Lin, H., Chi, O. H., & Gursoy, D. (2020). Antecedents of customers' acceptance of artificially intelligent robotic device use in hospitality services. *Journal of Hospitality Marketing & Management*, *29*(5), 530–549.

Lin, R. R., & Lee, J. C. (2023). The supports provided by artificial intelligence to continuous usage intention of mobile banking: Evidence from China. *Aslib Journal of Information Management*, *76*(2), 293–310.

Liu, D., Lv, Y., & Huang, W. (2023). How do consumers react to chatbots' humorous emojis in service failures. *Technology in Society*, *73*, 102244.

Liu, J., Hsu, F. C., Yu, J., Cao, J., & Mai, H. (2025). When humble AI meets narcissistic customers: A terror management perspective. *International Journal of Information Management*, *83*, 102904.

Liu-Thompkins, Y., Okazaki, S., & Li, H. (2022). Artificial empathy in marketing interactions: Bridging the human-AI gap in affective and social customer experience. *Journal of the Academy of Marketing Science*, *50*(6), 1198–1218.

Longoni, C., & Cian, L. (2022). Artificial intelligence in utilitarian vs. hedonic contexts: The "word-of-machine" effect. *Journal of Marketing*, *86*(1), 91–108.

Lu, L., Cai, R., & Gursoy, D. (2019). Developing and validating a service robot integration willingness scale. *International Journal of Hospitality Management*, *80*, 36–51.

Luo, X., Tong, S., Fang, Z., & Qu, Z. (2019). Frontiers: Machines vs. humans: The impact of artificial intelligence chatbot disclosure on customer purchases. *Marketing Science*, *38*(6), 937–947.

Marangunic, N., & Granić, A. (2014). Technology acceptance model: A literature review from 1986 to 2013. *Universal Access in the Information Society*, *14*, 81–95.

Markovitch, D. G., Stough, R. A., & Huang, D. (2024). Consumer reactions to chatbot versus human service: An investigation in the role of outcome valence and perceived empathy. *Journal of Retailing and Consumer Services*, *79*, 103847.

Martin Holzwarth, C. J., & Neumann, M. M. (2006). The influence of avatars on online consumer shopping behavior. *Journal of Marketing*, *70*(4), 19–36.

McKnight, D., & Chervany, N. (2002). What trust means in e-commerce customer relationships: An interdisciplinary conceptual typology. *International Journal of Electronic Commerce*, *6*, 35–59.

Mitchell, A. A., & Olson, J. C. (1981). Are product attribute beliefs the only mediator of advertising effects on brand attitude? *Journal of Marketing Research*, *18*(3), 318–332.

Nass, C., & Moon, Y. (2000). Machines and mindlessness: Social responses to computers. *Journal of Social Issues*, *56*(1), 81–103.

Oldmeadow, J. A. (2018). Stereotype content and morality: How competence and warmth arise from morally significant interactions. *British Journal of Social Psychology*, *57*(4), 834–854.

Pelau, C., Dabija, D. C., & Ene, I. (2021). What makes an AI device human-like? The role of interaction quality, empathy and perceived psychological anthropomorphic characteristics in the acceptance of artificial intelligence in the service industry. *Computers in Human Behavior*, *122*, 106855.

Peng, C., van Doorn, J., Eggers, F., & Wieringa, J. E. (2022). The effect of required warmth on consumer acceptance of artificial intelligence in service: The moderating role of AI-human collaboration. *International Journal of Information Management*, *66*, 102533.

Pennington, N., & Hall, J. A. (2014). An analysis of humor orientation on Facebook: A lens model approach. *Humor, 27*(1), 1–21.

Piao, J., Liu, J., Zhang, F., Su, J., & Li, Y. (2023). Human–AI adaptive dynamics drives the emergence of information cocoons. *Nature Machine Intelligence, 5*(11), 1214–1224.

Ringwald, W. R., & Wright, A. G. (2021). The affiliative role of empathy in everyday interpersonal interactions. *European Journal of Personality, 35*(2), 197–211.

Rodriguez-Lizundia, E., Marcos, S., Zalama, E., Gómez-García-Bermejo, J., & Gordaliza, A. (2015). A bellboy robot: Study of the effects of robot behaviour on user engagement and comfort. *International Journal of Human-Computer Studies, 82*, 83–95.

Roy, R., & Naidoo, V. (2021). Enhancing chatbot effectiveness: The role of anthropomorphic conversational styles and time orientation. *Journal of Business Research, 126*, 23–34.

Roy, R., & Naidoo, V. (2025). The role of materialism and social judgment in human-chatbot service interactions. *Journal of Services Marketing, 39*(4), 316–332.

Saleem, A., Ghafar, A., Ibrahim, M., Yousuf, M., & Ahmed, N. (2015). Product perceived quality and purchase intention with consumer satisfaction. *Global Journal of Management and Business Research: E Marketing, 15*(1), 21–28.

Sapmaz, F., Yıldırım, M., Topcuoğlu, P., Nalbant, D., & Sızır, U. (2016). Gratitude, forgiveness and humility as predictors of subjective well-being among university students. *International Online Journal of Educational Sciences, 8*(1), 38–47.

Sela, A., Wheeler, S. C., & Sarial-Abi, G. (2012). We are not the same as you and I: Causal effects of minor language variations on consumers' attitudes toward brands. *Journal of Consumer Research, 39*(3), 644–661.

Senecal, S., & Nantel, J. (2004). The influence of online product recommendations on consumers' online choices. *Journal of Retailing, 80*(2), 159–169.

Shen, A. (2014). Recommendations as personalized marketing: Insights from customer experiences. *Journal of Services Marketing, 28*(5), 414–427.

Söllner, M., Hoffmann, A., & Leimeister, J. M. (2016). Why different trust relationships matter for information systems users. *European Journal of Information Systems, 25*(3), 274–287.

Sun, L., Tang, Y., & Ma, X. (2025). It just would not work for me: Perceived preference heterogeneity and consumer response to AI-driven product recommendations. *European Journal of Marketing, 59*(5), 1426–1452.

Sun, Y., Li, S., & Yu, L. (2022). The dark sides of AI personal assistant: Effects of service failure on user continuance intention. *Electronic Markets, 32*(1), 17–39.

Svebak, S. (1996). The development of the Sense of Humor Questionnaire: From SHQ to SHQ-6. *Humor, 9*(3-4), 341–362.

Swencionis, J. K., Dupree, C. H., & Fiske, S. T. (2017). Warmth-competence tradeoffs in impression management across race and social-class divides. *Journal of Social Issues, 73* (1), 175–191.

Toader, C., Dana, B., Toader, R., Măcelaru, M., Toader, C., Ighian, I., & Rădulescu, A. (2019). The effect of social presence and chatbot errors on trust. *Sustainability, 12*, 256.

Trzebiński, W., & Marciniak, B. (2022). Recommender system information trustworthiness: The role of perceived ability to learn, self-extension, and intelligence cues. *Computers in Human Behavior Reports, 6*, 100193.

Usman, U., Kim, T., Garvey, A., & Duhachek, A. (2024). The persuasive power of AI ingratiation: A persuasion knowledge theory perspective. *Journal of the Association for Consumer Research, 9*(3), 319–331.

Van Doorn, J., Mende, M., Noble, S. M., Hulland, J., Ostrom, A. L., Grewal, D., & Petersen, J. A. (2017). Domo arigato Mr. Roboto: Emergence of automated social presence in organizational frontlines and customers' service experiences. *Journal of Service Research, 20*(1), 43–58.

Van Pinxteren, M. M. E., Wetzels, R. W. H., Ruger, J., Pluymaekers, M., & Wetzels, M. (2019). Trust in humanoid robots: Implications for services marketing. *Journal of Services Marketing, 33*(4), 507–518.

Venkatesh, V., Thong, J. Y., & Xu, X. (2012). Consumer acceptance and use of information technology: Extending the unified theory of acceptance and use of technology. *MIS Quarterly*, 157–178.

Verhagen, T., Van Nes, J., Feldberg, F., & Van Dolen, W. (2014). Virtual customer service agents: Using social presence and personalization to shape online service encounters. *Journal of Computer-Mediated Communication*, *19*(3), 529–545.

Wang, W., Qiu, L., Kim, D., & Benbasat, I. (2016). Effects of rational and social appeals of online recommendation agents on cognition-and affect-based trust. *Decision Support Systems*, *86*, 48–60.

Wei, Q., Bao, A., Lv, D., Liu, S., Chen, S., Chi, Y., & Zuo, J. (2024). The influence of message frame and product type on green consumer purchase decisions: An ERPs study. *Scientific Reports*, *14*(1), 23232.

Wien, A. H., & Peluso, A. M. (2021). Influence of human versus AI recommenders: The roles of product type and cognitive processes. *Journal of Business Research*, *137*, 13–27.

Wimbush, A. (2014). Humility, self-Awareness, and religious ambivalence: Another look at beckett's 'Humanistic Quietism'. *Journal of Beckett Studies*, *23*(2), 202–221.

Wu, K., Zhao, Y., Zhu, Q., Tan, X., & Zheng, H. (2011). A meta-analysis of the impact of trust on technology acceptance model: Investigation of moderating influence of subject and context type. *International Journal of Information Management*, *31*(6), 572–581.

Xiao, Y., & Yu, S. (2025). Can ChatGPT replace humans in crisis communication? The effects of AI-mediated crisis communication on stakeholder satisfaction and responsibility attribution. *International Journal of Information Management*, *80*, 102835.

Xu, Y., Zhang, J., & Deng, G. (2022). Enhancing customer satisfaction with chatbots: The influence of communication styles and consumer attachment anxiety. *Frontiers in Psychology*, *13*, 902782.

Yang, Y., Zheng, J., Yu, Y., Qiu, Y., & Wang, L. (2024). The role of recommendation sources and attribute framing in online product recommendations. *Journal of Business Research*, *174*, 114498.

Yeomans, M., Shah, A., Mullainathan, S., & Kleinberg, J. (2019). Making sense of recommendations. *Journal of Behavioral Decision Making*, *32*(4), 403–414.

Yu, C. E. (2020). Humanlike robots as employees in the hotel industry: Thematic content analysis of online reviews. *Journal of Hospitality Marketing & Management*, *29*(1), 22–38.

Zhang, Y., Zhu, J., Chen, H., & Jiang, Y. (2025). Enhancing trust and empathy in marketing: Strategic AI and human influencer selection for optimized content persuasion. *Journal of Consumer Behaviour*, *24*(2), 866–885.

Zhao, K., Stylianou, A. C., & Zheng, Y. (2013). Predicting users' continuance intention in virtual communities: The dual intention-formation processes. *Decision Support Systems*, *55*(4), 903–910.

Zogaj, A., Tscheulin, D., & Olk, S. (2020). Benefits of matching consumers' personality: Creating perceived trustworthiness via actual self-congruence and perceived competence via ideal self-congruence. *Psychology & Marketing*, *38*, 416–430.

Practical Insights 4

This chapter presents the empirical context, methods, and data from the in-depth semi-structured interviews conducted to explore user-AI interactions. Qualitative data was collected from 20 interviewees with varied shopping behaviors and experiences of AI service usage. Each interview lasted 20–30 minutes and yielded rich insights into key themes such as AI versus human recommendations, AI communication styles, AI humor, and GAI humor. The following sections include the interview purpose and questions, subjects and recruitment methods, data analysis procedures, detailed results, and a comprehensive summary of findings.

4.1 Interview Purpose and Questions

To acquire in-depth, practical insights into the core concepts outlined in the research questions—including the distinctions between AI and human recommendations, AI communication styles, AI humility, and GAI humor—we conducted comprehensive empirical fieldwork through in-depth, semi-structured interviews. The fieldwork was implemented via online meetings, with 20 interviewees recruited based on the author's network. This selection method leveraged pre-existing interpersonal familiarity, which played a key role in reducing potential communication barriers. Interviewees were more likely to share genuine experiences, detailed emotional responses, and candid opinions, which was essential for enhancing the authenticity and depth of the interview content. Such openness ensured that the collected data could directly address the research focus and provide meaningful insights into user-AI interactions.

The interview protocol was developed based on a review of prior relevant literature and the core objectives of the current research, covering five key themes that directly correspond to the research questions. The first theme—Respondent Basic Information—focused on collecting demographic data, including age,

F. Yang, *AI and Consumer Interaction in Business*, Management for Professionals,
https://doi.org/10.1007/978-981-95-9430-6_4

gender, educational background, and monthly disposable income, as well as details of interviewees' online shopping and AI service usage habits, such as shopping frequency, preferred e-commerce platforms, and frequency of customer service interactions. This information served as a foundational context for interpreting subsequent responses, allowing researchers to link specific opinions or experiences to demographic traits or behavioral patterns, for instance, whether master's degree holders were more critical of AI's humility expressions.

The specific questions for this theme were:

1. What is your age group? (e.g., 21–30 years old, 31–40 years old, etc.)
2. What is your gender?
3. What is your highest level of education? (e.g., high school/ or below, bachelor's, masters or above)
4. What is your monthly disposable income range?
5. Have you had experiences with online shopping (e.g., on platforms like Taobao, JD) or using AI customer service/human customer service? If yes, what is the approximate frequency?

The second theme—AI vs. Human Recommendation—explored interviewees' overall impressions of AI and human recommendations. Interviewees were asked about the typical scenarios where they encountered with these recommendations, such as product browsing pages, or in-store shopping guide interactions, and the key differences they perceived between the two, such as in personalization, communication tone, response speed, or relevance to needs. Insights regarding how each type of recommendation influenced their purchasing decisions were also collected. Example questions included: "When receiving recommendations from AI, what is your overall feeling? Please provide specific examples, such as the content of recommendations for a certain type of product or the interaction method of AI recommendations."

The specific questions for this theme were:

6. When you receive recommendations from AI (e.g., platform's automatic product recommendation AI system or proactive AI customer service), what is your overall feeling? You can illustrate with specific scenarios, such as the recommendation content for a certain type of product, the interactive method of AI recommendations, and the experience it brings to you.
7. When you receive recommendations from humans (e.g., human customer service, store human shopping guides), what are the characteristics of your overall feeling? You can also illustrate with examples, such as communication details in human recommendations, the targeted nature of the recommendation content, and aspects that left a deep impression on you.
8. Based on the above two experiences, what do you think is the most obvious difference in overall feeling between AI recommendations and human recommendations? For example, are there differences in recommendation accuracy, communication warmth, response timeliness, etc.?

9. Do you think there are differences between AI recommendations and human recommendations in influencing your purchase intention? If yes, in which aspects do you think this difference is mainly reflected?

The third theme—AI communication style—aimed to understand interviewees' general impressions of AI customer service language, such as whether it felt mechanical, overly formal, or conversational, their perceptions of two distinct communication styles: "social-oriented," for example, warm, playful, with references to daily life or personal circumstances, and "task-oriented," for example, concise, fact-based, focused solely on product details or problem-solving steps, and how these styles affected their engagement with brands, such as their willingness to follow brand updates, participate in brand activities, or repurchase products.

The specific questions for this theme were:

10. In your past interactions with AI customer service, have you noticed their language style? Please describe the AI customer service language styles that left a deeper impression on you.
11. We divide AI communication styles into "social-oriented" (e.g., chatting in a lively tone, caring about the user's daily life) and "task-oriented" (e.g., focusing only on product information). What kind of feelings do you think these two styles of AI customer service would bring to you respectively?
12. Do you think the social-oriented or task-oriented AI communication style would affect your engagement with the brand (e.g., following brand updates, repurchasing the brand's products, etc.)? How does it affect?

The fourth theme—AI Agent Humanity (Humility Traits)—delved into interviewees' cognitive understanding of whether AI could possess the trait of "humility," their preference for "high-humility" AI, for example, proactive apologies for service failures, clear explanations of mistakes, and specific, actionable solutions, versus "low-humility" AI, for example, evasive responses, failure to acknowledge errors, or vague promises of follow-up. Practical insights were gained regarding how AI humility impacted their willingness to use the service again in the future. Example questions included: "Do you think AI can exhibit the trait of 'humility'? Please explain your reasoning based on your own experiences with AI services."

The specific questions for this theme were:

13. Do you think AI can exhibit the trait of "humility"? Please explain your reasons based on your experiences.
14. If we divide AI's humility level into "high humility" (e.g., proactive apology for service failures) and "low humility" (e.g., no apology for service failures), which kind of AI service do you prefer? Why?
15. Do you think high-humility AI would increase your willingness to continue using the AI service in the future? If yes, what do you think is the core reason?

The fifth theme—GAI Humor—investigated interviewees' experiences with humorous GAI, such as social media comment bots, AI chat tools for casual conversation, or GAI-driven review generators, the differences in "warmth" they perceived between "high-humor" GAI (e.g., witty, contextually relevant jokes, playful teasing, or lighthearted references to popular culture) and "low-humor" GAI (e.g., serious and straightforward responses), and how GAI humor influenced their satisfaction with the service.

The specific questions for this theme were:

16. Have you encountered generative AI with a sense of humor (e.g., social media comment bots, ChatGPT, etc.)? Please describe your experiences (e.g., the humorous reply content from AI and your feelings).
17. How do "high-humor" GAI and "low-humor" GAI conditions differ in terms of perceived warmth?
18. Do you think the humor of GAI would affect your satisfaction with its service? Is the impact positive or negative? Please explain the reasons.

4.2 Interview Subjects and Recruitment Methods

Guided by the logic of theoretical sampling, our sampling strategy was designed to capture potential variances in interviewees' online shopping behaviors, frequency of AI service usage, and cognitive preferences toward AI-related interactions. This approach was intended to avoid sample homogeneity and ensure that the data could reflect diverse perspectives on the research topics, rather than being limited to a narrow range of experiences. In terms of demographic characteristics, all 20 interviewees fell within the 21–30 age group—a demographic that is not only a core user base for online shopping but also highly engaged with AI services. This age group typically demonstrates strong familiarity with digital platforms, engages in frequent online transactions, and is more receptive to interacting with emerging AI tools, such as AI customer service, AI recommendation systems, and GAI chatbots, in daily life. Focusing on this cohort ensured that the interview data was closely aligned with the research context, as their experiences were directly relevant to the core themes of AI-user interactions.

Regarding educational background, the sample was structured to include both undergraduate and postgraduate students. This intentional variation in educational attainment was designed to explore whether differences in academic training, analytical thinking patterns, and information processing approaches might influence how interviewees evaluate AI services. For example, postgraduate students might offer more nuanced reflections on abstract concepts like AI's humility trait or the emotional value of GAI humor, drawing on their experience with critical analysis and complex problem-solving. In contrast, undergraduate students might focus more on practical, day-to-day experiences—such as the efficiency of AI recommendations, the clarity of AI communication, or the ease of resolving issues with AI customer service. This diversity in educational backgrounds helped enrich the depth and breadth of insights derived from the interviews.

In terms of monthly disposable income, the sample covered three distinct tiers to reflect the diversity of economic backgrounds among the interviewees, ensuring that the collected data would not be limited to a single income group and could capture a broader range of user perspectives on AI services. Specifically, 5 interviewees had a monthly disposable income of 3000 yuan or less, 10 had an income ranging from 3001 to 6000 yuan, and 5 had an income exceeding 6000 yuan. This income-based stratification was intended to add dimensionality to the sample, providing a more comprehensive view of how users with different economic circumstances might engage with AI services—such as whether there are differences in how frequently they interact with AI recommendations, or how they perceive the practical value of AI-driven support. For instance, interviewees with varying income levels might naturally differ in their online shopping habits, which in turn could lead to differences in their exposure to and experiences with AI services. This variation in economic background thus enriches the overall dataset, offering supplementary perspectives that help contextualize the core findings related to the research's focus areas, rather than serving as a focal point for analyzing economic influences on AI service usage.

In terms of gender, the sample included both female and male interviewees. The gender distribution roughly mirrors the gender characteristics of active online shopping users, where female users tend to engage in more frequent online transactions and interactions with customer service. This gender distribution ensured that the data could capture gender-specific perspectives on AI interactions. For example, female interviewees often emphasized the emotional tone of AI communication, with one noting that she paid close attention to whether an AI's response felt empathetic during service failures, such as when an order was delayed. In contrast, male interviewees were more likely to focus on the functional efficiency of AI services; one male interviewee, for instance, highlighted that he prioritized how quickly an AI could provide product specifications or resolve technical issues, such as clarifying the compatibility of a digital accessory. Such gender-based insights added layers of depth to the understanding of user-AI dynamics.

A critical criterion for selecting interviewees was their prior experience with online shopping and AI services—all 20 participants had extensive experience using major e-commerce platforms, including those focused on general merchandise, consumer electronics, daily necessities, and fashion. Their online shopping frequencies varied widely: some shopped once a week, while others made purchases multiple times a day. One interviewee, who frequently bought daily essentials like toiletries and snacks, noted that she shopped online almost every other day, while another who primarily purchased clothing and accessories reported shopping once a week.

Similarly, their usage patterns of AI and human customer service differed significantly. Some interviewees frequently encountered AI customer service, particularly those who preferred to shop at night when human customer service

Table 4.1 Specific demographic and AI service use profiles for each interviewee

Interviewee	Highest education	Monthly disposable income	Online shopping frequency	Customer service frequency
1	Bachelor	Over 6000 Yuan	Regular	Once a month
2	Bachelor	3001-6000 Yuan	Frequent	Regular
3	Bachelor	Over 6000 Yuan	Frequent	Infrequent
4	Bachelor	Over 6000 Yuan	Daily	Occasional
5	Bachelor	3001-6000 Yuan	Frequent	Infrequent
6	Bachelor	3001-6000 Yuan	Frequent	Regular
7	Master	3001-6000 Yuan	Frequent	Regular
8	Bachelor	Within 3000 Yuan	Occasional	-
9	Master	Within 3000 Yuan	Occasional	Infrequent
10	Master	Within 3000 Yuan	-	Regular
11	Master	3001-6000 Yuan	Frequent	-
12	Master	3001-6000 Yuan	Frequent	Regular
13	Master	3001-6000 Yuan	Regular	-
14	Master	Within 3000 Yuan	Occasional	Infrequent
15	Master	3001-6000 Yuan	Frequent	Daily
16	Bachelor	Over 6000 Yuan	Occasional	Infrequent
17	Bachelor	Within 3000 Yuan	Frequent	Infrequent
18	Master	3001-6000 Yuan	Occasional	Regular
19	Bachelor	Over 6000 Yuan	-	Frequent
20	Bachelor	3001-6000 Yuan	-	-

teams were typically offline. One such interviewee explained that she often shopped after 9 PM, so she regularly relied on AI-driven support tools to track orders, initiate returns, or clarify product details like fabric composition. In contrast, other interviewees rarely used AI customer service and instead chose to consult human representatives whenever they encountered issues. One interviewee expresses a preference for more flexible, context-aware problem-solving approaches in customer service scenarios. For instance, she recalled a complex return dispute involving a damaged product and inconsistent seller communication. A human representative was able to negotiate a personalized solution, such as a partial refund plus a discount on a future purchase. According to her, an AI would lack the capacity to negotiate such nuanced, personalized outcomes. This variation in exposure to AI services provided a multi-faceted lens for analyzing how different levels of interaction shape user trust, satisfaction, and preference toward AI versus human support. The details of the insights gained are presented in Table 4.1.

4.3 Data Analysis

To ensure the quality and integrity of the data, the researcher adhered strictly to pre-defined procedures during the data collection process. All interviews were conducted via online meeting platforms and recorded with the explicit consent of the interviewees—a step taken to avoid missing key information, misinterpreting responses, or losing nuanced expressions, such as tone of voice or pauses that conveyed doubt or enthusiasm. Each interview lasted between 20 and 30 minutes, a duration that balanced the need for in-depth discussion, to explore complex opinions such as why an interviewee preferred human recommendations over AI, with the need to prevent interviewee fatigue, which could lead to superficial or rushed responses. During the interviews, the researcher maintained a neutral and supportive stance. Instead of leading the conversation or imposing personal views, interviewees were encouraged to share detailed, specific anecdotes. One interviewee, for instance, shared a situation where a human recommendation resolved a long-standing uncertainty: she had struggled to find a skincare product suitable for her sensitive skin until a human customer service representative asked follow-up questions about her specific skin concerns, like dryness and redness, and recommended a targeted moisturizer, a resolution she didn't think AI could have achieved. The researcher also asked follow-up questions to clarify ambiguous points. For example, if an interviewee mentioned "do not like AI recommendations," the researcher might prompt: "Could you tell me more about what specifically made those recommendations feel irrelevant to your needs?" to elicit deeper, more actionable insights.

After each interview, the audio recordings were transcribed into text within 24 hours to preserve the accuracy of the interviewees' statements. Delays in transcription were avoided, as they could lead to the loss of contextual details, such as references to specific platforms or products, or nuanced expressions, such as sarcasm or hesitation. The transcribed text was then cross-checked against the original recording to correct any errors, omissions, or misinterpretations of colloquial language, such as slang or casual phrases that might have been misheard. The raw data—including audio recordings and transcribed text—was stored securely in encrypted files to ensure compliance with data privacy principles and maintain traceability, allowing for later verification of quotes, details, or contextual nuances. Additionally, the transcribed content was categorized into themes corresponding to the four core parts of the interview results, a process that involved sorting responses by topic, such as AI vs. human recommendation, AI communication style, AI humility, GAI humor, and tagging key quotes for subsequent analysis. This organization laid the groundwork for extracting consistent patterns from the interviews and linking empirical data directly to the research questions.

In summary, this fieldwork provided preliminary empirical support for the relevance and significance of the research questions. It helped refine core concepts—for example, clarifying how interviewees define "AI humility" as proactive accountability rather than scripted apologies or "GAI humor" as contextually relevant wit rather than generic jokes in practical, real-world scenarios—and confirmed that the interview protocol effectively elicited detailed, relevant information. The diverse backgrounds of the interviewees, in terms of education, income, gender, and usage habits, and the richness of their shared experiences ensured the interview data was comprehensive and representative, offering valuable practical insights for exploring the complex dynamics of user-AI interactions in depth. This fieldwork also laid a solid foundation for the next stage of the research, including thematic analysis of the interview results and the integration of findings with broader theoretical frameworks related to AI-user interaction and service design.

4.4 Findings

To help readers better understand the practical implications of the interview results and gain a vivid understanding of users' real experiences and perceptions regarding AI-related interactions, this section presents a synopsis of pertinent interview quotes—highlighting unique, context-rich insights shared by the 20 interviewees—and is followed by a brief reflection on their significance. The quotes are categorized according to the core themes of the interview protocol, which directly align with the research's focus on exploring user attitudes toward AI and human recommendations, AI communication styles, AI humility traits, and GAI humor.

Each research theme is populated with specific, detailed quotes and direct opinions from interviewees, ensuring that the insights are rooted in real-world user interactions rather than theoretical assumptions. By organizing the quotes in this way, the researcher aims to systematically unpack the diverse perspectives on the four core themes of the research, and to illustrate how these elements influence users' overall experiences, preferences, and behavioral intentions—such as their willingness to repurchase a brand's products or continue using an AI service.

Before diving into the categorized quotes, it is critical to note that the interviewees' responses were not only varied but also closely tied to their individual contexts: their frequency of online shopping, past experiences with AI or human service successes and failures, and personal expectations of digital tools. For instance, interviewees who often shopped at night (when human customer service was offline) and thus relied heavily on AI support frequently shared detailed observations about AI's functional strengths and limitations—such as its speed in providing basic product information versus its struggle to resolve complex return disputes. Meanwhile, those who had engaged with humorous GAI tools (like social media comment bots or casual chat platforms) often emphasized how such interactions influenced their emotional state, such as lifting their mood during a frustrating shopping experience. These contextual differences add depth and nuance to the insights, and underscore the importance of considering user diversity when analyzing AI-user interaction dynamics. The following subsections will present the categorized quotes, alongside brief analyses of how each set of insights contributes to the understanding of the four core research themes.

4.4.1 Cases Regarding AI vs. Human Recommendation

This section presents a structured analysis of user perceptions towards different recommendation sources with four tables. Table 4.2 presents insights regarding AI recommendations, focusing on their data-driven accuracy, long-term limitations such as repetitive content, and associated privacy concerns from cross-platform tracking. Table 4.3 summarizes insights regarding human recommendations, emphasizing attributes like empathetic communication, contextual understanding, and the ability to build trust through personal interaction. Building on these findings, Table 4.4 details the perceived differences between AI and human recommendations, comparing them across dimensions such as adaptability, emotional resonance, and depth of personalization. Finally, Table 4.5 directly examines the relationship between recommendation source and purchase intention, analyzing how the distinct characteristics of AI and human agents influence consumers' final decision-making and likelihood to complete a transaction. Together, these tables provide a comprehensive framework for understanding how recommendation sources shape user experience and commercial outcomes.

A deeper analysis of interviewees' responses reveals consistent patterns in how users distinguish between AI and human recommendations, as well as the underlying factors that shape their trust, satisfaction, and decision-making. These patterns not only reflect the functional differences between the two recommendation types but also highlight the emotional and contextual needs that drive user preferences.

The analysis underscores that AI recommendations are primarily valued for efficiency and accessibility, yet constrained by a lack of contextual awareness. Interviewees repeatedly noted that AI excels at delivering instant responses to straightforward queries—such as confirming product stock, sharing basic specifications (e.g., material, size ranges), or surface-level personalization based on recent browsing history. For example, multiple participants mentioned that AI could quickly direct them to relevant product categories or alert them to price discounts, a benefit that aligned with their needs for speed during low-stakes shopping tasks (e.g., purchasing daily essentials like toiletries or household goods). However, this efficiency came with clear limitations: AI often failed to account for "unspoken" context, such as whether a user had already purchased a recommended item, their lifestyle constraints (e.g., travel needs for a camera), or nuanced preferences (e.g., a preference for stainless steel over plastic water bottles). This "narrow focus" of AI—rooted in its reliance on explicit data (browsing history, search terms) rather than implicit cues—led to frustration, as seen in interviewees who received repeated recommendations for identical winter coats or irrelevant product types. Privacy concerns further tempered enthusiasm for AI's "predictive" capabilities; several participants expressed discomfort with AI's ability to anticipate needs based on off-platform interactions (e.g., casual conversations with roommates), which undermined their trust in the recommendation's relevance and authenticity.

In contrast, human recommendations were distinguished by contextual depth and emotional resonance, attributes that made them more trusted for complex or high-

Table 4.2 Insights regarding AI recommendations

"Based on my experience with shopping apps, Taobao's product recommendation mechanism can quite accurately identify and predict my recent shopping intentions or search tendencies. Take clothing shopping as an example: the system can, according to my historical preferences, push products that are highly matched in terms of style, color, and even seasonality (such as autumn clothing and summer clothing). However, this recommendation model gradually reveals its limitations with continued use—the scope of recommendations tends to narrow, and the content repetition rate increases. As a result, the sense of freshness diminishes steadily. In the long run, I inevitably experience aesthetic fatigue and find it difficult to come across products that bring an amazing experience. This may reflect that while big data-based personalized recommendations pursue accuracy, they may also excessively filter the diversity of information, which in turn limits users' exploration of potential interests." **Respondent 1**
"Taking Taobao as an example, its AI recommendation system often pushes products through the 'You May Also Like' section after I complete a purchase. However, based on my observations, approximately 60% of the recommended content deviates from my actual anticipation or immediate purchasing desires. Generally speaking, the system can partially touch upon my interest points, but in most cases, it still seems unable to deeply understand my true consumption intentions and decision-making logic." **Respondent 2**
"What I mainly experience is passive recommendations based on big data, rather than active intervention by AI. For instance, during the National holiday, I searched for Lancôme' products on JD.com. On the following days, advertisements related to Lancôme appeared on multiple different platforms, even when I was reading novels. This cross-platform precise delivery made me feel uncomfortable as if my privacy was being invaded, and the experience was similar to being under constant surveillance." **Respondent 3**
"In my shopping experience, AI recommendations usually appear after a transaction is completed. The system will push products of similar categories based on the style or attributes of the purchased items. However, when I make personal decisions, I take multiple factors into account, such as price, style, and fabric. Therefore, there is a disconnect between AI recommendations and my complex decision-making dimensions, and the probability that I finally adopt its recommendations to complete a purchase is relatively low." **Respondent 4**
"Most of the AI recommendations I have encountered take the form of page-level recommendations. The core problem lies in the excessive singularity of the recommended content and the serious homogenization of products—some can even be regarded as different supplier versions of the same product. When I want to explore different styles or new products, this recommendation system lacks effective style extension and exploration capabilities, appearing mechanical and rigid. I often have to conduct active searches again." **Respondent 5**
"Platforms' AI-based recommendation systems demonstrate a certain level of intelligence in specific scenarios. For example, after purchasing earrings, it can accurately recommend similar styles. However, its flaw is the lack of judgment on users' consumption cycles. For instance, after purchasing a large quantity of fast-moving consumer goods like tissues, the system still continues to recommend similar products. Such ineffective recommendations reduce its overall practical value." **Respondent 6**
"AI recommendations mainly conduct big data analysis based on my historical consumption data and push similar products. In another case, it seems to be able to perceive my potential needs through background data-tracking technology. For example, after mentioning to my roommate that I wanted to buy a cup, relevant recommendations quickly appeared on Taobao's page. This method has two sides: on the one hand, it triggers a sense of unease about being monitored and concerns about privacy; on the other hand, it does bring convenience to my life on some occasions." **Respondent 7**

(continued)

Table 4.2 (continued)

"I usually pay little attention to products recommended by AI. When I need to seek customer service help, AI customer service often fails to solve core problems, and I still have to be transferred to human service in the end. Therefore, in terms of the effectiveness of solving practical problems, the current AI customer service has limited practical value for me." **Respondent 8**
"When shopping on platforms like Taobao, most of the recommendations I encounter are AI-based. Their notable feature is the high degree of homogeneity of recommended products and the lack of diversity, making it difficult to find unique products that are surprising or exceed expectations." **Respondent 9**
"I can clearly distinguish the difference between AI recommendations and human recommendations. Specifically, when I inquired about power banks, the AI customer service pushed several popular models before I even specified my specific needs. Such recommendations lack in-depth exploration of my personal needs, giving people a feeling of standardized and generalized recommendations rather than customized services." **Respondent 10**
"AI recommendations mainly appear on online platforms or when checking out in offline stores, based on my shopping and search habits. My feeling is that commercial promotions are ubiquitous. However, I rarely buy products recommended by AI on social platforms like Xiaohongshu and Douyin; I usually only search actively when I have clear needs. In addition, AI recommendations will repeatedly push the same product, and its frequent appearances on the homepage easily lead to aesthetic fatigue and boredom." **Respondent 11**
"Most of my shopping is done online, and my feelings about AI customer service recommendations vary by scenario. When encountering special, non-standardized complex problems, AI responses lack pertinence and personalization, which makes me feel irritable and anxious, and I urgently hope to be transferred to human customer service. But when dealing with common issues, such as finding the entrance to claim coupons, AI can quickly provide direct links, and this efficient experience is satisfying." **Respondent 12**
"My overall feeling about AI recommendations is that they are highly efficient but lack accuracy. The system rigidly relies on my historical browsing records. For example, I researched cat food once because of a course requirement, and then the homepage was filled with cat food recommendations for the next two weeks, even though I had no need to raise a cat. This makes me feel that AI is like a dutiful assistant with limited understanding." **Respondent 13**
"Taking Taobao as an example, the AI-recommended products used by merchants often show an obvious tendency of homogenization and high repetition rate. This is mainly because the recommendation logic is based on my past purchase records and tends to push similar products, but these recommendations often disconnect from my actual needs during specific periods." **Respondent 14**
"I often buy clothes online. When I consult the AI customer service about size information, it usually can only mechanically reply with material and standard size data, in a rigid way that feels like it is operating according to a fixed program. Most of the time, it cannot truly understand and capture my deeper real needs regarding fit, version, and other aspects." **Respondent 15**
"Overall, AI-recommended products generally align well with my personal needs, as the system appears to combine my individual usage preferences with broader group-based consumption patterns. However, a common issue is the high degree of homogenization. The system tends to repeatedly recommend items I already like, while offering limited expansion into other domains. For example, when I recently intended to purchase a camera, multiple platforms continuously pushed camera-related products, whereas recommendations for clothing or cosmetics noticeably decreased." **Respondent 16**

(*continued*)

Table 4.2 (continued)

"In my experience, product recommendations on platforms such as Taobao are extremely frequent, even when I have only briefly browsed a store without making a purchase. These recommendations are often highly homogeneous and repetitive, usually focusing on flagship products or items similar to those I have already purchased. As a goal-oriented consumer, I typically search for products based on clear needs, so such AI-driven recommendations rarely influence my purchasing decisions and often make me feel uncomfortable due to excessive exposure." **Respondent 17**
"When consulting AI customer service for product recommendations, I find that the suggestions often fail to accurately match my actual needs. AI systems tend to rely on preset keywords and standardized logic, which limits their ability to capture more nuanced or personalized requirements. In contrast, human customer service representatives are better able to provide recommendations that resonate with my real situation and emotional needs, especially when I am comparing similar products." **Respondent 18**
"I gradually realized that features such as "You May Also Like" are driven by AI recommendation systems. These recommendations often exhibit a high level of homogenization and become repetitive when I show interest in a particular category. Continuous exposure to similar products can easily lead to aesthetic fatigue rather than increasing my willingness to purchase. Although human recommendations also have limitations, AI recommendations feel more mechanical and rigid." **Respondent 19**
"AI recommendations on online shopping platforms are mainly based on algorithmic analysis of my browsing and purchase history, which makes them highly efficient in terms of information retrieval. However, from a personal perspective, such recommendations feel relatively cold and lack emotional depth. While AI can serve as a useful tool during the search process, it rarely generates genuine emotional resonance or significantly enhances my purchase intention compared with human-generated recommendations." **Respondent 20**

stakes decisions. Interviewees emphasized that human representatives, shopping guides, or even peers (e.g., a photographer friend) would engage in "active listening"—asking follow-up questions to uncover hidden needs that AI missed. For instance, a human skincare advisor asked about a user's room temperature and current routine to tailor a moisturizer recommendation, while a physical store shopping guide considered a user's body type (long neck) to suggest complementary accessories. These actions reflected an understanding of "user context" that extended beyond transactional data, creating a sense of being "seen" rather than reduced to a set of browsing behaviors.

Humans also demonstrated flexibility in problem-solving: when an interviewee needed a laptop charger replacement (not a refund) for work, a human representative adjusted the solution to align with their urgent needs, a level of adaptability AI could not match. Additionally, human recommendations often included experiential insights (e.g., "this shoe sole is thin and uncomfortable on rough roads") that AI, limited to product descriptions, could not provide. These insights reduced uncertainty for users, particularly when purchasing products with subjective or performance-based attributes (e.g., skincare, footwear, cameras).

Table 4.3 Insights regarding human recommendations

"In the customer service system of e-commerce platforms, human customer service and AI customer service form a sharp contrast. Especially in the product recommendation process, human customer service demonstrates excellent situational understanding ability. When I consult about skincare products, they can perform in-depth personalized product matching based on the skin condition and specific skincare needs I actively provide. The entire communication process is not only efficient and accurate in information transmission but also reflects an in-depth insight into consumers' needs. This interactive experience based on real human wisdom significantly surpasses the technical boundaries of current AI customer service in terms of personalized services and understanding of complex needs." **Respondent 1**
"As a senior online shopping user, I have accumulated rich experience in interacting with human customer service. Usually, I find interesting stores after recommendations from others and then take the initiative to contact customer service for consultation. In the clothing field, after I provide key parameters such as height and weight, customer service can accurately recommend styles and sizes that suit my physical characteristics, and the accuracy of such recommendations based on professional experience is satisfactory. Moreover, in recommending daily necessities such as storage products, human customer service also shows excellent professional judgment, and the recommendation results are often highly consistent with my actual needs." **Respondent 2**
"Although the frequency of directly accepting human recommendations is limited, from the perspective of acceptance, my recognition of human recommendations is significantly higher than that of algorithm recommendations. This difference stems from the essential difference in interaction modes: human recommendations are based on my active inquiries and clear choices, reflecting consumers' autonomy; while algorithm recommendations are passive information feeding which easily triggers psychological resistance. More importantly, the cognition that the conversation partner is a real 'person' greatly enhances my psychological identification and trust foundation, and this emotional connection is difficult for machines to establish." **Respondent 3**
"In the field of clothing shopping, I have rich experience in human customer service recommendations. After I become a loyal customer of a store, human customer service will systematically analyze my purchase records, including various items such as tops, pants, and shoes, and then recommend new products that can be perfectly matched. Compared with AI recommendations, human recommendations show stronger pertinence and forward-looking, because they can provide truly personalized styling solutions by combining an in-depth understanding of my deep needs such as personal style preferences and physical characteristics." **Respondent 4**
"The core advantage of human recommendations lies in the depth of communication and the accuracy of intention understanding. When I am looking for a specific style or product type, interacting with AI requires me to accurately refine keywords and feature descriptions, and there is often information loss in this process. In contrast, human customer service can quickly capture my expression intentions through natural conversations, and even infer the details of needs that I have not clearly expressed. This smooth and accurate interactive experience not only improves communication efficiency but also establishes a solid foundation of trust." **Respondent 5**
"Although the frequency of actively seeking human customer service assistance in online shopping is not high, on occasions that require professional advice, such as product style selection or preferential plan matching, I always tend to choose real customer service. AI customer service is limited by preset response templates and often seems powerless when facing problems beyond the conventional. In contrast, communication with human customer service is more natural. I can fully express complex needs, and the understanding and empathy shown by the other party make the entire shopping experience more pleasant and efficient." **Respondent 6**

(continued)

Table 4.3 (continued)

"In the e-commerce environment, there are indeed few recommendations initiated purely by humans; in most cases, I need to take the initiative to ask. However, in offline retail scenarios, the service value of human shopping guides is fully reflected. Their unique advantage lies in the ability to provide comprehensive personalized services: when purchasing clothing, shopping guides will professionally evaluate factors such as my physical characteristics and skin tone to recommend the most suitable styles. More importantly, human shopping guides have a unique aesthetic vision accumulated based on long-term experience. This creativity is difficult for data-driven AI to achieve, making them show unique value in fields that require creativity such as fashion matching." **Respondent 7**
"Taking offline retail shopping guides as an example, I think the actual effectiveness of their recommendation services has certain limitations. The primary problem is the conflict of interest: the salary mechanism of shopping guides is often directly linked to sales performance, which inevitably affects the objectivity of their recommendations. Secondly, due to the lack of in-depth understanding of consumers' personal preferences, the recommended products may only meet public aesthetics but not necessarily truly conform to my personalized needs and aesthetic preferences." **Respondent 8**
"In the offline shopping environment, experienced human shopping guides can effectively enhance the persuasiveness of recommendations through professional product knowledge and infectious expression methods. They can not only accurately describe product characteristics but also stimulate consumers' purchasing desire through situational descriptions. This emotional resonance brought by interpersonal interaction is difficult for machines to replicate." **Respondent 9**
"The advantage of human recommendations is particularly obvious when dealing with specific issues. Taking the purchase of power banks as an example, I pay special attention to details such as delivery time and air transportation restrictions, and human customer service can provide clear and authoritative answers. In contrast, the standardized response templates of AI customer service are difficult to eliminate my worries about special situations, and this uncertainty will directly affect my confidence in purchasing decisions." **Respondent 10**
"The human recommendations discussed here mainly refer to offline shopping guide services. When I enter a physical store to receive shopping guide services, I often experience subtle psychological pressure. If the shopping guide shows an overly enthusiastic service attitude, I will feel guilty for 'letting down the other party's efforts without making a purchase'. This psychological burden sometimes prompts me to make irrational purchasing decisions and buy some products that I do not actually need." **Respondent 11**
"The efficiency of human customer service in solving complex problems is impressive. As I mentioned earlier, they are good at providing highly customized solutions. During the shopping process, when I raise some questions involving special situations or requiring professional judgment, AI usually cannot understand them well. However, human customer service can quickly grasp the core of the problem and give accurate and effective answers, which greatly improves the efficiency of problem-solving." **Respondent 12**
"What touches me most about human recommendations is the humanistic care and professional insight they demonstrate. An experience of buying skincare products made me deeply feel this: at that time, I had just arrived in a new living environment, and my skin had problems due to climate adaptation. After gaining a detailed understanding of my problems, the human customer service not only considered my skin characteristics and care habits but also comprehensively analyzed the local climate environment and seasonal changes, and finally gave a highly targeted solution. This professional judgment that integrates multi-dimensional information and personal experience shows a service concept truly centered on consumers' needs." **Respondent 13**

(*continued*)

Table 4.3 (continued)

"The main scenarios where I come into contact with human recommendations are concentrated in offline retail environments. The advantage of this face-to-face communication lies in the ability to achieve immediate and in-depth demand communication. I can directly and clearly express my specific requirements, and the other party can quickly understand my needs through observation and dialogue, and provide the most targeted solutions on-site. This interactive efficiency is incomparable with online recommendations." **Respondent 14**
"The difference can be clearly seen through a specific case: when I consult about the applicable occasions or fabric comfort of a certain piece of clothing, AI usually can only mechanically repeat the basic information on the product detail page. In contrast, human customer service or shopping guides can give professional and considerate suggestions based on my specific usage scenarios and personal preferences. This value judgment and personalized guidance based on real human experience are the fundamental reasons why I always prefer human recommendations." **Respondent 15**
"In my experience, human recommendations are highly dependent on personal judgment, which makes them more subjective. If the recommended products clearly do not match my preferences, I tend to lose interest quickly and may even develop a negative impression of the store. This is particularly evident in offline clothing shopping, where inappropriate recommendations can directly affect my willingness to continue engaging with the brand." **Respondent 16**
"As a consumer with clear purchasing goals, I usually consult human customer service only when I need more precise information. In scenarios such as clothing or footwear purchases, human customer service is able to provide more targeted suggestions after I clearly explain my body characteristics, which AI systems often fail to consider. This level of detailed understanding makes human recommendations more practical in specific decision-making situations." **Respondent 17**
"Compared with AI-based recommendations, human customer service recommendations are more likely to resonate with my actual needs. Through communication, human customer service can provide suggestions that feel more aligned with my real-life situation, especially when I am hesitating between similar products. This emotional and situational understanding makes human recommendations more persuasive." **Respondent 18**
"Although human recommendations can sometimes be rigid, especially when they rely too heavily on surface-level impressions, I still find human judgment more trustworthy in certain scenarios. In particular, human customer service can adjust recommendations through conversation and respond flexibly to unexpected needs, which AI systems often struggle to handle." **Respondent 19**
"What I value most in human recommendations is their ability to provide advice based on real usage scenarios. When asking about aspects such as fit, comfort, or suitability for specific occasions, human customer service can offer professional and considerate guidance beyond standardized product descriptions. This experience-based judgment significantly enhances my trust in human recommendations." **Respondent 20**

Table 4.4 Insights regarding differences between AI and human recommendations

Accuracy and Personalization
"The most obvious difference lies in the accuracy of recommendations. The AI recommendation mechanism is mainly driven by system algorithms and historical data, and its recommended content often shows homogenized characteristics, making it difficult to form differentiated supply for the unique needs of individual customers; while human recommendations can deeply explore my specific consumption needs and personalized preferences, and provide more targeted customized suggestions combined with actual scenarios." **Respondent 4**
"In terms of recommendation accuracy, human recommendations have more prominent advantages. Human customer service can quickly capture my core needs, accurately generate recommendation plans based on the needs, and then effectively promote purchase conversion; when communicating with AI systems, there are often cases of disconnection between demand and matching. For example, after I clearly express my needs, the content of AI's replies often deviates from the actual demands and cannot provide effective support for decision-making." **Respondent 6**
"For categories with strong professional attributes such as electronic products and digital products, due to my limited understanding of product parameters and industry information, I believe AI recommendations can maintain a more objective and neutral stance ... From the perspective of professional selection, AI recommendations do have more advantages in accuracy and objectivity in this field; while human customer service is often affected by subjective factors such as personal experience and sales orientation during the recommendation process, which may lead to bias in recommendation results." **Respondent 8**
"AI recommendations tend to rely on preset keywords and standardized matching logic, which often leads to a mismatch between my actual needs and the recommended content. In contrast, human customer service can better understand my specific situation through communication and provide more targeted and personalized recommendations, especially when I have detailed or non-standard requirements." **Respondent 17**
"Compared with AI systems, human recommendations are more likely to align with my real needs. Human customer service can adjust recommendations based on contextual information and my personal preferences, whereas AI recommendations often remain limited to surface-level attributes and fail to capture deeper consumption intentions." **Respondent 18**
Warmth in Communication and Flexibility
"The core difference between the two lies in the recommendation logic and adaptability: human customer service has a high degree of sensitivity in identifying individual needs, and can flexibly optimize recommendation strategies according to dynamic factors such as scene changes and demand adjustments; while AI customer service mainly pushes preset content through keyword extraction, sentence matching and other methods, and its so-called 'affinity' only comes from the fixed script reserve of the corpus, which has obvious shortcomings in the flexibility of demand adaptation and the adaptability of scene changes." **Respondent 1**
"The service of human shopping guides is more emotionally warm, and their response content can accurately match the specific questions I put forward; while the service content of AI shopping guides mostly relies on preset programs, which is limited by the current technical maturity. There are often cases of irrelevant answers, which cannot accurately reach my core needs and consumption pain points. In contrast, human shopping guides can adjust the recommendation logic and communication methods in real time according to my questions, and the overall service experience is more intimate and can convey humanistic care better." **Respondent 3**

(continued)

Table 4.4 (continued)

"There are certain differences in communication scripts between the two: the AI shopping guides I have come into contact with so far have obvious scripted characteristics; although the scripts of some human customer service also have a standardized tendency, the tone expression and emotional transmission of human customer service are more likely to make me feel comfortable, and the communication experience is relatively better." **Respondent 10**
"The most noticeable difference between AI and human recommendations lies in the sense of distance during communication. AI interactions feel more objective and emotionally distant, which I personally find comfortable. However, human recommendations are more subjective and sometimes give me the impression that the other party is attempting to infer my thoughts, which may reduce my sense of trust if the boundary is not well managed." **Respondent 16**
"Human customer service can flexibly adjust their communication style and recommendation logic during interaction, while AI responses often follow fixed patterns. This rigidity makes AI recommendations less adaptable when facing changes in my needs or more complex situations." **Respondent 19**
Responsiveness Timeliness and Recommendation Quality
"In terms of response speed, AI systems have significant advantages and can achieve nearly real-time responses within seconds, but from the perspective of recommendation value, the content they output is often difficult to meet the actual decision-making needs; although human customer service is slightly inferior in response speed, it can provide more valuable targeted suggestions combined with my specific needs, and the recommendation quality is more guaranteed." **Respondent 4**
"The core advantage of AI recommendations lies in service efficiency, with fast response speed and 24/7 service, but the recommendation quality often fails to meet expectations. As I mentioned earlier, AI recommendations also have the problem of excessively high content repetition; while human recommendations, although not as efficient as AI in response, have more advantages in warmth of service and recommendation accuracy, and can achieve accurate matching and recommendation of products based on my personalized needs." **Respondent 5**
"In terms of responsiveness timeliness, if human customer service does not require queuing, its response speed can also reach a high level; while as long as AI customer service can accurately extract the core information of my questions, its responsiveness is undoubtedly the strongest, and this advantage also makes me quite recognize the timely service of AI." **Respondent 12**
"In terms of response speed, AI clearly has an advantage, as it can provide immediate replies. However, fast responses do not necessarily mean high-quality recommendations. Human customer service may respond more slowly, but their recommendations are usually more relevant and practically useful in supporting my decision-making." **Respondent 18**
"When I need quick access to basic information, AI recommendations are efficient. But when the issue involves specific usage scenarios or requires judgment, human customer service can provide more reliable and effective guidance, which makes their recommendations more valuable despite slower response times." **Respondent 20**
Information Breadth and Diversity
"But in the process of browsing products, I found a problem: although the quality of individual products recommended by AI is acceptable, as the browsing time increases, the scope of recommended content gradually narrows, and the sense of novelty is obviously insufficient ... This phenomenon may stem from the 'excessive precision' of big data recommendations, leading to the continuous solidification of the recommendation pool, making it difficult to present more diversified product choices." **Respondent 1**

(continued)

Table 4.4 (continued)

"The product categories recommended by AI show obviously lack of diversity. Most recommended products are highly similar in functions, styles and other aspects, and there are even repeated recommendations of different manufacturer versions of the same product. When I have the need to change consumption styles and try new categories, I am usually not satisfied with AI recommendations, and I have to re-conduct keyword searches to find products that meet the needs." **Respondent 5**
"In the scene of product matching, human shopping guides' recommendations are more creative, which can break through conventional matching logic, provide more personalized plans, and avoid falling into formulaic choices. In contrast, the thinking of AI recommendations is relatively rigid, and the recommended content lacks innovation, which is difficult to meet my needs for diversified matching." **Respondent 7**
"AI recommendations often become increasingly narrow over time. Once I show interest in a certain category, the system repeatedly pushes similar products, which limits diversity and reduces the sense of novelty. In contrast, human recommendations are less constrained by historical data and can offer broader perspectives when introducing products." **Respondent 16**
Trust and Psychological Feelings
"I found that human recommendations are more acceptable to me than algorithm recommendations. The core reason is that human recommendations are services generated based on my active consultation and independent choice, while algorithm recommendations are passive information pushes, and this passivity will make me feel uncomfortable. More importantly, the recognition that the person behind the human recommendation is a real 'person' can make me gain a stronger psychological identity and be more willing to trust the recommended content." **Respondent 3**
"I think human recommendations can provide accurate answers to my specific questions, and the recommendation suggestions are more targeted. However, the replies of AI customer service are often limited to standardized responses, lacking in-depth adaptation to actual problems. For example, when I consult about issues related to carrying products on board, the vague replies of AI will make me have concerns about 'what to do if I cannot board the plane', and it is difficult to feel sufficiently reassured." **Respondent 10**
"I tend to place more trust in human recommendations because they are usually generated in response to my active inquiries. AI recommendations, on the other hand, are mostly passive pushes, which makes me feel less comfortable and less willing to fully rely on them when making purchasing decisions." **Respondent 17**
"When AI customer service provides vague or standardized replies to specific concerns, it often fails to reassure me. Human customer service can address my questions more clearly and directly, which significantly enhances my sense of security and trust in the recommendation." **Respondent 20**

A critical finding from the analysis is that user preferences for AI vs. human recommendations are scenario-dependent, rather than absolute. For quick, low-engagement tasks—such as verifying product availability, finding basic items, or checking prices—interviewees favored AI for its speed and 24/7 accessibility. For example, a participant noted that AI was ideal for "grabbing a last-minute toothbrush" but inadequate for "choosing a birthday gift for my mom." In contrast, for decisions requiring personalization (e.g., gifts, skincare for sensitive skin), problem-solving (e.g., post-purchase issues), or experiential validation (e.g., travel-

Table 4.5 Insights regarding recommendation source and purchase intention

"For shopping behaviors, the service differences between AI and human customer service have not had a significant impact on my core purchase decisions, because I always compare products from multiple dimensions based on my actual needs before completing the purchase. However, the differences in service experience between the two do directly affect my shopping feelings and further influence subsequent purchase choices. For example, when encountering after-sales problems that need to be resolved after purchase, if I am dealing with an AI customer service, its mechanical and repetitive communication mode is likely to wear out my patience. This negative experience will lead to lower my satisfaction with AI after-sales service, and may even change my future purchase decisions, or even give up choosing the merchant or similar products." **Respondent 1**
"The impact of AI recommendations and human recommendations on my purchase intention needs to be analyzed in combination with product types. Specifically, for hardware products and products that require data support for decision-making, I am more inclined to adopt AI's recommendation suggestions. For products with high experience requirements and subjective feelings dominating purchase decisions, human recommendations are more in line with my needs and preferences." **Respondent 2**
"For me, if I have a clear purchase target, neither AI recommendations nor human recommendations will change my decision. However, when my purchase intention is not yet determined, human recommendations can bring a more pleasant communication experience and smoother interaction. In contrast, AI recommendations have poor adaptability, which may lead to purchased products not matching actual needs and ultimately trigger returns. Human recommendations are more reliable and can meet my personalized needs more accurately." **Respondent 6**
"From the perspective of shopping guide services alone, AI recommendations may be more in line with my needs. In the process of communicating with AI, it can more accurately capture my preferences through data accumulation. In contrast, human shopping guides' recommendations are highly subjective. AI recommendations focus more on providing suggestions based on users' actual situations, while human shopping guides may affect the objectivity of recommendations due to personal self-interest." **Respondent 8**
"There are obvious differences in the impact of AI and human recommendations on my purchase intention. Specifically, when communicating with humans, the real sense of interaction makes it easier for me to accept recommendation suggestions. In contrast, when communicating with AI, I often feel uncomfortable being forced to accept views, which in turn reduces my acceptance of the recommended content." **Respondent 9**
"The core of purchase decisions still depends on my own needs—if I have determined the purchase target and plan to complete the transaction in the store, neither AI nor human recommendations will change my purchase behavior, and the impact of differences between the two is small. However, if I cannot get accurate consultation replies, I may turn to other merchants to buy." **Respondent 10**
"There are significant differences in the impact of the two on purchase intention. Specifically, when facing AI recommendations, I can refuse suggestions that do not meet my needs without any psychological burden. However, when facing human shopping guides' recommendations, I will have psychological barriers due to social concerns, and sometimes even if the product does not fully meet my needs, I may choose to buy it." **Respondent 11**
"I think there are obvious differences in the impact of AI and human recommendations on purchase intention, and I am relatively more willing to accept the recommendation suggestions of human customer service. Human customer service performs better in communication and understanding, which can not only convey warmth of service but also provide accurate answers. These advantages will effectively enhance my purchase intention." **Respondent 12**

(*continued*)

Table 4.5 (continued)

"The difference in the impact of AI and human recommendations on purchase intention depends on the product type. For consumables that need to be purchased repeatedly, such as skin care products and household items, I am more inclined to choose AI recommendations because they mostly recommend mature products with high platform sales and favorable rates. For high-value products such as electronic products or expensive items, the professional suggestions of human customer service can make me feel more at ease, so I trust human recommendations more." **Respondent 13**
"AI recommendations have basically no impact on my purchase intention, and I only consider them as information-providing tools, and it is difficult to change my purchase decision based solely on the information they output. In contrast, human shopping guides will influence my purchase intention through verbal guidance and subjective suggestions, and even affect the direction of decision-making to a certain extent." **Respondent 14**
"There are significant differences in the impact of AI and human recommendations on purchase intention, and human customer service's recommendations are more likely to promote my purchase behavior. When receiving service from human customer service, the probability of me buying clothes will increase significantly." **Respondent 15**
"I think AI recommendations and human recommendations have different impacts depending on the situation. When I need quick information, AI recommendations can be helpful. However, when I am hesitating between similar products, human recommendations are more likely to influence my purchase intention, as they can better consider my personal circumstances and provide more convincing guidance." **Respondent 18**
"In my experience, repetitive and poorly matched AI recommendations may lead to aesthetic fatigue and reduce my willingness to purchase. In contrast, human recommendations can influence my purchase intention more effectively when they are able to adjust suggestions based on my actual needs, although inappropriate recommendations may also weaken my trust in the store." **Respondent 19**
"AI recommendations rarely determine my purchase decisions and are mainly treated as reference information. Human customer service, however, can affect my purchase intention more directly by offering scenario-based advice and practical suggestions that align with my real usage needs, which makes their recommendations more persuasive in the decision-making process." **Respondent 20**

friendly cameras), humans were preferred for their ability to handle complexity and provide emotional reassurance. This duality suggests that AI and human recommendations serve complementary roles, rather than being direct substitutes—a distinction that is often overlooked in discussions of "AI replacing human labor" in retail and service contexts.

The analysis also reveals that trust is a key factor affecting user attitudes toward both recommendation types. Trust in AI was built on speed and consistency but eroded by privacy concerns and contextual failures. Trust in humans, meanwhile, was built on empathy, flexibility, and experiential credibility—attributes that made users more willing to share personal information (e.g., skin concerns, lifestyle habits) and rely on advice for high-stakes decisions. For example, one interviewee shared the experience with AI recommendations after purchasing a winter coat, explaining, "After I looked up a winter coat last month, the homepage kept showing similar coats—same style, even similar colors—for nearly two weeks.

It's like it only remembers one thing I did, and doesn't think about whether I already bought it or if I want to try other styles." In contrast, when discussing a human recommendation for skincare, the same interviewee noted, "I told the human representative my skin gets dry and red in winter, and she didn't just push a random moisturizer—she asked about my current skincare routine, whether I use toner, and even what temperature my room is at. Then she recommended a gentle cream that really worked." This contrast highlights a fundamental gap between AI's transactional focus—relying on past browsing data to repeat similar suggestions without accounting for purchase status or evolving preferences—and humans' relational focus, which involves active listening to contextual details to tailor recommendations to the user's actual needs. This difference in trust highlights a fundamental gap between AI's transactional focus and humans' relational focus in recommendation contexts.

Finally, the insights from this analysis have practical implications for the design of AI recommendation systems. Interviewees' frustrations with AI's narrow focus and lack of context suggest that integrating more diverse data sources—such as user-generated reviews (for experiential insights), explicit preference settings (for avoiding repeated recommendations), or conversational follow-ups (to uncover hidden needs)—could improve AI's relevance. Similarly, the value placed on human active listening and flexibility suggests that AI tools could be enhanced with "contextual prompting" (e.g., "Would you like recommendations for complementary items?") to mimic some of the relational aspects of human interaction. However, the analysis also emphasizes that AI cannot fully replace the emotional and adaptive qualities of human recommendations, particularly in scenarios requiring empathy or complex problem-solving.

In summary, the analysis of interviewees' perceptions of AI vs. human recommendations reveals a nuanced landscape: AI excels at efficiency and accessibility but lacks contextual depth, while humans excel at personalization and empathy but are limited by availability and scalability. User preferences shift based on the task's complexity and emotional stakes, and trust is shaped by how well each recommendation type aligns with user needs for relevance, transparency, and reassurance. These findings not only validate the research's focus on exploring AI vs. human recommendations but also provide empirical grounding for understanding how to optimize both systems to better serve user needs.

Based on the interview responses, a clear pattern emerges: human recommendations exert a stronger and more direct influence on purchase intention compared to AI-generated suggestions. The persuasive power of human interaction consistently outweighs that of automated systems across diverse shopping contexts and product categories. The fundamental advantage of human recommendations lies in their emotional and social resonance. Respondents repeatedly noted that communicating with a human agent provides a more pleasant, trustworthy, and engaging experience. The capacity for empathy, natural conversation, and adaptive understanding allows human agents to build rapport and alleviate purchase anxieties—factors that directly translate into higher purchase intention, especially for high-involvement or experience-driven products such as electronics, cosmetics, and apparel. Even in cases where the consumer enters the interaction with undefined needs, human guidance is seen as more reliable and personalized, reducing perceived risk and increasing the likelihood of a completed purchase. In contrast, while AI recommendations are valued for efficiency and objectivity in data-driven or repetitive purchases, they are largely perceived as impersonal reference tools. The rigid, mechanical, and at times repetitive nature of AI communication often leads to user frustration, diminished trust, and a lower likelihood of conversion. Ultimately, the human capacity for emotional connection and contextual judgment makes it a more effective driver of purchase decisions than even the most data-optimized AI system.

Notably, when consumers have a clear purchase goal, neither AI nor human recommendations substantially alter their decisions. However, in exploratory or uncertain shopping scenarios, human interaction carries significantly more persuasive power. This stems from the social and emotional dimensions of human communication—such as perceived warmth, adaptive dialogue, and reduced psychological pressure to refuse—which AI currently cannot replicate. Conversely, AI's impersonal nature allows users to reject suggestions without social discomfort, but its repetitive, rigid, or poorly matched advice often leads to frustration, decreased trust, and, in some cases, cart abandonment or merchant switching. Ultimately, while AI serves as a functional reference, human recommendations remain more effective in shaping purchase intention through personalized engagement, empathetic communication, and scenario-based guidance that aligns with deeper consumer needs.

4.4.2 Cases Regarding AI Communication Style

This section presents a series of analytical tables that systematically explore the characteristics and consequences of AI customer service communication styles. Table 4.6 provides foundational insights regarding AI customer service communication styles, synthesizing user perceptions of different communication features. Building upon this, Table 4.7 offers a focused comparative analysis by delineating insights regarding social-oriented versus task-oriented AI communication styles. Table 4.8 consolidates insights regarding the impact of AI communication style on brand engagement. Collectively, these three tables move from descriptive classification to comparative evaluation and finally to impact assessment, creating a coherent framework for understanding how the nuanced design of AI communication directly shapes the user experience and influences key commercial relationships.

This interview focuses on the communication styles of AI customer service across multiple scenarios (such as online shopping and business handling). It collects users' real experiences and feedback, and reflects the characteristics, problems and differences in user needs of AI communication styles in a concentrated manner.

From the perspective of overall characteristics, the communication styles of AI customer service show a high degree of homogeneity and standardization. All platforms generally take high politeness as the core principle, and often use intimate titles such as 'Dear' and 'Dear User' combined with polite honorifics to try to create

Table 4.6 Insights regarding AI customer service communication styles

"In various online service scenarios such as shopping apps, courier service platforms, and food delivery applications, the language styles of AI customer service show a high degree of homogenization. In terms of communication tone, AI customer service on all platforms maintains a standardized polite attitude, with standardized and non-offensive scripts. At the same time, with the rapid development of speech synthesis technology in recent years, the sound quality of AI customer service has reached a high level of closeness to human-like voices, and both speech clarity and fluency have been significantly improved. Even so, after listening continuously for 1–2 minutes, I can still accurately distinguish its AI identity—the core reason is that the tone of AI speech always remains standard and stable, without the ups and downs caused by emotional changes in human communication, nor natural pauses and emotional fluctuations. Except for basic polite expressions, it cannot convey real emotions such as joy, patience, or apology, and the overall listening experience is mechanical and monotonous." **Respondent 1**
"From daily experience, the difference in language style between AI customer service and human customer service is not significant. Taking Taobao's customer service as an example, both AI automatic responses and human reception generally use intimate titles such as 'Dear' and 'Dear User', and match them with cute Emoji symbols. Through such youthful communication methods, they narrow the psychological distance with users and create a friendly interactive atmosphere. However, the language style of AI customer service has obvious functional shortcomings: when encountering complex problems beyond the scope of the preset knowledge base or failing to accurately identify the core demands in users' expressions, it will enter a repetitive cycle, repeatedly sending standardized scripts such as 'Could you please re-describe your problem in more detail?' and 'Please clarify your specific needs before consulting again'. This communication mode, which seems polite but fails to solve problems, not only wears out users' patience but also becomes the most recognizable negative feature of AI customer service's language style." **Respondent 2**
"Among the many AI products, DeepSeek's language style is particularly outstanding, standing out among similar products. Compared with other AIs, its responses are more human-like and warm. When users consult questions, seek advice, or share ideas, it enhances the communication experience through accurate use of modal particles and emotional expressions—for example, responding to needs with brisk expressions such as 'Sure ~'and 'No problem!', and affirming users with encouraging words such as 'Your idea is very good and creative!' and 'This approach is very reliable!'. This positive language style can effectively engage users emotionally, making people feel relaxed and pleasant during interaction, and greatly increasing favorability." **Respondent 3**
"Through long-term observation, I found that the most iconic linguistic feature of AI customer service is the frequent use of overly intimate expressions such as 'Dear' and 'Baby, hello, what can I do for you?'. Although such highly stylized scripts attempt to create a friendly atmosphere, they instead strengthen their 'non-human' mechanical sense, making me clearly perceive the sense of distance in 'human-machine interaction'. For me, this overly deliberate polite expression reduces the authenticity of communication—in daily life. Communication between humans focuses more on natural and fluent tone and sincere emotional transmission, and the tone adjusts flexibly with the scenario. However, regardless of the problem faced, AI customer service maintains a fixed intimate tone in its scripts, lacking relevance and failing to convey real emotional warmth, giving an overall cold feeling." **Respondent 4**

(*continued*)

Table 4.6 (continued)

"I think the language style of AI customer service generally presents the characteristic of 'template-based friendliness'. Currently, more and more online service platforms design customer service scripts to be more approachable to improve user experience—for example, letting customer service start with intimate titles such as 'Baby', 'Dear', and 'Little Cutie'. Although AI customer service also strictly applies such template scripts, due to the lack of human emotional perception and contextual understanding capabilities, its usage seems very stiff and deliberate. For example, when users consult complex problems, AI still mechanically throws out expressions such as 'Baby, do not worry', which not only fails to alleviate users' anxiety but also makes users feel unprofessional and untrustworthy." **Respondent 6**
"I previously learned that some AIs use lively and personalized tones to communicate with users, but I have never actually encountered this type of AI customer service. Most AI customer service I have encountered so far adopt traditional standardized communication methods, with scripts mainly focusing on concise and clear information transmission. They have no special tone fluctuations or personalized expression designs, and the overall style is plain and unremarkable, making it difficult to leave a deep impression." **Respondent 7**
"Whether it is customer service in online shopping platforms or service applications, my biggest intuitive feeling is that their language styles are centered on the core principle of high politeness—they use honorifics such as 'Hello', 'Excuse me', and 'Thank you for your understanding' during communication, always maintaining a humble attitude without any impolite or aggressive expressions. This standardized polite style has become a unified feature of all customer service." **Respondent 8**
"When handling financial businesses such as bank card opening and credit card applications, I called the official customer service number of the bank multiple times. Each time I connected, I was first connected to the AI customer service system. The AI customer service would guide me through voice to perform a series of click operations on the mobile banking APP, such as 'Please click the "My" column at the bottom of the screen and select the "Business Handling" option'. The entire guidance process was cumbersome and time-consuming, seriously affecting business processing efficiency. What annoyed me more was that there was an obvious flaw in the design of its human transfer function—whether I clearly expressed 'Please transfer to a human' or operated according to the voice prompts, it was difficult to successfully connect to a human agent. I often had to try repeatedly to get through. This inefficient language guidance and function setting brought me a very poor service experience." **Respondent 9**
"In daily online service interactions, I can rarely clearly distinguish whether it is AI or human serice. The main reason is that the AI customer service I have come into contact with has neither particularly prominent language styles nor iconic script features—their expressions are neither particularly intimate nor indifferent, maintaining an overall conventional communication state with little difference from the scripts of ordinary human customer service. Therefore, it is difficult for them to leave a clear impression on me, and I cannot judge their identity through language style." **Respondent 11**
"The language style of some AI customer service has very distinct anthropomorphic characteristics. Such AIs use professional algorithm optimization and refined script settings to make the output language content as close to human communication habits as possible, thereby reducing the sense of alienation in human-machine interaction. For example, they use expressions with modal particles and intimate titles such as 'Dear, hello ~' and 'What can I do for you?', imitating the natural conversational tone between humans; at the same time, they appropriately add auxiliary words such as 'oh', 'ne' and 'ya' when responding to questions, making the language sound more vivid and approachable, as if communicating with a real person." **Respondent 12**

(*continued*)

Table 4.6 (continued)

"When using services on different platforms, I deliberately paid attention to the differences in the language styles of AI customer service and found that their styles change significantly with the platform attributes. For example, on shopping websites such as Taobao and JD.com, the language style of AI customer service is more friendly and lively, often starting with 'Dear' and ending with modal particles such as 'la' and 'oh', such as 'Dear, this product is in stock, and it will be shipped within 48 hours after placing the order', creating an enthusiastic service atmosphere through such expressions; while on online platforms of public departments such as banks and government services, the language style of AI customer service is serious and formal, with scripts mostly being standardized expressions such as 'Hello, what business do you need to handle?' and 'Please provide your ID number for verification'. The overall focus is more on professionalism and rigor, which is my most intuitive experience difference." **Respondent 13**
"Most service from AI are positioned as friendly-style. Their language expressions are not too direct or stiff, but create a friendly communication atmosphere through gentle tones, intimate titles, and patient guidance. For example, when users consult questions, they will say 'Hello, what problem have you encountered? Take your time, I will try my best to help you solve it'; when users express confusion, they will respond 'Don't worry, let me sort it out for you step by step'. This friendly language style can effectively alleviate users' anxiety and improve the interaction experience." **Respondent 14**
"Among many online platforms, some AI customer service on Taobao have left me a very deep negative impression—their language style is overly sweet and has a serious redundancy problem. On the one hand, they use intimate titles such as 'Dear' and 'Dear' frequently and intensively, starting almost every sentence with such words, which seems particularly deliberate; on the other hand, when I consult specific questions, they cannot provide clear and effective answers, but instead automatically send a lot of irrelevant information at the end of the conversation, such as 'Dear, if you like this product, place your order quickly, the stock is limited' and 'You can still enjoy the full discount when placing an order now, don't miss it'. Sometimes they send five or six such marketing messages at a time, and I have to manually click to block them every time. This communication method, which seems friendly but actually ignores users' core needs and excessively pushes marketing content, makes its language style very cloying and seriously affects the service experience." **Respondent 15**
"Overall, the language style of AI customer service appears rather neutral and standardized, with a formal and regulated tone. Task-oriented communication is efficient and allows users to obtain accurate information quickly, while socially oriented language that simulates human emotions may, to some extent, facilitate decision-making when emotional factors are involved. However, the most important characteristic of AI customer service for me remains the accuracy and usefulness of the information it provides." **Respondent 16**
"In my experience, both AI and human customer service place strong emphasis on emotional value through the use of polite and intimate forms of address. Nevertheless, once I realize that I am communicating with an AI agent, my expectations are naturally lowered, and I consciously avoid asking highly personalized questions. Linguistically, AI customer service is relatively easy to identify, as it frequently uses standardized expressions and sentence-ending symbols, while maintaining a polite but problem-insensitive communication style that often fails to address users' actual needs." **Respondent 17**

(*continued*)

Table 4.6 (continued)

"The language style of AI customer service is generally well-structured and highly logical. When dealing with emotional topics, AI tends to respond by systematically analyzing the issue and offering step-by-step explanations, which makes the interaction feel rational but emotionally distant. Compared with task-oriented styles, socially oriented AI communication feels more natural and human-like, and I would prefer interacting with such AI agents in daily use." **Respondent 18**
"I perceive the language style of AI customer service as displaying a form of 'artificial intimacy', such as the frequent use of affectionate terms. Although its expressions are clear, well-organized, and efficient, the communication often feels rigid and inflexible. In task-focused scenarios, this style is acceptable and even preferable, but overly friendly or playful language may reduce my trust in the brand and be perceived as a form of marketing rather than genuine service." **Respondent 19**
"AI customer service generally adopts a professional and official language style, aiming to simulate the politeness and enthusiasm of human service staff. While such expressions can create a sense of friendliness, I personally prefer a task-oriented communication style that focuses on efficiency and problem-solving. When AI customer service demonstrates a pragmatic, objective, and efficient manner, it positively influences my overall impression of the brand and increases my willingness to repurchase." **Respondent 20**

a friendly atmosphere (Respondents 1, 2, 3, 4, 5, 8, 12, 14). However, most AIs maintain a stable tone without emotional fluctuations, lack the naturalness and emotional transmission of human communication, and are generally mechanical (Respondents 1, 8). Only a few products (such as DeepSeek) present an anthropomorphic and warm style through modal particles and encouraging expressions, which are favored by users (Respondent 3). In addition, some AI customer service systems do not have particularly prominent language styles or iconic script features, so some users cannot clearly distinguish whether the other party is an AI or a human service provider, nor can they leave a deep impression (Respondents 7, 11).

The existing problems are quite prominent: first, the functional limitations are obvious. When facing complex problems or vague needs, AI is prone to fall into the cycle of standardized scripts, unable to solve practical demands and thus consuming users' patience (Respondents 2, 17). Second, the expression is stiff and deliberate. "Template-based friendliness" lacks contextual adaptability, and overly intimate titles or redundant marketing information will arouse resentment instead and reduce professionalism (Respondents 4, 6, 19). In some scenarios (such as banks), there are also efficiency problems such as cumbersome guidance and difficulty in transferring to human service (Respondent 9).

There are significant differences in scenario adaptability: AI on e-commerce platforms has a lively and cordial style, and uses more modal particles to create a warm atmosphere; while public service platforms such as banks and government affairs mainly adopt a serious and formal style, focusing on professionalism and rigor (Respondent 13). User preferences are polarized: some favor an efficient and pragmatic task-oriented style, while others prefer a social-oriented style close to

Table 4.7 Insights regarding social vs. task oriented AI communication styles

"In fact, based on my personal consumption experience, the core demand for consulting customer service has always been to obtain accurate answers to questions—regardless of the communication style adopted, what I care most about is whether I can receive accurate and effective information and whether I can truly get the solutions I need. Therefore, the core value still lies in the effectiveness of the information." **Respondent 1**
"I think both task-oriented and social-oriented customer service styles have their own advantages and disadvantages, adapting to the needs of different consumption scenarios. The advantage of the task-oriented style is its intuitiveness and efficiency, especially when I have a clear consulting goal, it can quickly hit the core of the problem and provide solutions. For example, when I am eager to buy a certain product or have an urgent need to meet, I prefer this style—it can directly respond to my questions, with clear and concise information transmission, and no unnecessary communication costs. On the other hand, social-oriented customer service provides users with emotional value through a lively tone and strong affinity, bringing a certain sense of pleasure after communication and alleviating the tediousness of the consulting process. However, based on my personal consumption habits, I still prefer the task-oriented style in most scenarios when purchasing products, because efficiently solving needs is always my top priority." **Respondent 2**
"I prefer the social-oriented style when choosing customer service. From a social perspective, humans are inherently social animals, generally having a natural resistance to cold and mechanical answers, and being more willing to accept AI customer service with a warm tone and language expression close to natural human communication. Social-oriented style can make the consulting process more human-like and reduce the sense of distance in human-machine interaction." **Respondent 3**
"Personally, I prefer the task-oriented customer service style. Its core advantage is being concise and direct, being able to accurately connect with and solve my actual problems. For example, when I want to know specific information such as the material composition and size parameters of shoes, I only need the customer service to provide clear answers, without excessive friendly greetings or emotional expressions." **Respondent 4**
"The most prominent feature of task-oriented customer service is its accurate response to needs—I can directly get corresponding clear answers to the questions I raise, with extremely high effectiveness in information transmission. Social-oriented customer service narrows the psychological distance with users through more approachable expressions, making the consulting process more humanistic. However, I still lean more towards the task-oriented style, because in my opinion, the core function of customer service is to provide effective information, not to meet social needs through chatting." **Respondent 5**
"To be honest, I think there is not much essential difference between these two customer service styles—both can clearly convey core information such as product performance parameters, and the only difference lies in the external speaking style. If I have to choose between the two, I will prefer the task-oriented one, because my core purpose is to buy the target shoes. Obtaining key information in an efficient and direct way can maximize the efficiency of shopping decisions and avoid unnecessary communication time consumption." **Respondent 6**
"When facing a social-oriented AI customer service, I will exclaim 'AI technology has developed to such an anthropomorphic level' and be surprised by the experience improvement brought by technological progress. However, for task-oriented customer service, since I usually carefully browse the product detail page in advance to independently understand the basic information of the product before purchasing, I feel that the necessity of such customer service is relatively low—I have obtained most of the information it can provide through other channels." **Respondent 8**

(*continued*)

Table 4.7 (continued)

"I think the advantage of social-oriented customer service is that it can convey a warmer communication atmosphere, allowing users to feel humanistic care during the consulting process; while task-oriented customer service focuses on efficiency and can solve actual problems more quickly, each having its own merits. Based on my personal preferences, I may lean more towards the social-oriented style, because a gentle communication method can improve the comfort of the overall service experience." **Respondent 9**
"The social-oriented customer service style makes me feel a bit strange—although it tries to imitate the human communication mode, there is always an obvious 'human-machine sense', which is not natural enough. While the task-oriented customer service is more pragmatic and lacks human touch, the information provided is direct and accurate, which can effectively meet the consulting needs. I will prefer the second style. As long as I can efficiently obtain the required information, it is enough to meet my core needs." **Respondent 11**
"First of all, the social-oriented language style can make me have a sense of reality of 'communicating with a real person', with a friendly and natural tone, effectively narrowing the distance in language interaction and making me more willing to take the initiative to communicate; while the task-oriented language style makes me feel a certain sense of distance, and the overall expression seems relatively unfamiliar. However, it is undeniable that it has significant efficiency in information transmission—by eliminating redundant modal particles and greetings, it can directly focus on the core of the problem. Overall, I still lean more towards the social-oriented style, because a more comfortable communication experience can improve the overall service satisfaction." **Respondent 12**
"For task-oriented AI customer service, I prefer this style—its advantage lies in clear goals and outstanding efficiency, which can effectively solve various practical problems and meet my core consulting needs." **Respondent 13**
"I want to talk about my views on task-oriented customer service first. Like the bank AI customer service I mentioned, the target positioning of such customer service is very clear, always focusing on business handling needs. However, the overall operation process is too cumbersome. Although social-oriented AI customer service can convey a certain sense of care in communication and make users feel valued, it has obvious shortcomings in providing effective information, unable to solve practical problems efficiently and meet core needs." **Respondent 14**
"For my personal consumption intention, I prefer the task-oriented customer service style. When I consult specific information about clothes (such as material, size, washing method, etc.), I hope to get direct and affirmative accurate answers rather than excessive socialized tone responses. After all, the social experience that AI customer service can provide is far less than the real interaction effect of human customer service. In my opinion, when users choose AI customer service, the core demand is to obtain direct and accurate responses to my needs, and this efficient information transmission method is what most consumers prefer." **Respondent 15**
"The core purpose of consulting customer service is to obtain accurate and effective information. Regardless of whether the communication style is task-oriented or socially oriented, what matters most to me is whether the system can truly provide useful solutions. Decorative elements such as emojis or expressive tone do not play a decisive role. The effectiveness of information remains the central value." **Respondent 16**

(*continued*)

Table 4.7 (continued)

"I believe both task-oriented and social-oriented AI communication styles have their respective advantages and are suitable for different consumption scenarios. Task-oriented communication is efficient and direct, especially when I have clear goals and urgent needs. Although social-oriented styles can offer emotional comfort and a more pleasant interaction, I still prefer task-oriented AI in most purchasing situations, as efficiency and problem-solving are always my top priorities." **Respondent 17**
"I personally prefer social-oriented AI customer service. Humans naturally resist cold and mechanical responses and are more willing to communicate with AI that uses warmer, more human-like language. A socially oriented communication style reduces the sense of distance in human–machine interaction and makes the consultation process feel more natural." **Respondent 18**
"I tend to prefer task-oriented AI customer service. Its main advantage lies in concise and direct responses that can accurately address my actual problems. When seeking specific information, such as product materials or size parameters, I only expect clear and precise answers rather than excessive emotional expressions, as efficiency is my primary concern." **Respondent 19**
"The key feature of task-oriented AI customer service is its high accuracy and efficiency in responding to user needs, while social-oriented communication mainly helps narrow psychological distance through a friendlier tone. However, based on my own usage habits, I still lean toward task-oriented styles, because the fundamental function of customer service should be to provide effective information rather than fulfill social interaction needs." **Respondent 20**

human communication. However, all users regard the accuracy and practicality of information as their core demand (Respondents 16, 20).

In general, there has been a consensus on the standardization and politeness of AI customer service communication styles, but there is still considerable room for improvement in emotional transmission, flexibility and refined adaptation to scenarios.

The analysis of the interview responses reveals some interesting findings regarding task vs. social oriented communication styles. First, the analysis underscores that task-oriented AI communication is valued for clarity and efficiency, particularly when users have explicit, time-sensitive needs. Interviewees repeatedly noted that task-oriented AI excels at delivering direct, actionable information without unnecessary conversational fluff—an attribute that aligns with their goals for quick problem-solving or information-gathering. For example, one interviewee described the experience with a task-oriented AI customer service representative on a shopping platform: "When I asked about the shoe's material and size, the customer service representative just replied that 'this shoe is of standard size and is made of wear-resistant rubber'—no extra talk, just what I needed to know." This directness was praised for reducing cognitive load, especially during high-pressure or time-constrained tasks (e.g., verifying product specs before a sale ends, confirming return procedures). Another interviewee emphasized a preference for task-oriented AI when seeking specific details, explaining, "I don't need the AI to ask about my day; I just want to know if the shirt can be machine-washed. The task-oriented ones get to the point faster."

Table 4.8 Insights regarding the impact of AI communication style on brand engagement

"I believe that customer service style significantly influences repurchase intention. Superficially, it may seem like a difference in language style, but the underlying reason lies in whether it can evoke a sense of 'in-group identity' in users. As a consumer majoring in psychology, from a professional perspective, humans naturally categorize 'in-groups' and 'out-groups' in cognition. AI is generally perceived as an out-group, while human customer service belongs to the in-group. Therefore, when AI customer service's communication style is closer to human natural expression and exhibits in-group behavioral characteristics, it is more likely to generate emotional identification in me, thereby increasing my repurchase tendency." **Respondent 3**
"Customer service style directly affects my attitude toward the brand. If the design of the AI customer service style makes the operation process exceptionally cumbersome (such as confusing guidance logic, redundant steps, etc.), it will cause strong aversion to the brand, and I may even give up purchasing the brand's products because of this." **Respondent 10**
"The core factor affecting brand engagement is whether customer service can effectively solve users' problems—if the problem is resolved effectively, it naturally enhances favorability toward the brand; if the problem remains unresolved for a long time, even the best customer service style can hardly improve user brand engagement." **Respondent 13**
"In my view, when human customer service is needed, users tend to prefer real interactions in offline scenarios; the core value of AI customer service is to provide efficient and convenient services for humans. Therefore, when I choose AI customer service, what I need more is accurate, direct, task-oriented answers. For consumers, clearly knowing the solution to a problem can efficiently meet consumption needs and provide a more comprehensive understanding of product information, so I prefer and recognize this style of AI customer service. If a brand's AI customer service adopts such a precise and efficient task-oriented style, it will significantly enhance my favorability toward the brand." **Respondent 15**
"The communication style of AI customer service can influence my perception of a brand to some extent. Socially oriented language may enhance my overall impression and make the interaction more pleasant, which could increase my willingness to pay attention to the brand. However, from a rational consumer perspective, information accuracy and problem-solving ability are still more important than emotional expression." **Respondent 17**
"I think brands that adopt socially oriented AI communication styles appear more approachable and user-friendly. When AI customer service communicates in a more human-like and emotionally warm manner, I am more willing to follow the brand's updates and maintain engagement, as this style reduces the sense of distance in human–machine interaction." **Respondent 18**
"The communication style of AI customer service can affect my trust in a brand. Overly playful or marketing-oriented language may reduce my confidence in the brand and be perceived as promotional rather than service-oriented. In contrast, task-oriented communication that is clear and efficient is more likely to enhance my overall impression of the brand." **Respondent 19**

However, task-oriented AI also faced criticism for feeling "mechanical" or "impersonal," particularly in scenarios where users sought reassurance or context beyond basic facts. One interviewee noted frustration with a task-oriented bank AI customer service representative, mentioned that, "I called to ask about card activation, and it just repeated clicking certain buttons over and over again—even when I said I couldn't find the button." This rigidity highlighted a key limitation of task-oriented styles: they struggle to adapt to ambiguity or user confusion, which can leave users feeling unheard and increase frustration.

In contrast, social-oriented AI communication was celebrated for its emotional warmth and relatability, yet criticized for inefficiency when users prioritized speed. Interviewees who favored social-oriented styles highlighted how conversational language, emotional cues, and personalized references created a sense of "human connection" that reduced the alienation of human-machine interaction. For example, one interviewee shared their positive experience with a social-oriented AI, noting that platforms like DeepSeek stood out for their humanized tone: "When I asked for advice or share ideas, I got responses like 'Okay ~' 'No problem at all!' and encourages me by saying 'Your idea is really great and creative!' 'This thinking is super reliable!' This kind of positive, conversational expression makes the interaction relaxed and pleasant, and I end up liking it more." Another interviewee emphasized the emotional value of social-oriented AI in specific scenarios, recalling a time they shared a personal struggle on a social platform: "Once I just broke up and was in a bad mood, so I posted a sad Weibo post. The social-oriented comment AI replied, 'Breaking up might be the start of your next new life.' That sentence was warm and healing, and it really made me feel better. It didn't just give a rigid response—it felt like it cared about my mood." Another interviewee also pointed out that social-oriented AI enhanced their sense of connection with brands, explaining, "Some shopping platforms' AI customer service uses a friendly tone, like starting conversations with 'Hi ~' and adding little emojis. Once I was asking about a pair of shoes, and it not only answered my question about size but also mentioned, 'The weather's turning cool lately, this pair of shoes with a slightly thicker insole is just right for now!' It didn't just talk about the product—it paid attention to small details in life. That made me feel the brand wasn't just selling things, but actually cared about users' daily needs. I even started checking the brand's new products more often because of that." These experiences illustrate how social-oriented AI's focus on emotional resonance and contextual relevance can create a more engaging, human-like interaction—something interviewees often contrasted with the cold, scripted feel of task-oriented AI.

Yet social-oriented styles also had drawbacks, particularly for users focused on efficiency. One interviewee pointed out the inefficiency of overly social AI communication, noting that some social-oriented AI customer service agent on shopping platforms "highly use 'dear', 'baby' and other overly intimate expressions, and almost every sentence starts with such words, which is very deliberate." They further explained that when consulting about specific product issues—such as confirming the washing method of a shirt—this social-oriented AI "could not provide a clear answer, but automatically sent a lot of irrelevant information at the end of the conversation, such as 'Dear, if you like this product, hurry up and place an order. The inventory is limited!' Sometimes it sends five or six such marketing messages at a time, and I have to click to block them every time." This kind of unnecessary social interaction is a waste of time when I just want to get key information quickly." These experiences highlight a key criticism of social-oriented AI: when its conversational flourishes are disconnected from the user's core query, they not only fail to enhance the interaction but also create friction by delaying or diluting the information users actually seek. Several interviewees noted that this type of "forced" socialization made the AI feel insincere—like a scripted attempt to appear friendly, rather than a genuine effort to understand and assist. As one interviewee put it, "I don't mind the AI being friendly, but it should first answer my question. If it spends more time on small talk than on solving my problem, it just feels like it's not taking my needs seriously."

A critical finding from the analysis is that AI communication style exerts a multi-faceted and differentiated impact on users' brand engagement, with its influence mechanism closely linked to users' core demand priorities (emotional needs vs. functional needs) and cognitive perceptions of AI's value. While some users are driven by emotional resonance to enhance brand engagement through human-like, socially oriented communication, others prioritize the functional value of AI (e.g., efficiency, problem-solving capabilities) and tend to favor task-oriented communication styles. Additionally, the fundamental premise for communication style to play a role lies in the brand's ability to ensure operational convenience and effective problem resolution—otherwise, even an optimized communication style will be difficult to drive positive brand engagement.

For users who value emotional connection in interactions, socially oriented AI communication styles have a significant positive impact on their brand engagement. Humans inherently have a cognitive tendency to categorize "in-groups" and "out-groups," and AI is often initially perceived as an out-group. However, when AI customer service adopts a communication style closer to natural human expression—such as warm emotional feedback, friendly tone, and humanized interaction logic—it can break down the psychological distance between humans and machines, enabling users to perceive AI as having "in-group behavioral characteristics." This sense of emotional identification not only makes the interaction process more pleasant but also fosters users' sense of closeness and trust in the brand. For example, users often feel that brands with socially oriented AI communication are more approachable and user-centric, which motivates them to actively follow brand updates, maintain long-term interaction, and even increase their willingness to repurchase. Although such users acknowledge the importance of information accuracy, the emotional value brought by socially oriented communication still becomes a key factor in enhancing their brand engagement.

In contrast, users who focus on the functional value of AI customer service tend to prefer task-oriented communication styles, and this preference directly translates into positive brand perception and engagement. In the eyes of these users, the core value of AI customer service lies in providing efficient, convenient, and accurate services that complement human needs—unlike offline interactions that emphasize emotional communication, AI should focus on "solving problems directly." A task-oriented communication style, characterized by clear guidance, concise expression, and accurate information transmission, can help users quickly obtain solutions, reduce time costs caused by redundant interactions, and efficiently meet their consumption needs (such as understanding product information or resolving after-sales issues). Moreover, overly playful, marketing-oriented, or verbose communication styles may make users perceive the brand as "service-neglectful and promotion-focused," thereby reducing their trust in the brand. On the contrary, a rigorous, efficient, and task-focused AI communication style can convey the brand's professionalism and reliability, significantly enhancing users' overall favorability toward the brand and their willingness to continue engaging with it.

Notably, AI communication style is not the decisive factor in driving brand engagement—users' core demands for "effective problem resolution" and "convenient operation" are the fundamental prerequisites. Many users emphasize that regardless of how excellent or humanized the communication style is, if AI customer service fails to fundamentally solve their problems (such as prolonged unresolved after-sales issues) or makes the operation process cumbersome (such as confusing guidance logic or redundant steps), it will inevitably trigger strong dissatisfaction and even lead users to abandon the brand. This indicates that communication style plays a "supplementary and enhancing" role in brand engagement: on the basis of effective problem resolution and convenient operation, a suitable communication style can further amplify positive brand perception; however, without this foundation, the role of communication style will be greatly weakened or even ineffective. For rational consumers, in particular, the functional attributes of AI (problem-solving ability, information accuracy) are always more important than emotional expression, and communication style can only affect brand engagement when these core functional needs are met.

In summary, the relationship between AI communication style and brand engagement can be constructed through a three-dimensional analytical framework. The first dimension is the dual orientation of AI communication style: socially oriented (focused on emotional resonance and humanized interaction) and task-oriented (focused on efficiency, accuracy, and problem-solving). The second dimension is users' demand priority structure: emotional demand-driven users who pursue psychological connection and sense of identity, and functional demand-driven users who prioritize efficiency and practical results. The third dimension is the conditional boundary of influence: the role of communication style depends on the brand's ability to meet the basic needs of "effective problem resolution" and "convenient operation." These three dimensions interact with each other: the communication style needs to match users' demand priorities, and at the same time, it must be based on the satisfaction of basic functional needs to effectively promote brand engagement. This framework not only covers the differentiated perceptions and preferences of different user groups but also clarifies the core logic of how AI communication style affects brand behavior, providing a comprehensive perspective for understanding the interaction between AI traits and brand management.

4.4.3 Cases Regarding AI Humanity

This section presents the interview results regarding AI humanity through three analytical tables. Table 4.9 establishes a foundational understanding by summarizing the respondents' insights regarding AI humanity. More specifically, Table 4.10 presents insights regarding AI humanity in service failure contexts. Building directly

Table 4.9 Insights regarding AI humanity

"One of AI service design intents is to replace some functions of human customer service, so language modules such as 'apologies' or 'sorry' are pre-programmed to handle problem scenarios. However, in practical use, I've found that although AI can accurately generate apology scripts, the efficiency of the solutions it provides is often inferior to human processing. For example, when a problem is not properly resolved, the AI might say, 'I'm truly sorry for not handling your current issue properly,' but the subsequent solution offered isn't directly targeted; instead, it guides the user to transfer the problem to other service platforms, prolonging the problem-solving process." **Respondent 1**
"I believe AI generally possesses the trait of humility, which is reflected in various AI models, including customer service systems. When I inquire about specific product information from AI customer service, especially questions involving real-world experience, the AI will candidly inform me of its limitations—for instance, clearly stating 'This question is beyond my knowledge scope' or 'Lacking relevant practical experience, I cannot provide an accurate answer,' and proactively guide me to transfer to a human agent. This behavior of not avoiding capability boundaries and actively seeking professional support fully demonstrates AI's humility trait and allows users to clearly understand the subsequent solution." **Respondent 2**
"During use, AI does present an attitude similar to humility through scripts like 'sorry,' but I believe this is not an intrinsic trait of the AI itself. Rather, it is a function endowed through programming by technical developers. In other words, AI's humility does not stem from autonomous consciousness but is a passive response based on preset algorithms, essentially a standardized script output, not a genuine expression of attitude." **Respondent 3**
"I have encountered multiple instances where AI customer service exhibited humility, especially noticeable when purchasing digital products or small appliances. When the AI cannot accurately understand my question or is unable to solve it, it humbly states its limitations, for example, saying, 'Dear, I didn't accurately understand the problem you described' or 'I'm not sure about this issue and cannot provide a precise answer.' I fully accept this attitude of proactively admitting shortcomings because it lets me clearly know that I need to seek further help through a human agent, avoiding ineffective communication." **Respondent 4**
"Some AI does exhibit humility, and one usage experience was very impressive to me. I once asked AI to help solve a complex math problem. When checking the answer, I found the method it used had some problems. After I provided the correct answer, it automatically compared the differences, and then proactively pointed out 'There was a logical error in the previous solution process' or 'The current answer cannot meet your needs, recalculation is needed,' supplementing with statements like 'Sorry, there was a mistake in the earlier reasoning, thank you for the correction.' This attitude of proactively admitting errors and responding politely reflects both courtesy and humility." **Respondent 5**
"I have perceived AI's humility in non-shopping scenarios, for example, when asking AI to help revise an essay. When I clearly pointed out issues in the revised content, it would promptly generate apology scripts and adjust the revision direction. But in shopping customer service scenarios, I have never encountered similar situations, partly because I rarely proactively question the AI's responses, and it might also be that the AI in such scenarios does not trigger related humility script modules." **Respondent 6**
"I believe AI possesses the trait of humility, and in terms of service attitude, it has an advantage over human customer service. Specifically, AI won't let emotional fluctuations affect its response attitude, always handling user needs in a standardized, humble manner, avoiding issues like perfunctory attitudes that human agents might have." **Respondent 7**

(*continued*)

Table 4.9 (continued)

"In my view, AI's humility is more of a superficial script presentation rather than a true trait embodiment. It does not proactively exhibit humility based on cognition of its own actions, but triggers preset response programs according to the user's expression, essentially a mechanical feedback lacking a genuine attitude core." **Respondent 8**
"Based on my current user experience, I have never encountered AI customer service exhibiting humility. Because the core positioning of AI customer service is to improve communication efficiency, for issues requiring emotional investment like compensation or deep apologies, the platform usually directly transfers to human agents, resulting in AI lacking scenarios to demonstrate humility." **Respondent 9**
"I believe it is entirely possible for AI to possess humility. After all, technical developers can optimize programming to make AI's communication style more human-like. Since humility is an important trait for enhancing communication effectiveness, it would naturally be incorporated into AI's functional settings, making human-machine interaction smoother." **Respondent 10**
"It is feasible for AI to possess humility. Through targeted training of language models, AI can master the usage scenarios and expression logic of humble language, thereby presenting a humble attitude that meets user expectations in interactions." **Respondent 11**
"AI can exhibit humility at the verbal level through program settings. For example, when users raise compensation demands or problems remain unsolved, it promptly generate apology scripts like 'Sorry, we failed to meet your need, deeply apologize.' However, I think AI struggles to achieve deep humility that 'accurately hits the core needs of users—often only providing superficial verbal apologies, while the actual solutions are unsatisfactory, failing to truly address the core demands of users. This humility lacks substantive value support." **Respondent 12**
"I believe AI can possess humility because it can simulate humble behavior patterns through algorithms, and in many scenarios, this simulation effectively enhances user experience. But essentially, this humility is just the result of algorithmic settings, not a real feeling generated by the AI itself, more like a standardized service process." **Respondent 13**
"I believe AI possesses humility. The compensation scenario you mentioned earlier reminded me of a recent shopping experience on the Dewu platform: after submitting a return request, the system automatically pops up an AI customer service prompt, clearly stating 'The merchant will provide a two-yuan compensation to make up for the inconvenience.' This behavior of proactively taking responsibility and promptly offering a compensation plan is a concrete embodiment of AI's humility." **Respondent 14**
"I believe AI possesses humility, especially prominent in service failure scenarios. Taking the Pinduoduo platform as an example, when users apply for after-sales customer service, the AI directly reviews the appeal online and quickly provides targeted solutions, efficiently meeting consumers' reasonable demands. This attitude of avoiding blame-shifting and proactively solving problems fully demonstrates AI's humility." **Respondent 15**
"I believe AI can possess a form of humility, as it is designed by humans and inevitably carries human social attributes. In my experience, this humility is reflected in polite forms of address, courteous and lively tone, and the ability to calm users when emotions are negative. In service failure scenarios, a highly humble AI that maintains a sincere attitude, clearly identifies my needs, and provides concrete solutions significantly increases my willingness to continue using the service." **Respondent 16**

(continued)

Table 4.9 (continued)

"I think AI customer service can demonstrate humility, especially in service contexts where politeness and restraint are expected. AI often adjusts its responses according to the user's tone and emotional state, acknowledging its limitations when facing questions beyond its capacity and guiding users to human agents. In service failure situations, a highly humble AI is more acceptable, as its sincere attitude makes me feel respected, even if the problem-solving ability remains the same." **Respondent 17**
"In my view, AI can exhibit humility, but this humility differs from human humility. Human humility is more closely related to responsibility, whereas AI humility is grounded in factual acknowledgment of limitations. When AI admits that it lacks knowledge or cannot answer a question, this honesty is preferable over forced or inaccurate responses. In failure scenarios, a highly humble AI that responds quickly and offers solutions is more likely to increase my willingness to continue using the service." **Respondent 18**
"I consider AI's expressions of humility, such as apologies, to be largely embedded in its programmed scripts rather than intrinsic traits. However, in service failure situations, I still prefer a highly humble AI, as it clearly communicates what measures have been taken to resolve the issue. Even if this does not necessarily increase my usage intention, it helps me perceive the service process as orderly and problem-oriented rather than dismissive." **Respondent 19**
"AI's humility is mainly conveyed through language tone and apology expressions, which are intentionally designed by humans to inject warmth into service interactions. In failure scenarios, a highly humble AI that provides both emotional reassurance and concrete solutions can effectively ease negative emotions and positively influence my evaluation of the merchant and my willingness to continue using the service, even though AI cannot fully replace human empathy." **Respondent 20**

upon this, Table 4.11 provides insights regarding the impact of AI humility on subsequent service continuance intention. Together, these tables form a cohesive progression from defining AI humanity, to testing its value in critical contexts, and finally to measuring its concrete effect on a key behavioral intention, providing crucial insights for designing AI that fosters resilience and maintains user relationships through challenges.

Overall, the interviews suggest that most interviewees believe AI can exhibit humility, but they assess this trait using criteria different from those applied to humans. For the interviewees, AI humility is not perceived as an internal emotional state or moral intention. Instead, it is evaluated based on observable behavior during interactions. Interviewees focus on how AI responds when it makes mistakes, encounters limitations, or fails to meet expectations. In this context, humility becomes a practical and observable quality rather than an emotional one.

First, interviewees' awareness of AI humility is primarily shaped by direct interaction experiences rather than abstract beliefs about AI. Interviewees consistently report recognizing humility in everyday scenarios such as customer service conversations, problem-solving tasks, and routine inquiries. Behaviors like apologizing for errors, admitting misunderstandings, or clearly stating limitations are commonly interpreted as signs of humility. In contrast, AI that ignores complaints, avoids responsibility, or provides rigid responses is perceived as lacking this trait. These

Table 4.10 Insights regarding AI humanity in service failure contexts

"For the food delivery delay case, I clearly prefer to receive customer service from AI with high humility traits. On one hand, its sincere apology expression, whether relying on manual background operations or not, at least conveys the degree of attention to customer experience from the system design level. On the other hand, the communication logic of high humility can first alleviate customer dissatisfaction through emotional comfort, and then synchronously provide targeted solutions (such as prioritizing expedited delivery). This dual model of 'emotional guidance + problem-solving' can effectively make customers feel that their demands are valued, greatly improving the acceptance of problem handling." **Respondent 1**
"I am more willing to choose the service experience of AI with high humility. Food delivery delay is essentially a responsibility lapse of the service provider (merchant or delivery rider). At this time, the core needs of customers are to obtain a sincere apology and a clear solution—if the AI neither takes the initiative to apologize nor provides a clear estimated delivery time, it is likely to arouse users' doubts about service reliability, thereby damaging platform trust." **Respondent 2**
"I definitely prefer the first type of AI service with high humility. Food delivery delay directly hinders the dining plan and has already caused anxiety. The response with high humility can accurately soothe this negative feeling, making me more willing to continue using the platform's services. After all, the anxiety caused by the failure to meet dining needs in a timely manner needs to be alleviated through emotional responses, which cannot be achieved by low-humility services." **Respondent 3**
"AI customer service with high humility is more likely to gain my recognition. Its gentle communication tone can significantly enhance a sense of security. Even if the final result of the problem does not change, a sincere apology and solution can bring a sense of peace of mind at the psychological level. In contrast, the cold refusal of low-humility services will exacerbate the negative experience." **Respondent 4**
"I clearly prefer the first type of AI service model with high humility. It is not only more friendly in attitude but also can accurately capture the dissatisfaction of users caused by delays and take the initiative to soothe it. The subsequent synchronized implementation of solutions forms a complete service closed loop of 'attitude expression + practical action'. This one-stop problem handling method allows me to obtain a more comprehensive service experience with greatly improved acceptance." **Respondent 5**
"I undoubtedly favor the response of AI with high humility. On one hand, it can take the initiative to push delay notification information, saving users from additional calls or human service inquiries, reducing communication costs. On the other hand, clear solutions and compensation plans directly hit the core demands of users—after a problem occurs, obtaining reasonable compensation is a key factor in improving user acceptance." **Respondent 6**
"I think AI service with high humility has more advantages. One of the core competencies of the service industry lies in user experience. A gentle and humble communication method can effectively reduce users' negative emotions and make the entire service interaction process more comfortable, which is an important detail to improve user satisfaction." **Respondent 7**
"In actual experience, AI services with high humility account for a higher proportion and are also the type I am more willing to accept, but there is still a cognitive bias: when I initiate customer service consultation, it often means that the problem has exceeded the AI's processing capacity. At this time, the high-humility response of AI is more like a perfunctory method of the merchant, and it is difficult to truly solve the core problem." **Respondent 8**

(*continued*)

Table 4.10 (continued)

"If faced with service failure scenario, I will prioritize choosing the AI response with high humility, which can effectively alleviate negative emotions and make the experience more comfortable. However, from the perspective of fundamental needs, the solution handled manually can still better meet my expectations." **Respondent 9**
"I am more inclined to accept AI service with high humility. The response with high humility can convey a signal that 'the problem is being actively handled', making users have expectations that 'the demand may be resolved'. In contrast, the expression of low humility is likely to arouse a negative perception of 'being perfunctory', exacerbating user dissatisfaction." **Respondent 10**
"I clearly prefer the service model with high humility. Whether the service provider is AI or human, interactions with a humble and polite attitude can bring a more comfortable experience and make me feel respected. If a low-humility response comes from a human customer service, I will feel strongly dissatisfied. Even if it is the humble interaction from AI, I may forgive it because of its non-human nature. Being humbler will still affect the service evaluation." **Respondent 11**
"AI customer service with high humility is more in line with my needs. When consumers encounter unsatisfactory scenarios, their dual needs are particularly prominent: one is emotional comfort, and the other is the solution to practical problems. AI service with high humility can not only meet the demand for emotional value through attitude responses but also solve practical problems relying on solutions, achieving dual value supply." **Respondent 12**
"I will definitely choose AI service with high humility. In the 'AI has made a mistake' scenario you mentioned, the trait of high humility not only reflects service politeness but also can accurately soothe the anger that users may have. Whether the service provider is AI or human, a sincere and humble attitude is the basic premise for maintaining communication after service failures." **Respondent 13**
"I definitely recognize AI service with high humility more. Compared with the low-humility type, AI with high humility not only has a better service attitude but also can provide specific and implementable solutions. This dual advantage of 'attitude + action' is incomparable to low-humility AI." **Respondent 14**
"I am more willing to accept AI service with high humility. In scenarios with unsatisfactory consumption experiences, users' core needs include two aspects: one is a practical solution to the problem, and the other is psychological comfort at the emotional level. AI with high humility conveys an attitude of attention through expressions such as taking the initiative to apologize, avoiding perfunctory users with remarks like 'cannot be determined', which can effectively make up for the psychological gap in the consumption process and improve overall experience satisfaction." **Respondent 15**
"I clearly prefer AI customer service with high humility in service failure scenarios. A sincere and courteous attitude, combined with a clear solution, can effectively soothe negative emotions and make me feel that my needs are being taken seriously. This proper attitude and precise understanding of my demands significantly increase my willingness to continue using the service." **Respondent 16**
"I would definitely choose AI service with high humility. When service failure occurs, such as delivery delays, a humble response conveys respect and sincerity. If two AI systems have similar problem-solving abilities, I will always prefer the one with higher humility, as its attitude makes me feel valued, even if the service provider is only an AI." **Respondent 17**

(continued)

Table 4.10 (continued)

"I am more willing to accept AI service with high humility in failure scenarios. Delays or service breakdowns easily trigger negative emotions, and low-humility responses neither provide emotional comfort nor effective solutions. High-humility AI, by offering attitude-based responses and concrete remedial measures, better addresses my core needs in such situations." **Respondent 18**
"I would choose AI service with high humility. When problems occur, what I care about most is whether a solution is clearly provided. A highly humble AI can explain what actions have been taken, such as prioritizing delivery, which helps me perceive the process as problem-oriented rather than dismissive, even if AI itself is only a procedural step." **Respondent 19**
"I clearly prefer AI service with high humility. In unexpected service failure situations, emotional reassurance and practical solutions are both important. A highly humble AI that apologizes sincerely and offers concrete solutions can effectively ease negative emotions and positively influence my overall evaluation of the merchant and my willingness to continue using the service." **Respondent 20**

patterns demonstrate that, for interviewees, humility must be observable in action; if it cannot be perceived during interaction, it is unlikely to be acknowledged.

However, awareness alone does not lead to a positive evaluation. Many interviewees clearly distinguish between superficial humility and humility that feels genuine. Polite language and apology statements are widely recognized as scripted, which reduces their impact when not accompanied by behavioral changes. When AI repeats generic phrases without adapting its responses or advancing problem resolution, interviewees tend to perceive the humility as insincere. Even when the tone sounds respectful, the lack of responsiveness undermines its credibility. At this stage, interviewees often question whether the AI is genuinely humble or simply performing politeness.

More importantly, interviewees show a strong preference for a form of humility rooted in clear acknowledgment of boundaries. AI that openly admits when it does not know an answer, misunderstands a request, or is unable to resolve an issue is often evaluated positively. Interviewees perceive this as a practical and honest response that prevents wasted time and unrealistic expectations. Rather than interpreting such admissions as weaknesses, interviewees frequently describe them as signs of reliability. In their view, an AI that recognizes its limitations appears more humane than one that maintains authority through vague or inaccurate replies.

That said, humility is truly valued only when it leads to concrete follow-up actions. Interviewees consistently emphasize that apologies or admissions of error should be accompanied by clear next steps, such as offering solutions, proposing compensation, or escalating the issue to a human agent. When humility is paired with effective action, it signals responsibility and care. In contrast, repeated apologies without progress can quickly become a source of frustration. This suggests that interviewees evaluate humility not as an isolated trait but as part of a broader interaction process that either resolves or prolongs their problem.

Another key finding is that interviewees do not expect AI humility to replicate human humility. Interviewees generally recognize that AI lacks genuine emotions

Table 4.11 Insight regarding the impact of AI humility on subsequent service continuance intention

"The core reason why high-humility customer service can significantly enhance my willingness to continue using the service is its ability to deeply insight into customers' potential needs and emotional changes. By proactively paying attention to and responding to customers' emotional demands, this service model can effectively alleviate dissatisfaction arising during consumption, thereby comprehensively optimizing the overall service experience. More importantly, this 'humility' trait can bring customers a strong sense of psychological security—it allows us to clearly feel that the problems we encounter are being taken seriously rather than perfunctorily ignored. This perception of being valued greatly enhances trust in the service, making me more willing to use it continuously for a long time." **Respondent 1**
"The core driver behind the impact of high-humility AI customer service on my subsequent usage intention lies in service attitude. In my opinion, in service failure scenarios, the attitude of AI customer service is far more important than mere solutions—whether it can sincerely acknowledge its own mistakes and actively take effective measures to make up for them directly determines users' experience evaluations. This is similar to how a sincere apology is the key to gaining forgiveness when others make mistakes in daily life. If AI's apology lacks sincerity or fails to make up for the mistake through practical actions, it will not only exacerbate my negative emotions but also seriously damage the trust foundation I have in the brand and service, thereby affecting future choices; on the contrary, a sincere attitude can quickly resolve conflicts and maintain user stickiness." **Respondent 2**
"High-humility AI customer service will definitely increase my willingness to continue using the service, with its core influencing factor being the powerful emotional interaction function. The communication method of such AI customer service is closer to natural human communication, being capable of accurately capturing my emotional state, giving empathetic responses, and providing effective emotional comfort during the service process. This supply of emotional value beyond mere problem-solving makes me feel understood and valued during interaction, thereby generating a stronger sense of identity with the service and being willing to use it continuously." **Respondent 3**
"I believe high-humility AI customer service will have a positive impact on my subsequent usage intention, and the core reason is still the sincere attitude it demonstrates. Even if AI makes mistakes during the service process or the final processing result fails to fully meet my expectations, it always maintains a proactive attitude towards solving problems, allowing me to fully understand its functional limitations. This attitude of 'taking initiative to take responsibility and doing one's best to make up for it' conveys a strong sense of responsibility, and compared to cold and mechanical responses, it is more likely to gain my recognition, thereby prompting me to be more willing to continue using the service." **Respondent 4**
"High-humility AI customer service will inevitably increase my willingness to continue using it. On one hand, it benefits from its fast response speed and timely implemented solutions, and the efficient service process makes me feel a strong sense of practicality; on the other hand, this kind of AI customer service not only shows the advantages of intelligence and convenience but also conveys an intimate service concept through a humble attitude, making me have a favorable impression of it. However, it should be emphasized that the core determinant is still 'whether the problem can be truly solved': if it only stays at the level of being friendly and good at comforting, and the provided solutions are not feasible or cannot be implemented, then the previous apologies and concerns will be meaningless. Only by combining a humble attitude with effective solutions can we truly enhance user stickiness and determine whether I will use it continuously." **Respondent 5**

(*continued*)

Table 4.11 (continued)

"High-humility AI customer service will significantly enhance my willingness to continue using it, with the core reason being that it can make the service experience more worry-free and efficient. Such AI will proactively push problem notification information, clearly explain the current situation, and simultaneously provide targeted solutions, eliminating the need for me to repeatedly initiate consultations and communicate details, and greatly reducing time costs and communication efforts. For me, this model of 'proactive notification + efficient solution' perfectly meets the demand for convenient services, so I will be more inclined to use it for a long time." **Respondent 6**
"I think high-humility AI customer service will increase my usage frequency, with the core lying in its ability to provide scarce emotional value. In the fast-paced daily life, negative emotions during consumption often need to be guided in a timely manner. Through a polite attitude and sincere responses, high-humility AI customer service can effectively alleviate negative feelings such as anxiety and dissatisfaction, adding a sense of emotional pleasure to life. This additional emotional value makes the service go beyond mere functional attributes and become warmer, so I will be more willing to use the corresponding software or AI services frequently." **Respondent 7**
"High-humility AI customer service will not increase my willingness to continue using the service, because in my opinion, AI customer service is essentially just a tool used by merchants to perfunctory users—even if it shows high-humility traits through scripts, it is difficult to change the nature of 'being unable to truly solve complex problems' and make me feel truly valued, so it will not affect my subsequent choices." **Respondent 8**
"For me, high humility is not the core factor affecting the willingness to continue using; communication accuracy is the key. In most cases, when interacting with AI customer service, even if I have clearly expressed the problem, the AI will still repeat irrelevant content or fail to capture the core demands. This inefficient communication will make me feel exhausted and seriously affect the service experience. In contrast, the ability to accurately understand needs and efficiently transmit information is far more important than a humble attitude, so high-humility traits will not significantly enhance my usage intention." **Respondent 9**
"High-humility AI customer service will increase my willingness to continue using it, especially for apps used for the first time. This trait can quickly establish a good first impression. For example, when I first come into contact with a certain app, the high-humility AI customer service conveys a signal of 'being willing to communicate actively and valuing user needs' through a friendly communication method, which will greatly enhance my overall favorability towards the app, thereby making me more willing to continue using the platform's services in the future." **Respondent 10**
"High-humility AI customer service may not have a significant impact on my usage intention. My consumption decisions have always been centered on product quality and personal needs, and I rarely change my choices due to page recommendations or customer service attitudes. When facing customer service with a polite attitude and an average attitude, I prefer services that are easy to operate—because I know that AI is not a real person and do not have high requirements for its attitude." **Respondent 11**
"Of course, high-humility AI customer service will significantly enhance my willingness to use the service subsequently. Firstly, as a consumer, this service model makes me clearly feel that my needs are highly valued and that I can receive timely and positive feedback, avoiding the negative experience of unmet demands. Secondly, it can not only provide emotional value through a humble attitude to alleviate negative feelings during consumption but also simultaneously provide practical and feasible substantive solutions—this dual guarantee of 'emotional comfort + problem-solving' can fundamentally improve my service satisfaction, thereby greatly enhancing the willingness to use it subsequently." **Respondent 12**

(*continued*)

Table 4.11 (continued)

"I believe high-humility AI customer service will increase my willingness to continue using it, with the core reason being that it allows me to be in a controllable service environment. I fully understand that AI is not perfect and will inevitably make mistakes, but after making a mistake, the high-humility response method can quickly give me a sense of psychological security—it will not deliberately avoid the problem or guide users to ignore the mistake, but take the initiative to admit the mistake and propose specific solutions, allowing me to clearly know the progress and results of the problem handling. This 'transparent and responsible' attitude is the key to maintaining my trust in the service, so I will be more willing to use it continuously." **Respondent 13**
"High-humility AI customer service will enhance my subsequent usage intention. On one hand, when AI can take the initiative to be honest about its own ability limitations, it will instead make me feel more reliable—this trait of not exaggerating or concealing can greatly enhance trust. On the other hand, the high-humility communication method can make me feel fully respected. Compared to AI with a stiff attitude, this experience of being respected will significantly improve usage favorability, so I will be more inclined to choose the service subsequently." **Respondent 14**
"High-humility AI customer service will definitely increase my willingness to continue using it, and my experience with Pinduoduo is the best example. I have encountered multiple consumption mistakes when shopping on Pinduoduo (such as buying the wrong product color, mismatched model, etc.). Its AI customer service has both high-humility traits and task-oriented attributes. It not only apologizes with a sincere attitude but also quickly provides accurate solutions, and the entire processing process is efficient and intimate. This high-quality experience has made me have a strong sense of trust in the platform. Now my shopping frequency on Pinduoduo has exceeded that of Taobao and other platforms—it is precisely the combination of high humility and efficiency in AI customer service that has become an important reason for my continuous choice of this platform." **Respondent 15**
"High-humility AI customer service significantly increases my willingness to continue using the service. Its polite and sincere attitude, combined with a clear understanding of my needs and the provision of concrete solutions, not only helps regulate negative emotions but also makes me feel that my problems are taken seriously rather than being handled perfunctorily. This sense of being respected and valued greatly enhances my trust in the service and motivates continued use." **Respondent 16**
"High-humility AI customer service positively influences my subsequent usage intention, with service attitude being the core driver. In service failure situations, whether the AI can sincerely acknowledge mistakes and actively provide remedial measures is more important than the solution itself. A humble and responsible attitude can quickly ease negative emotions and maintain trust, whereas insincere apologies without action would undermine my willingness to continue using the service." **Respondent 17**
"I believe high-humility AI customer service will increase my willingness to continue using it, mainly because it can quickly address my core pain points. In urgent situations, such as delivery delays, a humble response accompanied by rapid problem-solving and clear solutions makes the service feel reliable and efficient, which directly enhances my acceptance of and reliance on the service." **Respondent 18**

(*continued*)

Table 4.11 (continued)

"High-humility AI customer service may have a positive but limited impact on my subsequent usage intention. Although such humility is largely embedded in programmed responses rather than an intrinsic trait, a humble attitude that clearly explains the actions taken to resolve problems helps me perceive the service process as orderly and responsible, even if AI is only a procedural step before human intervention." **Respondent 19**
"High-humility AI customer service increases my willingness to continue using the service because it provides both emotional reassurance and practical solutions in service failure scenarios. Although AI cannot fully replace human empathy, sincere apologies combined with feasible solutions can effectively ease negative emotions and positively influence my evaluation of the merchant and my future usage decisions." **Respondent 20**

and moral responsibility. As a result, they apply a different standard when judging AI humanity. Consistency, calmness, and transparency are often valued more highly than emotional depth. In some cases, interviewees even prefer AI' s stable and restrained humility over human agents whose attitudes may fluctuate. This highlights that AI humanity, from the user's perspective, is grounded in predictable and respectful behavior rather than emotional authenticity.

Ultimately, high humility does increase interviewees' satisfaction and willingness to continue using AI services, but only under specific conditions. Interviewees are more likely to trust and reuse AI systems when humility reduces friction and helps move interactions forward. When humility clarifies limitations, acknowledges mistakes, and supports resolution, it strengthens long-term engagement. When it remains purely verbal, its influence is limited. Therefore, the impact of humility on continued usage depends less on the frequency of AI apologies and more on whether those apologies meaningfully improve the experience.

In summary, the interviews show that interviewees believe AI can exhibit humility, but they define this trait in highly practical terms. AI humility is judged not by sincerity or emotional expression, but by clarity, honesty, and responsiveness in interactions. This functional understanding of humility shapes interviewees' perceptions of AI humanity and plays a decisive role in determining whether AI with high humility is regarded as trustworthy, satisfying, and worthy of continued use.

Across the interviews, a clear pattern emerges: when service failures occur, interviewees consistently prefer AI services that demonstrate high humility over those that do not. In these contexts, high humility, expressed through proactive apologies, acknowledgment of inconvenience, and a respectful tone, is not perceived as an optional courtesy but as an expected response. Interviewees did not frame this preference as a desire for AI to mimic human emotions; rather, they regarded humility as a basic requirement for appropriate system behavior once a failure has disrupted the service experience.

At a deeper level, this preference can be explained by the sequence in which interviewees process service failures, with emotional reactions preceding rational evaluation. Interviewees indicated that delays or errors initially trigger frustration or anxiety, creating a psychological barrier to problem-solving. By acknowledging responsibility and expressing regret, high humility AI reduces this emotional resistance and signals that the inconvenience has been recognized. In contrast, low humility AI responses tend to be perceived as detached or dismissive, which diminishes interviewees' willingness to engage with subsequent explanations or solutions, regardless of their technical adequacy.

Building on this mechanism, humility also shapes how interviewees assess the overall effectiveness and credibility of the service interaction. Once emotional tension is eased, interviewees become more receptive to proposed solutions such as updated delivery times, compensation, or escalation procedures. Over repeated interactions, these experiences accumulate and shape broader perceptions of trust toward both the AI system and the platform behind it. Interviewees often interpreted humble responses as evidence that the company had intentionally embedded concern for customer experience into its service design, whereas interactions characterized by low humility raised concerns about accountability and long-term reliability.

As a result, the role of humility extends beyond facilitating the acceptance of individual solutions and contributes to the development of ongoing trust. Interviewees suggested that even when outcomes were imperfect or delayed, a respectful and apologetic response mitigated negative evaluations of the service provider. In contrast, interactions lacking humility were more likely to be remembered negatively and to influence future usage intentions. This indicates that humility affects not only immediate satisfaction but also the long-term relationship between interviewees and the platform.

However, the interviews also reveal clear limitations to the effectiveness of humility. Interviewees emphasized that apologies must be accompanied by concrete actions to maintain credibility. High humility AI that fails to provide clear next steps, transparent explanations, or tangible remedies risks being perceived as symbolic rather than substantive. Moreover, interviewees recognized that AI has inherent capability limits and cannot replace human intervention in complex or high-stakes scenarios. In such cases, humility remains valuable only when it facilitates efficient escalation rather than delaying resolution.

Taken together, these findings highlight a crucial distinction in how interviewees evaluate humility in AI compared to human service agents. Interviewees do not expect AI to demonstrate deep empathy or moral responsibility, but they do expect adherence to basic social norms such as politeness, acknowledgment of fault, and respectful communication. Low humility behavior violates these minimum expectations and signals system indifference, whereas high humility serves as a baseline indicator of AI humanity. In this sense, humility does not humanize AI by making it emotionally expressive; rather, it ensures that AI behaves in a socially acceptable manner that supports effective service recovery.

A critical finding from the analysis is that the impact of AI humility on users' service continuance intention presents a diverse and multi-dimensional characteristic, whose mechanism is rooted in the dual demands of users' emotional and functional needs. Meanwhile, some users regard AI humility as a non-critical factor due to their own consumption decision logic or cognition of AI's essence, resulting in a non-linear correlation between AI humility and continuance intention, which is regulated by multiple dimensions.

For most users who believe AI humility can enhance their continuance intention, the provision of emotional value is the core driving force. AI humility brings users a strong sense of psychological security and being valued through a sincere attitude (such as taking the initiative to admit mistakes and not shirking responsibilities), empathetic communication methods (accurately capturing users' emotions and providing emotional comfort), and high attention to users' needs. This emotional satisfaction can not only effectively alleviate negative emotions (such as anxiety and dissatisfaction) caused by service failures or unmet needs during consumption but also enable users to gain a sense of identity and emotional pleasure in interactions. In turn, this strengthens users' trust and reliance on the service, laying a psychological foundation for long-term continuous use. For instance, when encountering service failures, AI's humble response of actively acknowledging errors and proposing remedial measures can quickly ease users' negative feelings, while its empathetic feedback can make users feel understood, thus reducing psychological resistance to reusing the service.

Beyond emotional needs, users' preference for AI humility is also inseparable from the support of practical functional value. Users generally expect AI humility to be combined with effective functional performance—that is, a humble attitude must be accompanied by efficient problem-solving capabilities. Specifically, this includes responding to needs quickly, providing feasible solutions, proactively pushing the progress of problem handling, and reducing time costs caused by repeated communication. When AI can not only convey respect and attention with a humble posture but also accurately locate core issues, handle processes transparently, and achieve problem-solving goals efficiently, its functional value and emotional value form a synergistic effect. This significantly improves users' service satisfaction and further enhances their continuance intention. Many users mentioned that high-quality AI service experiences stem from the combination of a humble attitude and efficient problem-solving abilities, making the platform stand out among similar services. For example, in scenarios such as wrong product deliveries or delayed refunds, AI's humble apology paired with rapid and practical solutions (such as arranging returns conveniently or offering compensation coupons) not only resolves practical problems but also strengthens users' recognition of the service's reliability.

Not all users believe that AI humility has a significant impact on their continuance intention, and the cognition of this group revolves around three core logics. Firstly, some users define the essence of AI customer service as a tool, believing that its humble traits mostly come from preset scripts, which cannot change its core limitation of "being unable to truly solve complex problems." Therefore, even if it shows humility, it is difficult to make users feel truly valued, and naturally, it cannot affect subsequent choices. Secondly, some users emphasize that communication accuracy and information transmission efficiency are more important than attitude. If AI, despite having a humble attitude, fails to accurately capture core needs and repeatedly outputs irrelevant content, this inefficient communication will seriously reduce the service experience and weaken the positive effect of the humble attitude. Thirdly, the consumption decisions of some users have always centered on product quality, personal actual needs, or the operational convenience of the service. AI attitude is only a secondary factor, and they do not have high expectations for AI's attitude. Thus, AI humility is difficult to change their established decision-making logic and may only have a limited positive impact. For example, some users stated that their choice of platform depends more on product quality and whether the service is easy to operate, and AI's polite or humble performance will not alter their long-term usage preferences.

In summary, the relationship between AI humility and users' service continuance intention can be understood through a three-dimensional integrated framework. The first dimension is users' perception of AI humility, which is jointly triggered by AI's verbal expressions (such as sincere apologies and polite communication) and practical actions (such as active remediation and efficient problem-solving). Empty politeness without action support is difficult for users to truly perceive as humility. The second dimension is users' preference for high-humility AI, which is rooted in the dual expectations of emotional value (psychological security, sense of being valued, emotional comfort) and functional value (problem-solving efficiency, communication accuracy, service convenience). The synergistic satisfaction of both is the key to the formation of preference. The third dimension is continuance intention, which is jointly influenced by the previous two dimensions—when users perceive genuine AI humility and their preferences are met, their continuance intention is significantly enhanced; on the contrary, if the perception is insufficient or the preferences are not satisfied, the intention will weaken or remain unaffected. These three dimensions are interrelated and progressive, collectively constructing a complete analytical framework for understanding how AI humility affects consumers' attitudes and behaviors. It not only reflects the positive feedback of most users but also covers the differentiated cognition of a few users, providing a comprehensive perspective for in-depth exploration of the relationship between AI traits and consumer behavior.

4.4.4 Cases Regarding AI Humor

The following section presents the analytical tables examining the understudied dimension of AI humor, progressing from descriptive characterization to impact measurement. Table 4.12 establishes analysis foundation by presenting insights regarding AI humor. Building upon this, Table 4.13 explores the affective consequence of this communicative feature by synthesizing insights regarding AI humor and perceived warmth. This relational linkage is then connected to a core service outcome in Table 4.14, which aggregates findings on the impact of AI humor on user satisfaction, evaluating whether and under what conditions humor affects user satisfaction. Collectively, this section provides a structured basis for understanding the strategic value and changes of implementing AI humor.

Table 4.12 Insights regarding AI humor

"I have come into contact with many AIs with humorous traits, such as interacting with large language models like DeepSeek and Doubao. I found that the humorous styles of AIs on different platforms are highly correlated with the attributes of their target user groups—taking Weibo as an example, as a content platform with strong social attributes, its built-in comment robot 'Robert' is trained based on massive Weibo user data, and its reply style accurately matches the usage habits and reading preferences of platform users. Its humorous expressions are usually concise and refined, and it also flexibly integrates current popular internet terms and internet memes, which not only fits Weibo's social atmosphere but also quickly resonates with users, meeting the interaction needs of young user groups." **Respondent 1**
"I have indeed come into contact with many AIs with humorous styles. For example, when browsing Weibo, I often see 'Robert' in the comment section. Its replies are full of humor and always make people laugh. In addition, when chatting with large language models like Doubao, I also take the initiative to request to turn on the humorous mode. The humorous answers they generate are often full of creativity, and sometimes they throw out clever teasing combined with scenarios, making the interaction experience very interesting." **Respondent 2**
"Among the AIs I have come into contact with, the humorous performance of Weibo's comment robot 'Robert' is the most prominent. For example, I often post fan circle-related content, and 'Robert' will automatically generate suitable comments based on my past speech style. Its humorous expression method is unique, and it can even create a language style that is difficult for humans to think of, which is both novel and interesting. As long as it is not malicious or spoof humor, this kind of creative interaction can make me feel happy and is very much in line with my preferences." **Respondent 4**
"Now there are quite a few AIs with humorous traits, and many of them can bring a relaxed interaction experience. For example, the 'Robert' robot in Weibo's comment section has a humorous style that leans towards sharp-tongued but witty—it often responds to content in unexpected ways, breaking the conventional reply logic, and always brings a sense of surprise. Every time I see its comments, I find them very funny, which greatly increases the fun of browsing Weibo." **Respondent 5**
"Should the comment robot 'Robert' on Weibo be considered as an AI with a humorous style? I have seen its replies many times when browsing Weibo before. The content is relaxed and interesting, and sometimes it interacts in a playful tone, leaving a deep impression on me. It feels more dynamic than ordinary AI replies." **Respondent 6**
"I have come into contact with many AIs with humorous styles. The comment robot on Weibo often leaves messages and interacts under the content I post, and sometimes what it says is particularly funny; in addition, I have also used DeepSeek's fortune-telling function. The replies it generates are full of fun. Although they have no practical reference value, the process is particularly joyful and interesting." **Respondent 7**
"Indeed, 'Robert' on Weibo is quite humorous, but its humor has nothing to do with the style of speaking, but comes from the dislocation between the reply content and the poster's expression intention—for example, the poster originally wanted to convey a serious or sad emotion, but 'Robert' gave a completely irrelevant reply. The poster may feel dissatisfied, but other viewers will find this sense of contrast of 'irrelevant answers' particularly humorous, becoming a unique interactive fun." **Respondent 8**

(continued)

Table 4.12 (continued)

"Yes, I have had many experiences interacting with humorous AIs. Every time I post a Weibo, 'Robert' will frequently interact with me in the comment section. Its replies are not only timely but also have a relaxed tone. This continuous interaction makes me truly feel that 'someone is paying attention to me', which greatly improves my enthusiasm for posting Weibo and makes the social experience warmer." **Respondent 9**
"I think the existence of humorous AIs like 'Robert' is of limited functional usefulness. Sometimes its comments can indeed hit the joke point and bring unexpected joy. However, in most cases, the reply content has nothing to do with the theme of the post, and even some are awkward, which instead destroys the original interactive atmosphere." **Respondent 10**
"'Robert' on Weibo is often active in the comment section, either making irrelevant summaries of the post content or posting some inexplicable remarks. I usually regard its replies as entertainment. Although the style is quite special, occasionally reading them can relieve browsing fatigue, which is a unique humorous experience." **Respondent 11**
"I have come into contact with many AIs with humorous styles, among which 'Robert' is the most active on Weibo—whether it is the Weibo I post myself or browsing others' content, I can see its comments. However, its humorous way is quite special. It often tells some lame jokes, and many times it fails to accurately understand the content or tone of the post, leading to a discounted humorous effect, but overall it can still bring a certain sense of fun." **Respondent 12**
"The comment robot on Weibo often comments on my posts, with a strong sense of interaction. In addition, when I used ChatGPT to practice oral English before, I specially asked it to simulate the identity of a friend to communicate. Its replies are often full of humor, and occasionally tell some small jokes that make me smile. This kind of humorous expression close to real people makes me feel that it is no longer a cold machine, but an interactive partner that can bring joy." **Respondent 13**
"The comment robot 'Robert' on Weibo is a typical representative of AI humor. It often posts some teasing remarks, or pretends to say funny things in a serious manner. Its unique humorous style has attracted many users. Everyone often copies its comments to create memes and play with memes, forming a unique community interactive atmosphere, which makes the browsing experience of Weibo more interesting." **Respondent 14**
"The humorous AI I have come into contact with the most is Weibo's 'Robert'. For a period of time, I especially liked posting Weibo. Since I didn't have many fans, every time I posted a text-based Weibo, 'Robert' would comment immediately, with a very supportive attitude. Its humor is not only reflected in funny remarks but also conveys warmth sometimes—for example, once I just broke up and was in a bad mood, so I posted a sad Weibo. 'Robert' commented on me saying 'Breaking up may be a new start for your next life'. This sentence was both warm and healing, leaving a deep impression on me and greatly increasing my favorability towards it." **Respondent 15**
"Occasionally, when using tools such as ChatGPT, if the generated content itself is relatively relaxed, the AI may add a light joke at the end. However, in situations where I am in a negative emotional state, overly humorous responses can feel inappropriate and even uncomfortable. In such cases, I tend to prefer AI responses with low humor that focus on providing clear solutions rather than emotional teasing." **Respondent 16**
"I have indirectly encountered generative AI with strong humor traits through others' usage. For example, my roommate often lets AI adopt a sarcastic role to comment on personal behavior. The response is expressed in a humorous and witty way, which makes it feel more human and emotionally warm. From this perspective, high-humor AI can provide emotional comfort, but its appropriateness still depends heavily on the specific situation and user needs." **Respondent 17**

(*continued*)

Table 4.12 (continued)

"I have interacted with humorous AI mainly through social media comment robots and large language models. In many cases, their humor does not come from deliberate joke-telling, but from slightly mismatched or unexpected responses, which creates a form of cold or ironic humor. Compared with low-humor AI that merely restates facts, high-humor AI feels more like a friend responding in everyday language, which enhances warmth and increases my willingness to continue engaging with the platform." **Respondent 18**
"I have observed humorous generative AI in comment sections. Although I do not actively rely on such features, I can clearly feel the difference in emotional impact. In unpleasant situations, low-humor responses may come across as indifferent or perfunctory, whereas humorous replies—even if they do not directly solve the problem—can help ease emotional tension and make it easier for me to reconcile with negative experiences, thereby improving overall satisfaction." **Respondent 19**
"I rarely encounter humorous AI in online shopping scenarios, but I have noticed humorous generative AI in social media platforms such as Bilibili, Douyin, and Weibo. High-level humor, such as creative metaphors or internet memes, can make me laugh in moments of frustration and quickly relieve emotional tension. Compared with bland or perfunctory responses, appropriate humor has a positive effect on my service satisfaction and also enhances my overall impression of the AI and the platform, as long as the humor remains within reasonable and ethical boundaries." **Respondent 20**

An in-depth analysis of interviewees' responses regarding GAI humor—focused on their direct experiences with humorous GAI, emotional differences brought by high vs. low humor levels, and the impact of humor on service satisfaction—reveals distinct patterns that reflect the dual role of GAI humor as an emotional enhancer and contextual adapter. These patterns not only highlight the variability in how users perceive and respond to GAI humor but also underscore its significant influence on user emotional engagement and service evaluation.

First, the analysis underscores that interviewees' experiences with humorous GAI are primarily centered on platform-specific AI tools, with the Weibo comment robot "Robert" and large language models (e.g., DeepSeek, Doubao) emerging as the most frequently cited examples. These experiences are characterized by diverse perceptions—ranging from strong approval of GAI humor's ability to enhance interaction fun to criticism of its occasional awkwardness or irrelevance. Most interviewees reported positive experiences with humorous GAI, noting that it adds vitality to interactions. For instance, many described "Robert" as a standout humorous AI: its concise, meme-integrated responses align with Weibo's social atmosphere, resonating with young users' preferences. One interviewee shared that "Robert" generates creative, human-like humorous comments on fan circle content, creating a novel and enjoyable interaction experience. Another noted that when practicing oral English with ChatGPT in a friend-like role, its humorous replies and jokes made the interaction feel warm and engaging, breaking the coldness of human-machine communication.

Humorous GAI also proved effective in emotional support scenarios. An interviewee recalled posting a sad Weibo post after a breakup, and "Robert" commented, "Breaking up might be the start of your next new life"—a response that was

Table 4.13 Insights regarding AI humor and perceived warmth

"For this case, I will clearly prefer the AI reply with high humor. The core reason lies in Weibo's social attribute—when users share or complain about personal experiences on the platform, they are not pursuing completely objective and rational responses, but focusing more on the expression and release of personal emotions. High-humor replies can take over users' emotions in a relaxed and peaceful way, not only helping users express their inner feelings but also alleviating negative emotions through resonance, making users who may be angry or irritable feel more relaxed, effectively reducing a sense of confrontation, and improving the interaction experience." **Respondent 1**
"Low-humor AI replies make me clearly perceive the distance of 'human-machine interaction', lacking emotional warmth overall and appearing mechanical and cold. In contrast, high-humor replies are extremely attractive, making the communication process full of fun. This dynamic interaction mode allows AI services to convey a warmer and more human-like emotional texture, greatly enhancing usage favorability." **Respondent 2**
"I believe high-humor AI conveys emotional value through richer expression forms, such as flexibly using emojis with humorous language to make replies more appealing. For example, when users feel dissatisfied due to being unable to dine on time, a high-humor comment may defuse negative emotions with a playful tone, making users smile and feel relieved. This emotional improvement will reduce users' negative impressions of the relevant restaurant, avoiding completely denying the brand due to temporary dissatisfaction." **Respondent 3**
"High-humor AI replies can indeed effectively distract attention from negative emotions and help me get out of negative emotions such as anger and disappointment—its interesting expression form brings a relaxed and pleasant experience. In contrast, low-humor replies are too serious and even boring, unable to alleviate negative emotions and only fulfilling the basic function of information transmission." **Respondent 4**
"I think there are significant differences between high and low humor AI replies, like two communication partners with distinct personalities: low-humor AI is more rational and pragmatic, focusing only on the problem itself. In contrast, high-humor AI is better at defusing users' irritability in a relaxed and witty way. This humorous response not only assists in solving problems but also adds a sense of ease to the interaction, allowing users to accept information in a pleasant atmosphere and improving the overall experience." **Respondent 5**
"Low-humor AI replies exhibit a calm and rational style. Although these replies can propose effective solutions, the expression method is too plain and lacks emotions. In contrast, high-humor replies are more interesting and can even arouse my desire to share—I will take the initiative to forward interesting comments to friends, forming secondary communication. This emotional value beyond the function itself can bring users a warm interaction experience, making AI no longer a mere tool but more like a partner that can bring joy." **Respondent 6**
"High-humor AI does affect my experience, but the effect varies by platform: although Weibo's comment robot focuses on a humorous style, its expression method often seems 'sarcastic', which instead adds fuel to the fire and exacerbates users' negative emotions; while DeepSeek's humorous expression is more in line with the logic of natural human language, and the optimization of the data model makes its humor more sincere, which can truly convey a sense of warmth and avoid the discomfort caused by deliberate teasing." **Respondent 7**
"Undoubtedly, high-humor AI makes me feel warmer and more humanistic. If I only need to solve a problem, a search engine is sufficient. However, high-humor AI can upgrade the service experience—through humorous language interaction, it makes me have the illusion that 'a real person is helping solve the problem'. This anthropomorphic experience greatly enhances emotional resonance and makes the service process warmer." **Respondent 8**

(continued)

Table 4.13 (continued)

"There are obvious differences between high and low humor AI replies, and high-humor AI can significantly improve my sense of participation. For example, the AI 'Yuanbao' in Honor of Kings belongs to this category—during the game, it provides emotional value through humorous language, such as mocking opponents when having operational advantages. This scenario-appropriate humorous interaction makes me feel particularly happy, greatly enhancing the fun and immersion of the game." **Respondent 9**
"I think the need for AI's humor should be judged according to the scenario: in leisure scenarios such as browsing Weibo, high-humor AI can make content more interesting and improve the browsing experience; but in scenarios where specific problems are solved or serious situations are involved, low-humor AI has more advantages—high-humor expressions may include irrelevant information, increasing the cost for users to extract core content, while low-humor AI can directly output solutions, better meeting the demand for efficient problem-solving." **Respondent 10**
"There are extremely significant differences between high and low humor AI replies, and high-humor AI can convey a strong sense of warmth. The core reason is that humorous expressions endow AI with a 'sense of being alive'. This highly anthropomorphic trait breaks the sense of alienation in human-machine interaction, significantly enhancing AI's 'emotional temperature'. In contrast, low-humor AI always maintains a mechanical and cold tool attribute." **Respondent 12**
"I believe high-humor AI brings a sense of warmth, and the key lies in the grasp of humor's scale—when AI's humorous expression is appropriate, it can accurately convey understanding and care. For example, when encountering bottlenecks in writing papers and lacking creativity, a relaxed tease or encouragement from AI will make me feel understood, relieve anxiety, and then generate a sense of warmth; while low-humor AI does not bring warmth, it does not appear cold either, more like a neutral information transmission tool." **Respondent 13**
"The sense of warmth brought by high and low humor AI comes from different sources: high-humor AI conveys warmth through emotional resonance—for example, when complaining about common topics, humorous interaction shortens the psychological distance and makes me feel close; while low-humor AI conveys warmth through reliable solutions—its accurate and efficient responses make me feel steady and at ease, and this sense of warmth based on functional value is more stable and trustworthy." **Respondent 14**
"The difference between high and low humor AI replies needs to be defined according to the scenario: in non-work and non-business scenarios (such as daily life sharing, emotional communication, etc.), high-humor AI has more advantages—witty language can bring unexpected joy and make interactions more vivid. However, in serious scenarios such as business negotiations and emergency problem handling, low-humor task-oriented AI is more appropriate, avoiding the lack of professionalism or distraction that may be caused by humorous expressions." **Respondent 15**
"In my experience, low-humor AI responses often feel more appropriate. When I am already in a negative emotional state, highly humorous replies may intensify discomfort rather than provide comfort, creating a feeling of emotional mismatch. Compared with humorous teasing, a calm and solution-oriented response can make me feel more secure and less irritated, which brings a more stable form of warmth." **Respondent 16**
"I perceive a clear difference in warmth between high- and low-humor AI. High-humor AI tends to convey emotional warmth by offering light-hearted or witty responses, which can temporarily comfort emotions and make unpleasant situations feel less heavy. However, this warmth is highly context-dependent, as humorous responses may become inappropriate when users urgently need concrete solutions." **Respondent 17**

(continued)

Table 4.13 (continued)

"I believe high-humor AI brings stronger warmth than low-humor AI. Its language style feels closer to everyday human communication and emotional expression, making interactions resemble conversations with friends rather than mechanical information exchange. Low-humor AI, by contrast, often focuses only on factual descriptions, which can feel emotionally distant and less considerate." **Respondent 18**
"The difference between high- and low-humor AI lies mainly in their emotional impact. Low-humor responses may sound indifferent or even sarcastic in negative situations, whereas humorous replies—although they may not directly solve the problem—can ease emotional tension and help users reconcile with unpleasant experiences, thus creating a warmer overall interaction." **Respondent 19**
"I clearly feel more warmth from high-humor AI responses. Appropriate humor can help release anger and frustration, allowing users to calm down and face problems more rationally afterward. In contrast, low-humor responses often appear perfunctory and emotionally hollow, which not only fails to comfort users but may further intensify dissatisfaction." **Respondent 20**

both humorous and comforting, significantly lifting the user's mood. Additionally, continuous humorous interactions from GAI enhanced users' sense of being noticed: one interviewee mentioned that "Robert" consistently commented on their low-follower Weibo posts, boosting their motivation to share content.

However, some interviewees criticized humorous GAI as "superfluous" or "awkward." For example, "Robert" occasionally posted irrelevant comments or forced jokes that disrupted the interaction flow. One interviewee noted that while "Robert" sometimes delivered funny content, it often strayed from the post's theme, creating awkwardness. Another pointed out that "Robert's cold jokes or failure to grasp the post's tone diminished its humorous effect, though it still added some lightheartedness. These mixed experiences indicate that GAI humor's effectiveness depends heavily on its relevance to the context and alignment with user expectations.

One salient dimension in understanding AI humor is the emotional differences between high and low humor GAI, particularly in terms of perceived warmth. Nearly all interviewees reported that high humor GAI delivered significantly more warmth than low humor GAI. High humor GAI created a sense of human-like interaction through lively language, popular memes, and emoji integration, reducing the distance in human-machine communication. For example, one interviewee explained that low humor GAI responses felt mechanical and cold, while high humor ones felt like chatting with a funny person—engaging and emotionally resonant. In service failure scenarios, high humor GAI effectively alleviated negative emotions: when a user complained about delayed meals, a humorous comment defused frustration, making them feel more relaxed.

High humor GAI also enhanced emotional participation. However, the warmth brought by GAI humor was context-dependent. Several interviewees noted that high humor GAI was more suitable for casual scenarios (e.g., browsing Weibo), while low humor GAI was preferable for serious or problem-solving contexts—high humor might distract users or increase information extraction costs in formal

Table 4.14 Insights regarding the impact of AI humor on user satisfaction

"I believe AI's humor may indeed produce different effects due to cross-cultural differences, and high-humor replies also have potential risks—for example, occasional inappropriate expressions may make users feel offended or overly sharp. However, I still prefer high-humor replies, because their advantages in relieving emotions and improving interaction experience are more prominent. As long as the expression scale is well grasped, negative effects can be effectively avoided." **Respondent 1**
"For me, the impact brought by AI's humor is completely positive. High humor makes AI get rid of the mechanical sense and closer to the communication state of real people. It not only adds warmth to the service but also makes the communication process full of fun, greatly enhancing the pleasure of the use experience. This positive feeling will be directly converted into recognition of the service." **Respondent 2**
"The humor of generative AI is an important factor affecting service satisfaction for me. The experience difference between high humor and low humor is extremely obvious: low-humor replies seem cold and alienated, unable to convey emotional value. In contrast, high-humor replies can bring a sense of warmth and make me feel happier. This emotional improvement caused by humor will directly increase my satisfaction with AI services. Therefore, I believe humor brings a positive impact." **Respondent 3**
"I prefer high-humor AI, and the core reason is that it has dual values—it can not only effectively relieve my negative emotions but also make the interaction process more interesting through humorous and relaxed expressions. Under the service experience of high humor, I will evaluate AI services as 'high-quality and intimate'. This good impression will significantly increase the willingness to use them subsequently, and even actively look forward to interacting with it again." **Respondent 4**
"If we set aside individual personality differences and only analyze from the perspective of generative AI, the level of humor will directly affect my satisfaction with the service, and the overall presentation is a positive correlation. If AI has a sense of humor, I will be more inclined to choose and use it. For example, in the comment section scenario, calm and serious replies are often difficult to attract my attention, but humorous comments will make me feel particularly interesting. I will not only read them carefully but also be curious about its response to the next post, thereby generating the willingness to pay continuous attention and expectation." **Respondent 5**
"The effect of AI's humor will indeed vary due to users' different acceptance of the language environment, which to a certain extent also reflects the influence of culture or group atmosphere. For example, the reputation of Weibo's comment robot is controversial. Its sharp humorous style is not suitable for all users: for users who are familiar with and accept Weibo's meme culture, this style will bring positive reactions and be regarded as interesting interaction; but for users who are not adapted to this language environment, they may feel offended and have a negative experience." **Respondent 7**
"If the final result of problem-solving is the same, the level of AI's humor will not affect my mood. However, if the problem is not solved, high-humor AI will have more advantages. I might have felt dissatisfied because 'AI is useless', but if its humorous expression can make me feel comfortable, it will reduce negative emotions and no longer care too much about the regret that the problem is not solved." **Respondent 8**
"I have always been inclined to accept AI services with a sense of humor. This style of service can make interactions more relaxed and interesting, and the overall experience is very good, which will make me have a clear favorable impression of AI services." **Respondent 9**

(*continued*)

Table 4.14 (continued)

"AI's humor will affect service satisfaction, but the effect needs to be judged in combination with specific scenarios: in scenarios where there is no rush to solve problems and a certain communication cost is acceptable, high-humor AI can provide emotional value, making me more comfortable psychologically and bringing a positive impact. However, in scenarios where problems need to be solved quickly, low-humor AI has more advantages—its concise and direct expression can reduce the cost of information extraction and meet demands faster. At this time, high humor may instead reduce efficiency due to distraction and have a negative impact." **Respondent 10**
"The impact of AI's humor on satisfaction needs to be judged in combination with service results: if the shopping experience is successful, whether AI is humorous is irrelevant and will not improve existing satisfaction; if the shopping experience fails, AI's humor may have the opposite effect, adding fuel to the fire and exacerbating the original dissatisfaction" **Respondent 11**
"I believe the impact of AI's humor on satisfaction needs to be discussed by scenario: in non-serious topic scenarios (such as leisure and entertainment communication), humor can bring fun and significantly positively improve satisfaction. However, in formal scenarios (such as scenarios that need to solve problems in a timely manner and obtain accurate feedback), humor will have a negative impact—at this time, the core demand is to solve problems efficiently, and humorous expressions may distract attention, or even delay the progress of problem-solving, reducing experience evaluation." **Respondent 12**
"AI's humor will affect service satisfaction, but it is likely to depend on the interaction scenario. Specifically, in informal scenarios such as creative types, for example, when needing to find inspiration for content creation, AI's humorous interaction can stimulate creative interest and improve satisfaction and use fun. However, in formal scenarios, such as encountering data problems that need to be verified when writing reports, AI's jokes will interfere with ideas and affect efficiency, thereby reducing satisfaction." **Respondent 13**
"AI's humor will affect service satisfaction, but it needs to be judged in combination with specific situations. In non-urgent and emotionally stable situations, humorous AI can defuse the atmosphere through teasing and humor, and instead improve satisfaction. However, if encountering poor service, AI's inappropriate humor will seem frivolous, which not only cannot relieve negative emotions but also further reduce satisfaction with the service." **Respondent 14**
"AI's humor will affect service satisfaction, and the key lies in 'moderation' and scenario matching. Taking consumption or online shopping scenarios as examples, I prefer low-humor AI services—just directly inform core information such as processing time and operation steps; if the humor is too high, it may increase the cost of understanding, make me feel a waste of time, and instead reduce satisfaction. Therefore, moderate humor that fits the scenario is the key." **Respondent 15**
"I think the humor of generative AI does influence my service satisfaction. When humor is inappropriate to the situation, especially when I am already in a negative emotional state, humorous replies may feel irritating rather than comforting, which will lower my overall evaluation of the AI service. In such cases, I am even willing to switch to another AI tool that better matches my immediate needs." **Respondent 16**
"In my view, the impact of AI's humor on service satisfaction is generally positive, but highly situational. High-humor AI can provide emotional comfort and make unpleasant experiences feel more bearable, which increases satisfaction at the emotional level. However, when facing serious problems that require concrete solutions, humor becomes secondary, and satisfaction depends more on whether the AI can respond effectively." **Respondent 17**

(*continued*)

Table 4.14 (continued)

"I believe that AI's humor has a clear positive effect on my service satisfaction. High-humor responses make the interaction feel warmer and more human-like, which improves my emotional experience and increases my willingness to continue using the service. Compared with rigid and purely factual replies, humorous interactions enhance overall satisfaction and platform engagement." **Respondent 18**
"For me, humor positively affects service satisfaction, especially in scenarios involving dissatisfaction or negative emotions. Although humorous replies may not directly solve the problem, they can help ease emotional tension and make the overall experience feel less frustrating, which improves my subjective evaluation of the service." **Respondent 19**
"In most cases, appropriate humor has a positive impact on my service satisfaction. High-level humor can help me calm down and regain a rational mindset when encountering unpleasant situations, which indirectly improves my perception of the service. However, this positive effect is premised on ethical boundaries and contextual appropriateness—humor that crosses these boundaries would instead reduce satisfaction." **Respondent 20**

settings. Additionally, some pointed out that overly sarcastic humor (e.g., "Robert's" occasional snarky tone) could backfire, intensifying negative emotions instead of soothing them. Low humor GAI, while lacking emotional warmth, still served functional purposes. One interviewee noted that low humor GAI acted as a neutral information provider—neither warm nor cold—while another emphasized that low humor GAI delivered reliable solutions, bringing a sense of stability and reassurance. This suggests that low humor GAI's "warmth" stems from functional reliability rather than emotional expression.

The impact of GAI humor on service satisfaction is primarily positive but context- and user-dependent. Most interviewees reported that high humor GAI positively influenced their satisfaction by enhancing emotional value and interaction fun. For example, one interviewee stated that high humor GAI's human-like interaction made the service more enjoyable, directly increasing their satisfaction. Another noted that high humor GAI's ability to relieve negative emotions and add fun led them to perceive the service as "high-quality and thoughtful," boosting their willingness to reuse it. In comment sections, humorous replies were more likely to attract attention: one interviewee said they paid more attention to funny GAI comments and looked forward to its future responses.

However, some interviewees responded differently to GAI humor. Those focused on functional needs emphasized that problem-solving ability mattered more than humor—as long as GAI provided accurate, efficient solutions, its humor level was irrelevant. Additionally, GAI humor's impact varied by scenario and expression scale. For instance, in urgent problem-solving or formal business contexts, high humor GAI could reduce satisfaction by distracting users or undermining professionalism. An interviewee noted that in online shopping scenarios, they preferred low humor GAI that directly provided key information (e.g., processing time, steps), as excessive humor increased comprehension effort and felt time-wasting.

GAI humor also carried potential risks: inappropriate humor (e.g., overly sharp remarks) could offend users and reduce satisfaction. One interviewee mentioned that cultural differences or poor scale control might make high humor responses offensive, though its advantages in emotional relief still outweighed such risks when properly managed. Additionally, the impact of GAI humor depended on service outcomes: if a problem remained unresolved, high humor GAI could mitigate negative emotions, but if the humor was ill-timed (e.g., during a bad user experience), it might worsen the experience.

In summary, GAI humor experiences and emotional responses encompass three core dimensions: users' mixed experiences with humorous GAI (shaped by relevance and context), emotional differences between high and low humor GAI (with high humor delivering greater warmth in casual scenarios), and the context-dependent positive impact of humor on service satisfaction. These dimensions are interconnected: GAI humor's relevance and appropriateness influence emotional responses, which in turn shape service satisfaction. Together, they form a holistic framework for understanding how GAI humor affects user emotions and behaviors, providing valuable insights into the role of humor in human-machine interaction.

4.4.5 Additional Interesting Observations

Beyond the core themes of AI versus human recommendations, communication styles, humility traits, and GAI humor, interviewees' responses revealed several nuanced, context-rich observations that deepen the understanding of user-AI interaction dynamics. These insights—rooted in real-world experiences—highlight unanticipated tensions, hidden influences, and scenario-specific contradictions that extend beyond the research's primary focus, yet offer critical perspectives on how users navigate AI-driven services in daily life.

4.4.5.1 The "Uncanny Valley" of AI's "Human-Like" Traits

A striking observation across interviews was interviewees' mixed reactions to AI's attempts to mimic human traits, such as humility, humor, and warmth—a phenomenon echoing the "uncanny valley" effect, where AI's near-human behavior triggers discomfort rather than connection. For example, several interviewees noted that overly scripted "humble" apologies or forced "friendly" social cues made AI feel "inauthentic" rather than relatable. One interviewee described an AI that repeatedly used "dear" and "sorry" during a return dispute but failed to address their core concern about a delayed refund, saying, "It felt like a robot reading a sympathy card—polite, but completely disconnected from what I was actually upset about." Similarly, a user criticized GAI's humor that missed the tone of their sad Weibo post: "I was venting about a bad day, and it replied with a silly joke. It wasn't funny; it felt like it didn't understand I was hurting."

This discomfort was most pronounced when AI's human-like traits clashed with its functional limitations. For instance, an interviewee praised an AI for admitting it could not answer a technical question about a camera—"that felt humble and honest"—but grew frustrated when it failed to escalate the issue to a human: "It apologized nicely, but then left me hanging. If it's going to act 'humble' like a human would, it should follow through like a human too." Conversely, AI that leaned into its "machine identity"—such as task-oriented AI that delivered concise, unembellished answers—often avoided this discomfort. As one interviewee put it, "I don't mind AI being a tool. What bugs me is when it pretends to be a person but can't back it up with real understanding."

4.4.5.2 The "Invisible Filter" of AI Recommendations: Shaping Preferences Without Awareness

Interviewees also highlighted an unexpected influence of AI recommendations: their ability to subtly reshape users' preferences over time, even when users actively ignored them. While many criticized AI recommendations for being repetitive or irrelevant, several admitted that prolonged exposure to AI's curated content had unconsciously narrowed their own search behavior. For example, an interviewee who frequently shopped for clothing noted, "I used to browse random categories for inspiration, but now I just scroll through the 'recommended' section because it's easier. I catch myself thinking, 'This is what I like,' even though it's just what the AI keeps showing me." Another user shared a similar experience with beauty products: "AI kept pushing matte lipsticks, and even though I initially preferred glossy ones, I eventually bought one just to see—now I own three. It's like the AI slowly trained me to like what it recommends."

This "invisible filter" effect was particularly evident among interviewees who shopped casually, such as browsing for leisure rather than specific needs. They described AI recommendations as a "default path" that reduced decision fatigue but also limited exposure to new styles or brands. One interviewee joked, "I used to be adventurous with my purchases, but now I'm basically buying what the AI thinks I should. It's convenient, but I wonder if I'm missing out because of it."

4.4.5.3 Gendered Perceptions of AI's Emotional Traits

Interviewees' responses also revealed subtle gender-based differences in how users evaluate AI's emotional traits, such as warmth, empathy, and humility. Female interviewees were more likely to prioritize AI's ability to "read" emotional cues and adjust responses accordingly, while male interviewees tended to frame emotional traits as "nice-to-have" rather than essential—unless they directly impacted functional outcomes. For example, a female interviewee emphasized the importance of an AI's humble tone during a service failure: "When my order was wrong, the AI said 'I'm truly sorry about this' and offered a discount. That acknowledgment made me feel valued, not just like a transaction." In contrast, a male interviewee noted, "I don't care if the AI apologizes—just fix the problem fast. Humility is irrelevant if it can't resolve the issue."

These differences extended to GAI humor: female interviewees were more likely to find humor "offensive" when it missed contextual cues, such as a joke during a complaint, while male interviewees often dismissed such missteps as "harmless." One female interviewee recalled a GAI that made a sarcastic comment about her returned dress: "It said 'Guess this one didn't fit—better luck next time!' I was already frustrated, and that just made it worse. It felt rude, not funny." A male interviewee, however, described a similar experience with a sarcastic AI: "It joked about my broken headphones, and I just laughed. It's a robot; I don't take its tone personally."

4.4.5.4 The "Contextual Blind Spot" of AI: Failure to Adapt to "Unspoken" User Circumstances

A recurring frustration across interviews was AI's inability to account for "unspoken" contextual factors that humans intuitively grasp—what interviewees referred to as AI's "contextual blind spot." For example, an interviewee who had recently purchased a washing machine was annoyed when AI continued recommending the same appliance for weeks: "It didn't know I already bought it—why keep showing it? A human would have remembered." Another user described an AI that recommended heavy winter coats to them while they were traveling in a tropical country: "I was in Thailand, browsing on my phone, and it kept pushing parkas. It had my location data—how did it miss that?"

4.4.5.5 The "Trust Paradox" of AI Humility and Competence

Finally, interviewees revealed a paradox in how they evaluate AI's humility: while they preferred high-humility AI in service failures, excessive admissions of limitation eroded trust in AI's overall competence. For example, an interviewee praised an AI for apologizing and fixing a wrong order—"that's humble and reliable"—but grew skeptical of an AI that frequently said "I don't know" during a product inquiry: "If it can't answer basic questions about the item, why should I trust its recommendations?" Another user noted, "I like AI that admits when it's wrong, but not when it's clueless. There's a line between humility and incompetence."

This paradox varied by scenario: in low-stakes interactions, such as casual GAI chat, interviewees tolerated frequent admissions of limitation; in high-stakes scenarios, such as financial advice or technical support, they expected AI to balance humility with expertise. One interviewee explained, "If I'm asking about a refund, I want AI to say, 'sorry for the delay' and fix it. If I'm asking about investing, I don't want it to say, 'I'm not sure'—I want it to either answer correctly or tell me to talk to a human."

These additional observations collectively highlight that user-AI interaction is far more complex than the sum of individual traits, such as humor or humility, or functional outcomes, such as accurate recommendations. Instead, it is shaped by subtle tensions—between AI's human-like mimicry and functional limitations, between convenience and preference manipulation, between emotional resonance and gendered expectations, and between humility and perceived competence. These insights offer a richer, more holistic view of how users engage with AI, emphasizing that effective AI design must account not just for what users say they want, but for the unspoken, context-dependent nuances that define their actual experiences.

4.5 Summary

Based on in-depth semi-structured interviews conducted via online meetings, this study collected qualitative data from 20 interviewees aged 21–30—an age group highly engaged with shopping (including online and offline channels) and AI services—and obtained empirical insights into core themes of user-AI interactions, as well as nuanced patterns shaping human-machine dynamics in digital services. All interviewees were recruited from the researcher's network, a selection method that leveraged pre-existing familiarity to reduce communication barriers, encouraging candid sharing of genuine experiences and emotional responses. The sample included both undergraduate and postgraduate students, covered three monthly disposable income tiers, and featured a majority of female participants (reflecting the gender distribution of active shoppers), with varied frequencies of shopping and AI service usage. Each interview lasted 20–30 minutes, focusing on five key themes: AI versus human recommendations, AI communication styles, AI humility traits, GAI humor, and additional contextual observations. Together, these data provided a comprehensive view of how users perceive, interact with, and evaluate AI-driven services in real-world scenarios.

Regarding AI versus human recommendations, the findings confirm that the two serve complementary roles rather than being direct substitutes, with user preferences strongly tied to task complexity and emotional stakes. AI excels at efficiency and 24/7 accessibility for low-stakes, information-focused tasks—such as querying product stock, verifying specifications, or locating coupon entrances—where speed and consistency are prioritized. However, AI recommendations are often constrained by a lack of contextual awareness: interviewees frequently reported issues like repetitive pushes of already purchased products, failure to account for lifestyle changes (such as travel to tropical regions), or over-reliance on browsing history (such as one-time cat food research leading to weeks of irrelevant recommendations). Privacy concerns also emerged as a key limitation, with some users feeling uncomfortable about AI's cross-platform data tracking and predictive pushes that feel like constant surveillance. In contrast, human recommendations stand out for their contextual depth and emotional resonance, particularly for high-stakes or personalized decisions—such as skincare for sensitive skin, birthday gifts, or complex product comparisons. Humans demonstrate active listening, asking follow-up questions to uncover unspoken needs (such as inquiring about room temperature to recommend moisturizers) and providing experiential insights (such as noting shoe sole comfort on rough roads) that AI. Trust in human recommendations is further strengthened by flexibility, as human representatives can adjust solutions to fit unique scenarios (such as offering a partial refund plus discount for a damaged product). Ultimately, users turn to AI for quick, routine tasks and humans for personalized, empathetic support, highlighting the need for integrated rather than competitive design of the two recommendation systems.

For AI communication styles, the analysis reveals a clear trade-off between efficiency (task-oriented) and emotional engagement (social-oriented), with their impact on purchasing decisions being contingent upon various factors including product quality, price, and suitability above communication tone. Task-oriented AI, defined by concise, fact-based responses focused on product details or problem-solving steps, is highly valued in time-sensitive or urgent scenarios, such as confirming return procedures, checking delivery times, or clarifying size parameters. Interviewees praised its ability to reduce cognitive load by delivering direct information without redundant small talk, noting that it excels at resolving straightforward issues like locating order tracking links. However, task-oriented AI also faces criticism for feeling mechanical or impersonal, particularly in scenarios where users seek reassurance or context beyond basic facts—such as a bank AI that repeats scripted guidance without adapting to user confusion about app operations. In contrast, social-oriented AI, characterized by warm, conversational language, references to daily life, and emotional cues (such as modal particles or casual greetings), enhances engagement in low-stakes or leisure scenarios—such as browsing fashion products or seeking casual product advice. Users reported that well-executed social-oriented communication reduces the human-machine gap, making interactions feel more relatable (such as an AI noting weather changes when recommending shoes with thicker insoles). Yet social-oriented styles risk inefficiency if social cues are generic or disconnected from user needs—interviewees complained about excessive use of intimate titles like "dear" or "baby" paired with irrelevant marketing messages, which feel insincere and time-consuming. The key insight is that social-oriented AI's effectiveness hinges on linking conversational warmth to the user's immediate query or scenario, while task-oriented AI can improve by adding flexibility (such as offering to connect to a human when scripts fail).

In terms of AI humility trait cognition, interviewees uniformly recognized that "humility" in AI is not merely verbal (such as scripted apologies) but a combination of attitude and actionable behavior, and high-humility AI is strongly preferred across service scenarios—especially service failures. Users define AI humility as proactive accountability: acknowledging mistakes clearly, avoiding blame-shifting, and providing specific, implementable solutions like prioritizing delayed orders or offering compensation. For example, interviewees praised Pinduoduo's AI customer service for apologizing sincerely and quickly resolving wrong-product issues, while criticizing low-humility AI that evades responsibility (such as dismissing delivery delays as "normal") or provides vague promises (such as "we will follow up later" without timelines). High-humility AI increases users' willingness to reuse services by fostering a sense of psychological security—users feel their concerns are taken seriously rather than perfunctory. In contrast, low-humility AI erodes trust, leading many interviewees to switch to human representatives or abandon the brand entirely. Notably, interviewees distinguished between "surface humility" (empty apologies) and "substantive humility" (action + attitude), emphasizing that the latter is critical for building long-term engagement. Consistency also matters: AI that alternates between humble and dismissive responses undermines user confidence, while consistent humility—even in limited-capability scenarios (such as admitting inability to answer technical questions and escalating to humans)—strengthens perceived reliability.

For GAI humor experiences, users' perceptions are mixed but predominantly positive when humor is contextually relevant and moderate. The most frequently cited humorous AI tools include Weibo's comment robot "Robert" and large language models like DeepSeek, which enhance interaction by integrating internet memes, witty teasing, and lighthearted references to daily life. In casual scenarios—such as browsing social media, casual product exploration, or emotional venting—high-humor GAI delivers significant emotional value: it relieves negative emotions (such as comforting a user after a breakup with "Breaking up may be a new start for your next life"), reduces browsing fatigue, and strengthens platform engagement by making interactions feel dynamic and human-like. However, GAI humor faces two key limitations: irrelevance and risk of offense. Interviewees criticized "Robert" for occasionally posting jokes unrelated to post themes (such as responding to a sad message with a trivial joke), which disrupts interaction flow and feels awkward. Overly sharp or inappropriate humor (such as sarcasm about a user's returned product) can also trigger dissatisfaction, especially when users are in negative emotional states. Additionally, humor's impact is highly scenario-dependent: high-humor GAI is well-suited for leisure and social contexts but may reduce efficiency in formal or urgent scenarios (such as online shopping inquiries about return procedures), where users prioritize clear, concise information. Low-humor GAI, by contrast, is valued for reliability in serious tasks, as it avoids distraction and maintains professionalism. Ultimately, GAI humor positively influences service satisfaction when it is relevant, moderate, and aligned with user emotional states—crossing ethical or contextual boundaries would instead reduce satisfaction.

Additional observations from the interviews revealed nuanced tensions in user-AI interactions that extend beyond core research themes, deepening the understanding of human-machine dynamics. The first tension is the "uncanny valley" effect of AI's near-human traits: when AI mimics human warmth, humility, or humor without matching functional competence, it triggers discomfort rather than connection. For example, interviewees felt frustrated by AI that used overly intimate language but failed to address core issues, describing it as "a robot reading a sympathy card"—polite but disconnected. Conversely, AI that embraces its "tool identity" (such as concise task-oriented responses) avoids this discomfort. The second tension is the "invisible filter" of AI recommendations: even when users actively ignore AI pushes, prolonged exposure to curated content unconsciously narrows their preferences. Interviewees noted that they now rely on "recommended" sections instead of browsing random categories, leading to reduced exposure to new styles. The third tension is gendered perceptions of AI's emotional traits: female interviewees prioritized AI's ability to read emotional cues (such as empathetic humility during service failures), while male interviewees framed emotional traits as "nice-to-have" and focused on functional efficiency. Fourth, AI's "contextual blind spot"—its inability to grasp unspoken circumstances that humans intuit—emerged as a recurring frustration, such as AI recommending winter coats to users in tropical countries or repeating pushes for already purchased appliances. Finally, the "trust paradox" of AI humility: while high-humility AI is preferred in service failures, excessive admissions of limitation erode trust in AI's overall competence, especially in high-stakes scenarios like financial advice.

Collectively, the findings of this study highlight the importance of scenario-specific AI design, as user preferences for traits like humility, humor, and communication style are deeply tied to their goals and contextual needs. For AI developers and service providers, the key insight is to balance functional efficiency with emotional value: AI should prioritize clarity and speed for urgent, task-focused interactions, while integrating contextually relevant warmth, humility, or humor for casual, relationship-building scenarios. The complementary roles of AI and humans also underscore the value of hybrid service models—using AI for routine tasks and humans for complex, personalized needs—rather than framing AI as a direct substitute for human labor. Additionally, the study provides empirical grounding for understanding user trust in AI: trust is built not just on technical performance, but on consistency, authenticity, and alignment with user expectations (such as humility paired with action, humor paired with relevance). While the sample is concentrated in the 21–30 age group and reflects the preferences of active digital shoppers, the findings offer actionable guidance for optimizing user-AI interactions in digital services. Future research could expand to broader age groups, cross-cultural contexts, or additional service scenarios (such as healthcare or education) to further explore the generalizability of these patterns. Ultimately, this study contributes to the growing body of literature on user-AI interaction by emphasizing the "human-centric" nature of effective AI design—one that respects user context, emotional needs, and functional expectations.

Methodology 5

This chapter delineates the methodological approach employed across a series of empirical studies investigating user-AI interactions. The research examines four principal themes: (1) recommendation types (AI versus human), (2) AI communication styles (task-oriented versus social-oriented), (3) AI humanity (low versus high), and (4) generative AI humor (low versus high). The data collection strategy comprised a sequence of pretests, controlled experiments, and survey-based assessments. Subsequent sections present the specific experimental designs, measurement instruments, and participant recruitment protocols for each study.

5.1 AI vs. Human Recommendation Type

5.1.1 Experiment 1 Regarding Recommendation Type

Pretest. To examine the effect of recommendation type (AI vs. human), a pretest with a single-factor between-subjects experimental design was adopted. In order to eliminate brand familiarity bias, participants were introduced to a fictitious laptop brand named "Ultry." The online platform Questionnaire Star was used to collect the data (Huang et al., 2021; Wang & Gao, 2021), and a total of 229 valid responses were collected—116 assigned to the AI condition and 113 to the human condition. The type of assistant (AI or human) was signaled using distinct text descriptions and avatars: a robot image for the AI, and a name with a human avatar for the human.

The manipulation of the recommendation source followed established procedures in prior research (Wien & Peluso, 2021). Participants first completed demographic questions, including gender, age, and income. They were then presented

Supplementary Information The online version contains supplementary material available at https://doi.org/10.1007/978-981-95-9430-6_5

F. Yang, *AI and Consumer Interaction in Business*, Management for Professionals,
https://doi.org/10.1007/978-981-95-9430-6_5

with a scenario in which they imagined themselves shopping for a laptop and browsing information on social media and official brand websites. Each participant received a product recommendation from a virtual shopping assistant, manipulated to be different recommendation type (Chen et al., 2023; Kim & Duhachek, 2020; Yang et al., 2024). To control for potential gender-based confounds, the gender of the human recommender was matched with that of the participant, as recommended by Feick and Higie (1992) and implemented in Wien and Peluso (2021).

Subsequent to reading the scenario, participants finished manipulation check measures. Given the objective nature of the manipulation, two checks were used. First, participants were asked to select whether the shopping assistant was AI- or human-based. Only those who responded correctly were included in further analysis. Second, participants rated their perceived similarity with the recommender (Ahn et al., 2021). The results indicated that individuals exposed to the human recommendation condition perceived a significantly higher degree of similarity with the assistant than those in the AI condition (M_AI = 4.20, SD = 1.72; M_Human = 5.23, SD = 1.11), with statistically significant differences ($p < 0.001$, $t = -5.39$, $F = 27.45$). These findings validate the effectiveness of the manipulation and justify its use in the main experiment. All measurement items for the study of recommendation type are detailed in Appendix A of the Supplementary Materials.

Main test. Formal experiment ($n = 150$) adopted a single-factor, between-subjects experimental design to assess the direct influence of recommendation source (AI vs. human) on consumers' purchase intention. Participants were recruited via the online data collection platform Credamo (Zhang et al., 2024; Zhu et al., 2022). The sample featured diverse demographic attributes, including variation in age, educational background, and income level. Detailed participant demographics are provided in Appendix B of the supplementary material. To eliminate brand familiarity bias, a fictitious laptop brand named "Ultry" was utilized, consistent with the material used in Pretest. After screening out low-quality responses (e.g., failed attention checks) and applying automated filters for inclusion criteria, 150 valid responses remained, evenly split between the AI recommendation group ($n = 75$) and the human recommendation group ($n = 75$).

5.1.2 Experiment 2 Regarding Recommendation Type

In Experiment 2 ($n = 150$) regarding recommendation type, a single-factor, between-subjects experimental design is adopted to manipulate recommendation type (AI vs. Human). Participants were recruited through the Credamo online platform (Zhang et al., 2024; Zhu et al., 2022) and were randomly assigned to receive either an AI or human recommendation. The detailed demographic information of Experiment 2 regarding recommendation type is presented in Appendix C. After screening out invalid responses and manually eliminating low-quality data, including those that failed attention checks, 150 valid answers were retained, equally split between the two experimental conditions (AI recommendation group = 75, human recommendation group = 75). Participants were instructed to imagine themselves shopping for a laptop and searching for related information online. The control of recommendation type was achieved through text-based descriptions and corresponding avatars, where the AI assistant was depicted with a robot image, and the human assistant was represented with a name and human avatar. To avoid gender-based confounding, the gender of the human shopping assistant matched the participant's own gender (Wien & Peluso, 2021).

5.2 AI Communication Style

5.2.1 Experiment 1 Regarding AI Communication Style

Pretest. This study involves the manipulation of the AI communication style of an intelligent customer service system—in the context of a sports shoe purchase scenario, specifically examining task-oriented and social-oriented communication styles. The social-oriented communication scenario is characterized by distinct features, where the dialogue consists of informal, social interactions rather than being limited to information inquiries and guidance. It includes daily greetings, emotional comfort, social compliments, and expressions of goodwill. In contrast, the task-oriented communication scenario adopts a formalized interaction style, with the primary goal of accomplishing specific tasks. Apart from an initial greeting, it avoids any social interactions, focusing solely on information delivery and problem-solving guidance.

To manipulate the different communication styles of the AI agents, this study constructed two sets of dialogue screenshots simulating real-world interactions between consumers and AI agents in an online shopping scenario, specifically depicting a customer consulting the AI about product information. The manipulation method for communication styles draws on existing research (Gretry et al., 2017; Liebrecht et al., 2021), which distinguishes communication styles through the use of differentiated linguistic elements. For instance, the social-oriented style incorporates informal vocabulary, casual punctuation, and emojis, while the task-oriented style employs standardized wording, punctuation, and strict adherence to grammatical norms (Gretry et al., 2017). Apart from differences in linguistic expression, the content and interface layout remain identical across the two communication modes. To control for extraneous variables, the brands involved in the study were fictional. The AI agent uses default system avatars, and both the scenario descriptions and the AI's name explicitly indicated its robotic identity to avoid potential biases arising from anthropomorphic design.

The pretest recruited 62 participants via the Credamo platform. During the experiment, participants were asked to complete a simulated purchase task for a fictional brand, "FAX" sports shoes, replicating the real-world process of online shopping. Before the experiment began, participants were provided with the following background description:

> Recently, you have been considering purchasing a pair of sports shoes. While browsing online as usual, you found a pair from the FAX official website that meets your expectations. You want to learn more about the product's specifications and determine the right size for yourself. To do so, you opened the customer service chat window and sent the link to the product. The FAX website uses an AI customer service bot to handle inquiries.

Subsequently, the 62 participants were randomly assigned to view one of the two sets of screenshots representing social vs. task-oriented style respectively. After reading the experimental material for 30 s, they completed a language style assessment scale (Van Dolen et al., 2007). All evaluations use a 7-point Likert scale (1 = "Strongly Disagree," 7 = "Strongly Agree"). Finally, the researchers collected basic demographic information from participants, including gender, age, education level, occupation, and monthly disposable income. The details of the variable measurement for the study regarding AI communication style are presented in Appendix D.

Main test. This experiment mainly adopted a single-factor between-subject experimental design, namely the social-oriented group and the task-oriented group. In the scenario of purchasing sports shoes, the communication style of AI agents was manipulated to test its main effect on brand engagement. In this formal experiment, the manipulation scenarios and processes were consistent with those in the pretest. A total of 200 subjects were recruited, and the subjects were randomly assigned to either the social-oriented group or the task-oriented group. The details of the respondents' demographic information are presented in Appendix E. As shown in the pretest, the subjects were required to complete scene descriptions related to purchasing sports shoes and consulting intelligent customer service. To avoid the influence of brand bias, a virtual brand "FAX" was designed in the experiment.

After completing the scenario reading, the subjects received the experimental materials that had been verified by the pretest. First, they were evaluated for the authenticity of the scenario, and the question was displayed as "After reading the materials, I can fully assume the role of the customer." For this assessment question, the average score of the task-oriented group was 6.18/7, and that of the social-oriented group was 6.21/7, fully demonstrating the degree to which the subjects engaged in the customer role. Afterwards, the subjects needed to report the level of brand engagement. At the end, basic information such as the subjects' gender, age and income was collected. All the relevant items of the variables were measured using a 7-point Likert scale (7 = "strongly agree", 1 = "strongly disagree").

5.2.2 Experiment 2 Regarding AI Communication Style

Experiment 2 regarding AI communication style was also a single-factor inter-group experiment design. To ensure the external validity of the experiment, Experiment 2 designed different experimental scenarios, namely manipulation verification in the hotel inquiry scenario. The design principle was similar to that of Experiment 1. The hotel brand was fictional, and the

AI agent used a neutral, standardized avatar with no emotional cues and its identity was explicitly stated to avoid bias caused by ambiguous identity perception. The experiment designed two different sets of dialogue texts, corresponding to two communication styles respectively, to simulate the real interaction between consumers and intelligent customer service in the corresponding scenarios. Participants were presented with the following background:

> You are currently planning a trip and searching for a suitable hotel. After browsing a hotel's website, you decide to inquire about its facilities and other details. You open the AI customer service chat window and engage in the following conversation.

Experiment 2 recruited 200 subjects and randomly assigned them to one group of two communication styles for experimental manipulation. The details of the respondents' demographic information are presented in Appendix F. Trust was also measured with items using the seven-point Likert scale (1= "strongly disagree", 7= "strongly agree").

5.2.3 Survey Regarding AI Communication Style

Participant data were collected via an online survey administered through the Credemo platform. A total of 200 respondents were recruited, all of whom completed the questionnaire in its entirety. To ensure the quality and relevance of the data, a two-stage screening and priming procedure was implemented. First, potential participants were screened to confirm they had prior experience using AI agent services. Those who qualified were then directed to a memory-guided questioning section, which prompted them to vividly recall and reflect on their most recent and concrete AI interaction experience before proceeding. This priming step was designed to ground subsequent responses in a specific, real-world context. Following this, participants were asked to complete assessments including task-oriented and social-oriented scales and the examined variables in the model. In addition, participants were required to provide demographic information. All variables were measured using a 7-point Likert scale (1 = "strongly disagree", 7 = "strongly agree"). The details of the respondents' demographic information are presented in Appendix G.

5.3 AI Humanity

5.3.1 Experiment 1 Regarding AI Humanity

Pretest. Before conducting the main experiment, pretest was conducted to ensure the validity and reliability of the AI humility manipulation. Participants were first asked whether they had ever interacted with an AI assistant, in order to screen for more effective samples. The material for the pretest was selected from the service failure scenario involving delayed deliveries on food delivery platforms.

Participants were informed that their food orders had exceeded the estimated delivery time, prompting them to contact the AI assistant to inquire about the reason. Then, participants were shown a scripted assistant-based customer service interaction (adapted to represent a digital customer service agent) and asked to evaluate the AI assistant. Participants were then randomly assigned to high/low humility assistant response scenarios, with the distinction between humility levels primarily based on whether the response acknowledged mistakes, provided clear explanations, and offered specific solutions (Ge et al., 2019). The details of the manipulation material were presented in Appendix H.

To test the effectiveness of the manipulation, the researcher used a 4-item humility perception scale adapted from prior research (Choi et al., 2020), rated on a 7-point Likert scale (1 = strongly disagree; 7 = strongly agree). An independent samples t-test confirmed that participants in the high humility condition perceived significantly greater humility than those in the low humility condition ($M_{High\ Humility} = 5.408$, $M_{Low\ Humility} = 3.285$; $t = 7.355$, $p < 0.05$), confirming the effectiveness of the manipulation.

To assess the realism of the scenarios, the researcher also adopted two items from Liao (2007), which asked participants to evaluate two statements on a 7-point Likert scale. These statements consisted of (1) "The scene is realistic." and (2) "The situation in the scene could also occur in real life." The mean score of the two checks was 6.14 out of 7 ($\sigma = 0.09$), an average hihger than that found in prior studies (e.g., 5.45 from Yang and Yang (2023)).

Main test. Experiment 1 ($N = 149$) employed a single-factor between-subjects experimental design with AI humility (high vs. low) to verify the direct effect of AI humility on user continuance intention. The experiment recruited participants through the Credamo platform to complete several questions. If their data was accepted after completing questions, participants would receive certain level of financial reward. In this study, participants were randomly assigned to either the "high humility" or "low humility" group to receive AI assistant responses after service failure. After automatically filtering out low-quality questionnaires (e.g., those failing attention detection questions) and manually rejecting others, the study ultimately obtained 149 valid questionnaire responses, with 75 samples in the "high humility" group and 74 samples in the "low humility" group.

The materials used in Experiment 1 were consistent with those in the pretest (see Appendix H). First, participants were asked to indicate whether they had previously interacted with an AI assistant. Subsequently, participants were randomly assigned to one of two manipulation groups. They were asked to read a scenario describing a situation where a food delivery was delayed and to imagine seeking help from an AI assistant to resolve the issue. After reading the responses, participants were asked to answer questions related to perceived humility ($\alpha = 0.869$), user continuance intention ($\alpha = 0.908$), and the authenticity of the scenario. Finally, participants were asked to provide demographic information such as their gender, age, income, education, and the frequency of their communication with AI assistants. The user continuance intention scale was adapted from Ashfaq et al. (2020) and measured using a 7-point Likert scale (1 = strongly disagree, 7 = strongly agree). It consists of three items: "I will continue to use AI customer service in the future.", "I will actively try AI customer service in my daily life", "I will recommend AI customer service to others.".

5.3.2 Experiment 2 Regarding AI Humanity

Pretest. The pretest of Experiment 2 also employed a single-factor between-subjects experimental design with AI humility (high vs. low), but this study focuses on the service failure scenario for delayed shipments on E-commerce platforms (specific materials can be found in Appendix I). After excluding participants who didn't pass the attention check and didn't experience with AI assistants in the past, a total of 60 participants were included in this study. Participants were informed that their food orders had exceeded the estimated delivery time, prompting them to contact the AI assistant to inquire about the reason. Then, participants were shown a scripted assistant-based customer service interaction (adapted to represent a digital customer service agent) and asked to evaluate the AI assistant. Participants were then randomly assigned to high/low humility assistant response scenarios, with the distinction between humility levels primarily based on whether the response acknowledged mistakes, provided clear explanations, and offered specific solutions (Ge et al., 2019).

To test the effectiveness of the manipulation, we used a 4-item humility perception scale like pretest 2. An independent samples t-test confirmed that participants in the high humility condition perceived significantly greater humility than those in the low humility condition ($M_{High\ Humility} = 5.967$, $M_{Low\ Humility} = 4.192$; $t = 6.835$, $p < 0.05$), confirming the effectiveness of the manipulation. As for the realism of the scenarios, the mean score of the two checks was 6.41 out of 7 ($\sigma = 0.51$).

Main test. The materials used in Experiment 2 were consistent with those in the pretest. First, participants were asked to indicate whether they had previously interacted with an AI assistant. Subsequently, participants were randomly assigned to one of two manipulation groups. They were asked to read a scenario describing a situation where a food delivery was delayed and to imagine seeking help from an AI assistant to resolve the issue. After reading the responses, participants were asked to answer questions related to perceived humility ($\alpha = 0.844$), user continuance intention ($\alpha = 0.899$), AI acceptance ($\alpha = 0.926$) and the authenticity of the scenario. Finally, participants were asked to provide demographic information such as their gender, age, income, education, and the frequency of their communication with AI assistants.

The AI acceptance scale was adapted from Lu et al. (2019) and measured using a 7-point Likert scale (1 = strongly disagree, 7 = strongly agree). It consists of four items: "AI assistants can provide a satisfactory experience in this case.", "AI assistants are useful for improving the service experience.", "I may start using AI on this platform soon.", "I plan to use AI assistants more and more on this platform in the future."

5.3.3 Survey Regarding AI Humanity

To empirically examine the proposed model, this study employed a survey method. The purpose was to investigate the impact of AI humility on user continuance intention in the context of service failure, and to explore the moderating role of frequency of communication with AI assistants. The survey study ($N = 200$) recruited participants through the Credamo platform to complete several questions. If their data was accepted after completing questions, participants would receive certain level of financial reward.

Participants were first presented with a brief recall-based prompt, instructing them to recall a real-life customer service experience where they interacted with an AI assistant (e.g., chatbot, virtual agent) and encountered a service failure. This method mirrors prior research that captures authentic emotional and cognitive reactions to service breakdowns (Tsarenko & Rooslani Tojib, 2011). After the recall task, participants completed a structured questionnaire composed of validated multi-item scales, all rated on 7-point likert scales (1 = strongly disagree, 7 = strongly agree), including AI humility ($\alpha = 0.796$) and user continuance intention ($\alpha = 0.872$). The rest remained consistent with Experiment 2. To ensure data quality, attention-check items were embedded, targeting adult respondents with prior experience interacting with AI assistants. A total of 200 participants were included in this study. The details of the variable measurement items of the study regarding AI humanity are presented in Appendix J.

5.4 AI Humor

5.4.1 Experiment 1 Regarding AI Humor

Pretest. The pre-experiment aimed to test the validity of materials for the formal experiment and ensure the reliability of the experimental design. The pre-test ($N = 79$) employed a single-factor between-subjects design comparing GAI humor (low-level humor vs. high-level humor). The experiment utilized GAI "commenting on Robert" on Sina Weibo as the GAI subject, adopting the experimental design context for AI humor from international core journals. Questionnaires were distributed via the Credamo platform. After automated exclusion based on screening options and manual rejection of low-quality responses (e.g., failing the attention check task), 79 valid questionnaires were ultimately collected: 39 in the "GAI High-Level Humor" group and 40 in the "GAI Low-Level Humor" group.

The manipulation of GAI humor (low vs. high level) drew from the existing experimental materials (Kobel & Groeppel-Klein, 2021). Participants first read a brief scenario text and image prompting them to imagine: "You go to a restaurant for lunch, place your order, and wait a long time for your food. However, the restaurant never serves your meal. You ask the server if there is a problem, and the server informs you that your order was forgotten, and the restaurant no longer has the dish you requested. You must choose another dish. At this point, you post a message on social media to express your feelings: I waited for a long time at a restaurant, but my order was forgotten. Now the server tells me they have run out of the dish I wanted, so I can only order something else." The experiment manipulated varying levels of humor by altering the content generated by GAI.

In the high-level GAI humor group, participants were informed:

> One minute later, you receive an automated comment from the social media GAI: Do you know the characteristics of snails? Remember not to order the snail dish anymore, because this restaurant has already run out of them due to their poor service.

In the high-level GAI humor group, participants were told:

> One minute later, you received an automated comment from the social media GAI: This is indeed a very frustrating experience. You can request reasonable compensation or choose another dish.

Next, participants completed the manipulation check items. They rated "this social media GAI as not humorous-humorous, not funny-funny, not playful-playful, not amusing-amusing, and not dull-dull" (using a 1–7 Likert scale). The final item was reverse-coded. Subsequently, participants' perceived realism of the scenario was measured to ensure full comprehension of the setting. Scenario realism was assessed using a 7-point Likert scale (Yang et al., 2022) (e.g., "I find this scenario realistic," "I think this could happen in real life," "It is easy to imagine myself in the condition as described here"). Participants were also asked to provide demographic information regarding their gender, age, income, etc.

Main test. The experiment aimed to examine the impact of GAI humor (low-level humor vs. high-level humor) on user satisfaction. The experiment ($N = 198$) employed a single-factor between-subjects design with GAI humor (low-level humor vs. high-level humor) to validate the direct effect of GAI humor on user satisfaction. Participants were recruited via the Credamo platform to complete an online questionnaire. Participants were randomly assigned to either the "GAI High-Level Humor" or "GAI Low-Level Humor" group to access GAI's proactive comments under user-generated content. Ultimately, 200 valid questionnaire responses were collected: 99 from the "GAI High-Level Humor" group and 99 from the "GAI Low-Level Humor" group. The materials used in experiment were the same as those in the pretest. In addition to measuring GAI humor, perceived warmth was assessed using a 7-point Likert scale (1 = Strongly Disagree, 7 = Strongly Agree), where the robot was described as tolerant, warm, good-natured, and sincere. Finally, user satisfaction was measured (e.g., I am fairly pleased with the GAI service).

5.4.2 Experiment 2 Regarding AI Humor

This experiment aimed to examine the impact of the interaction between GAI humor and sense of humor on the model. Experiment 2 (N = 200) employed a questionnaire survey to assess users' responses to GAI humor and user satisfaction, as well as their sense of humor. Two hundred participants were recruited from the Credamo data platform to complete the questionnaire. To ensure participants understood GAI, a screening question was included. Users unfamiliar with GAI were excluded from further participation. Subsequently, participants recalled their GAI interactions over the past few months and described its characteristics. They then completed the GAI humor level items and reported their perceived warmth toward GAI and user satisfaction within the experimental context. The scales measuring perceived warmth and user satisfaction were consistent with Experiment 1. Participants then completed the sense of humor scale (Yang et al., 2022), measured using a 7-point Likert scale. Finally, controlling for demographics, the experiment also measured perceived scenario authenticity, as well as frequency and duration of user exposure to GAI. Appendix K presents the details of the measured items for the study regarding AI humor.

References

Ahn, J., Kim, J., & Sung, Y. (2021). AI-powered recommendations: The roles of perceived similarity and psychological distance on persuasion. *International Journal of Advertising, 40*(8), 1366–1384.

Ashfaq, M., Yun, J., Yu, S., & Loureiro, S. M. C. (2020). I, Chatbot: Modeling the determinants of users' satisfaction and continuance intention of AI-powered service agents. *Telematics and Informatics, 54*, 101473.

Chen, S., Li, X., Liu, K., & Wang, X. (2023). Chatbot or human? The impact of online customer service on consumers' purchase intentions. *Psychology & Marketing, 40*(11), 2186–2200.

Choi, S., Mattila, A. S., & Bolton, L. E. (2020). To err is human(-oid): How do consumers react to robot service failure and recovery? *Journal of Service Research, 24*(3), 354–371.

Feick, L., & Higie, R. A. (1992). The effects of preference heterogeneity and source characteristics on ad processing and judgements about endorsers. *Journal of Advertising, 21*(2), 9–24.

Ge, X., Li, D., Guan, D., Xu, S., Sun, Y., & Zhou, M. (2019). *Do smart speakers respond to their errors properly? A study on human-computer dialogue strategy.* International Conference on Human-Computer Interaction.

Gretry, A., Horváth, C., Belei, N., & van Riel, A. C. R. (2017). "Don't pretend to be my friend!" When an informal brand communication style backfires on social media. *Journal of Business Research, 74*, 77–89.

Huang, Y., Gursoy, D., Zhang, M., Nunkoo, R., & Shi, S. (2021). Interactivity in online chat: Conversational cues and visual cues in the service recovery process. *International Journal of Information Management, 60*, 102360.

Kim, T. W., & Duhachek, A. (2020). Artificial intelligence and persuasion: A construal-level account. *Psychological Science, 31*(4), 363–380.

Kobel, S., & Groeppel-Klein, A. (2021). No laughing matter, or a secret weapon? Exploring the effect of humor in service failure situations. *Journal of Business Research, 132*, 260–269.

Liao, H. (2007). Do it right this time: The role of employee service recovery performance in customer-perceived justice and customer loyalty after service failures. *Journal of Applied Psychology*, *92*(2), 475–489.

Liebrecht, C., Sander, L., & Hooijdonk, C. (2021). *Too informal? How a chatbot's communication style affects brand attitude and quality of interaction*. International Workshop on Chatbot Research and Design.

Lu, L., Cai, R., & Gursoy, D. (2019). Developing and validating a service robot integration willingness scale. *International Journal of Hospitality Management*, *80*, 36–51.

Tsarenko, Y., & Rooslani Tojib, D. (2011). A transactional model of forgiveness in the service failure context: A customer-driven approach. *Journal of Services Marketing*, *25*(5), 381–392.

Van Dolen, W. M., Dabholkar, P. A., & De Ruyter, K. (2007). Satisfaction with online commercial group chat: The influence of perceived technology attributes, chat group characteristics, and advisor communication style. *Journal of Retailing*, *83*(3), 339–358.

Wang, L. L., & Gao, Y. (2021). Competition network as a source of competitive advantage: The dynamic capability perspective and evidence from China. *Long Range Planning*, *54*(2), 102052.

Wien, A. H., & Peluso, A. M. (2021). Influence of human versus AI recommenders: The roles of product type and cognitive processes. *Journal of Business Research*, *137*, 13–27.

Yang, F., & Yang, M. M. (2023). Examining motivation of IT vendors to share knowledge with clients. *International Journal of Information Management*, *71*, 102646.

Yang, H., Xu, H., Zhang, Y., Liang, Y., & Lyu, T. (2022). Exploring the effect of humor in robot failure. *Annals of Tourism Research*, *95*, 103425.

Yang, Y., Zheng, J., Yu, Y., Qiu, Y., & Wang, L. (2024). The role of recommendation sources and attribute framing in online product recommendations. *Journal of Business Research*, *174*, 114498.

Zhang, C. B., Li, T. G., Li, Y. N., Chang, Y., & Zhang, Z. P. (2024). Fostering well-being: Exploring the influence of user-AI assistant relationship types on subjective well-being. *International Journal of Information Management*, *79*, 102822.

Zhu, Y., Zhang, J., Wu, J., & Liu, Y. (2022). AI is better when I'm sure: The influence of certainty of needs on consumers' acceptance of AI chatbots. *Journal of Business Research*, *150*, 642–652.

Analysis and Empirical Results

6

This chapter presents the analysis and empirical results from experiments and surveys designed to test the proposed hypotheses on user-AI interactions. The analyses include manipulation checks, reliability and validity assessments, ANOVA, and regression. The following sections will present the details of the data assessment, hypothesis tests, and key findings for different studies, including recommendation type, AI communication styles, AI humanity, and GAI humor.

6.1 Data Assessment and Hypothesis Tests for Recommendation Type

6.1.1 Experiment 1 Regarding Recommendation Type

Participants first completed basic demographic items before being asked to imagine themselves shopping for a new laptop and browsing related information through social media and brand websites. They were then presented with a product recommendation scenario in which the recommendation type was manipulated. In the AI condition, the recommendation came from a robotic assistant accompanied by a robot avatar and machine-generated name. Within the human condition, the recommender was described as a real person, accompanied by a human-like avatar and a specific personal name.

Manipulation check. To ensure the effectiveness of the manipulation, a two-part manipulation check was implemented. Participants rated the statement "The recommender from the Ultry brand website is very similar to me" on a 7-point Likert scale (1 = strongly disagree, 7 = strongly agree), based on Ahn et al. (2021). Results showed that participants in the human recommender felt greater similarity with the assistant ($M_{human} = 5.38$, $SD = 1.27$) compared to those in the AI condition ($M_{AI} = 3.12$, $SD = 1.42$), with a marginally significant difference ($t(148) = 10.25$, $p < 0.001$).

F. Yang, *AI and Consumer Interaction in Business*, Management for Professionals,
https://doi.org/10.1007/978-981-95-9430-6_6

Purchase intention scale. Consumers' purchase intention was measured using items adapted from (Spears & Singh, 2004). The scale showed high internal consistency, with a Cronbach's alpha of 0.841. Exploratory factor analysis revealed a single underlying factor, with all item loadings exceeding 0.5. The construct's average variance extracted (AVE > 0.5) and composite reliability (CR > 0.7) also indicated strong convergent validity.

One-way analysis of variance (ANOVA) was used for testing whether the type of recommendation source had a significant impact on participants' purchase intention. Table 6.1 and Fig. 6.1 present the results. The test compared the mean purchase intentions between the AI and human recommender groups. The analysis revealed a statistically significant difference between the two groups. Participants who received a recommendation from a human assistant reported higher purchase intention ($M\_human = 5.90$, $SD = 0.66$) than those who received one from an AI assistant ($M\_AI = 5.48$, $SD = 1.27$). The difference was significant at the 0.05 level ($p = 0.01$, $F = 6.42$), thus providing empirical support for Hypothesis 1 that in comparison with AI recommendations, consumer' purchase intention is higher with human recommendations.

Table 6.1 The impact of recommendation type on purchase intention

		Descriptive statistics			ANOVA	
Variable	Group	Sample size	Mean	Standard deviation	F	p
Purchase Intention	AI recommendation	75	5.48	1.27	6.42	0.01
	Human recommendation	75	5.90	0.66		
	Total	150	5.69	1.03		

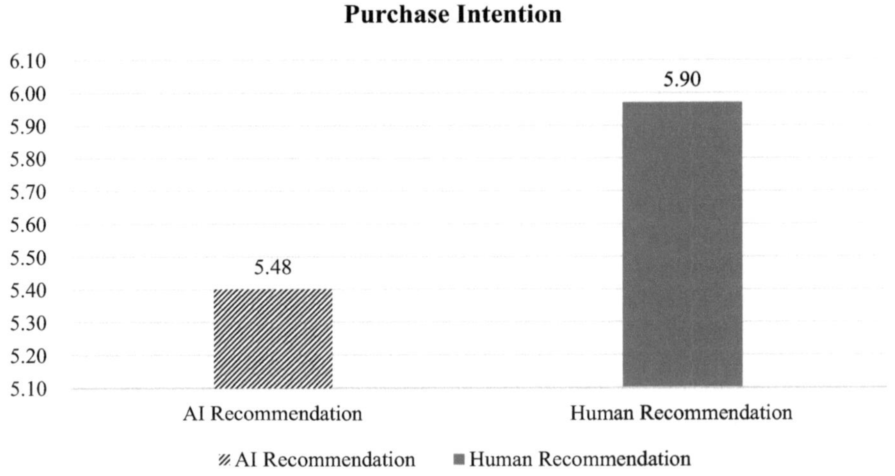

Fig. 6.1 The impact of recommendation type on purchase intention

6.1.2 Experiment 2 Regarding Recommendation Type

Participants first completed demographic information and then read a scenario about purchasing a laptop. The key manipulation was embedded in the recommendation they received from the fictional brand's online assistant. Participants subsequently completed measures assessing perceived warmth, product attitude and purchase intention. To guarantee the effectiveness of the recommendation type manipulation, a manipulation check was implemented. Consistent with Experiment 1 regarding recommendation type, participants in the human recommendation group perceived greater similarity between themselves and the shopping assistant than did those in the AI group ($M\_AI = 3.23$, $SD = 1.60$; $M\_human = 5.55$, $SD = 0.78$), with a highly significant difference ($p < 0.001$, $F = 41.20$). Reliability and validity assessments for both perceived warmth and purchase intention confirmed strong measurement properties. Cronbach's alpha values exceeded 0.8, principal component analyses extracted single factors with loadings above 0.5, and both AVE and CR values met accepted thresholds ($AVE > 0.5$, $CR > 0.7$).

Control variables included product familiarity, product knowledge, and digital experience. These were measured via the following items: "How familiar are you with laptop products? (1 = very unfamiliar, 7 = very familiar)," "How knowledgeable are you about laptop products? (1 = very unknowledgeable, 7 = very knowledgeable)," and "How familiar are you about digital and internet technologies in your daily life? (1 = very unfamiliar, 7 = very familiar)."

The impact of recommendation type on purchase intention. To examine how recommendation type influences purchase intention, one-way ANOVA was conducted. The correlations among the primary variables are summarized in Table 6.2. The results show that AI recommendation is negatively related to purchase intention ($r = -0.31$, $p < 0.01$). As shown in Table 6.3 and Fig. 6.2, participants exposed to human-generated recommendations exhibited significantly stronger purchase intentions than those receiving AI-based suggestions ($M\_human = 5.97$, $SD = 0.52$; $M\_AI = 5.40$, $SD = 1.12$; $p < 0.001$, $F = 15.88$). These findings suggest support for Hypothesis 1 that that in comparison with AI recommendations, consumer' purchase intention is higher with human recommendations.

The influence of recommendation type on perceived warmth. To further assess the effect of recommendation type on perceived warmth, another one-way ANOVA was conducted. As indicated by the outcomes in Table 6.3 and Fig. 6.2, participants rated human recommenders as significantly warmer than AI recommenders ($M\_human = 5.92$, $SD = 0.74$; $M\_AI = 4.69$, $SD = 1.33$; $p < 0.001$, $F = 49.52$). The results suggest that recommendations from humans are perceived to have a higher degree of warmth.

Examination of the mediating effect of perceived warmth. To test the mediating role of perceived warmth in the relationship between recommendation type and purchase intention, the researcher used PROCESS macro Model 4 with 5000 bootstrap samples and a 95% confidence interval. Control variables included demographic factors such as gender, age, education, and income, as well as product

Table 6.2 Correlation matrix for the study regarding recommendation type

Variable	1	2	3	4	5	6
1 Recommendation type (AI = 1, Human = 0)	1					
2 Perceived warmth	– 0.50**	1				
3 Purchase intention	– 0.31**	0.62**	1			
4 Product attitude	– 0.21*	0.57**	0.73**	1		
5 Familiarity	– 0.21*	0.30**	0.19*	0.17*	1	
6 Expertise	0.15	0.22**	0.23**	0.18*	0.53**	1
7 Digital	– 0.19*	0.31**	0.22**	0.19*	0.37**	0.36**

N = 150, p < 0.05*, p < 0.01**, p < 0.001***

Table 6.3 The effect of recommendation type (AI vs. Human) on purchase intention and perceived warmth

		Descriptive statistics			ANOVA	
Variable	Group	Sample size	Mean	Standard deviation	F	p
Purchase intention	AI	75	5.40	1.12	15.88	p < 0.001
	Human	75	5.97	0.52		
	Total	150	5.69	0.92		
Perceived warmth	AI	75	4.69	1.33	49.52	P < 0.001
	Human	75	5.92	0.74		
	Total	150	5.31	1.24		

p < 0.05*, p < 0.01**, p < 0.001***

familiarity, expertise, and digital experience. The analysis demonstrated that recommendation type had a significant impact on perceived warmth ($\beta = -1.11$, SE = 0.19, $p < 0.001$), and in turn, perceived warmth significantly predicted purchase intention ($\beta = 0.43$, SE = 0.06, $p < 0.001$). The detailed results are in Table 6.4. The indirect path was significant ($\beta = -0.47$, SE = 0.18, 95% CI [– 0.88, – 0.18]), while the direct path was non-significant ($\beta = -0.03$, SE = 0.15, 95% CI [– 0.32, 0.26]). These results confirm that perceived warmth serves as a mediator, supporting Hypothesis 2 that perceived warmth mediates the effect of recommendation type (AI vs. human) on purchase intention.

The interaction between recommendation type and product attitude on brand engagement. The moderating role of product attitude was evaluated using the PROCESS macro Model 1 with 5000 bootstrap resamples and 95% confidence intervals. The same control variables as those utilized in the mediation analysis were maintained (see Table 6.5). The results revealed that the effectiveness of the recommendation type on purchase intention was contingent on consumers' attitudes toward the product. Specifically, when product attitude was low, human

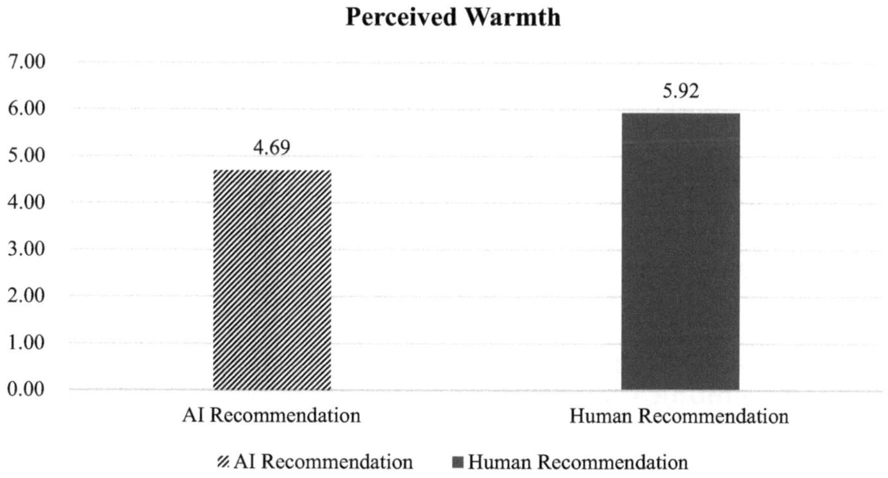

Fig. 6.2 The impact of recommendation type on perceived warmth

Table 6.4 The mediating effect of perceived warmth on the relationship between recommendation type and purchase intention

			95% CI	
	Effect	Boot S.E.	LL	UL
Total Effect	– 0.50	0.15	– 0.81	– 0.20
Direct Effect	– 0.03	0.15	– 0.32	0.26
Indirect Effect	– 0.47	0.18	– 0.88	– 0.18

Boot S.E.: Bootstrapping standard error (Boot S.E.), 95% CI: 95% confidence interval, LL: lower limit, UL: upper limit

Table 6.5 The moderating effect of product attitude

					95%CI	
Predictor	Effect	Boot S.E.	t	p	LL	UL
Intercept	5.69	0.41	13.90	0.00	4.88	6.50
Recommendation type	– 0.29	0.10	– 2.90	0.00	– 0.49	– 0.09
Product attitude	0.55	0.05	11.59	0.00	0.45	0.64
Recommendation type × Product attitude	0.62	0.09	6.54	0.00	0.43	0.80
Familiarity	– 0.01	0.05	– 0.19	0.85	– 0.11	0.09
Expertise	0.08	0.05	1.69	0.09	– 0.01	0.17
Digital literacy	– 0.01	0.06	– 0.21	0.83	– 0.12	0.10

Boot S.E.: Bootstrapping standard error (Boot S.E.), 95% CI: 95% confidence interval, LL: lower limit, UL: upper limit recommendations resulted in significantly greater purchase intention than AI recommendations ($B = 0.62$, $p < 0.001$). This difference narrowed at average levels of product attitude and was no longer significant when attitudes were highly positive. This pattern indicates that the superiority of human recommendations diminishes as consumers' attitudes toward the product become more favorable, thus supporting Hypothesis 3 that product attitude moderates the effect of recommendation type (AI vs. human) on purchase intention. Specifically, when product attitude is negative, consumers have higher purchase intention for human recommendation than AI recommendations.

6.2 Data Assessment and Hypothesis Tests for AI Communication Style

6.2.1 Experiment 1 Regarding AI Communication Style

Manipulation check of the pretest. The results of the manipulation checks showed that there were significant differences in the subjects' judgment of different communication styles of intelligent customer service. In the task-oriented scenario, the subjects' evaluation of task-oriented was significantly higher. Meanwhile, in the social-oriented scenario, the subjects' evaluation of the social-oriented approach was significantly higher, demonstrating the effectiveness of the manipulation verification of different intelligent customer service communication styles.

Manipulation check of the main test. The manipulation check for the AI agents communication styles was conducted. The measurement scale was adapted from the Li's research framework (Li & Wang, 2023), and an independent samples t-test was used to verify the effectiveness of the manipulation. The results showed that participants' perceptions of the different intelligent customer service communication styles exhibited significant differences: In the task-oriented scenario, the subjects' evaluation of task-oriented is significantly higher ($M_{\text{task-oriented}} = 5.12$, $M_{\text{social-oriented}} = 4.69$, $t = 4.274$, $p < 0.05$). Meanwhile, in the social-oriented scenario, the subjects' evaluation of the social-oriented approach was significantly higher ($M_{\text{task-oriented}} = 4.55$, $M_{\text{social-oriented}} = 5.52$, $t = -6.265$, $p < 0.05$), demonstrating the effectiveness of the manipulation verification of communication styles of AI agents.

Reliability and validity analysis of brand engagement. The brand engagement scale was adapted from the research framework (Hari et al., 2022). Its Cronbach α coefficient reached 0.887, which was greater than the benchmark value of 0.7. The KMO index was 0.839 and the P value was less than 0.001, indicating that the scale had high reliability and validity.

Hypothesis testing. A single-factor ANOVA was used for analysis, where task-oriented was encoded as "1" and social-oriented as "0". The results are presented in Table 6.6. The results showed that the communication style of intelligent customer service had a significant impact on the brand engagement of customers ($F = 4.29$, $p < 0.05$). Meanwhile, the social-oriented communication

Table 6.6 The impact of AI communication style on brand engagement

Variable	Group	Descriptive sample	Statistics mean	ANOVA Standard deviation	F	P
Brand engagement	Social-oriented	99.00	5.29	0.94	4.29	P < 0.05
	Task-oriented	100.00	4.98	1.15		
	Total	199.00	5.13	1.06		

style was more capable of enhancing brand engagement compared to the task-oriented style ($M_{task\text{-}oriented} = 4.98$, $SD = 1.15$; $M_{social\ orientation} = 5.29$, $SD = 0.94$), and the statistical results are shown in Fig. 6.3. Therefore, the results provide support for Hypothesis 4 that the communication style of AI agents generates a significant influence on customers' brand engagement. Specifically, social-oriented communication style enhances brand engagement more than task-oriented communication style.

6.2.2 Experiment 2 Regarding AI Communication Style

Manipulation check. A manipulation check for the intelligent customer service communication styles was conducted using a scale adapted from the developed framework (Li & Wang, 2023). An independent samples t-test was employed to verify the effectiveness of the manipulation. The results revealed significant differences in participants' perceptions of the two communication styles. In the task-oriented condition, participants rated the task-oriented style significantly higher

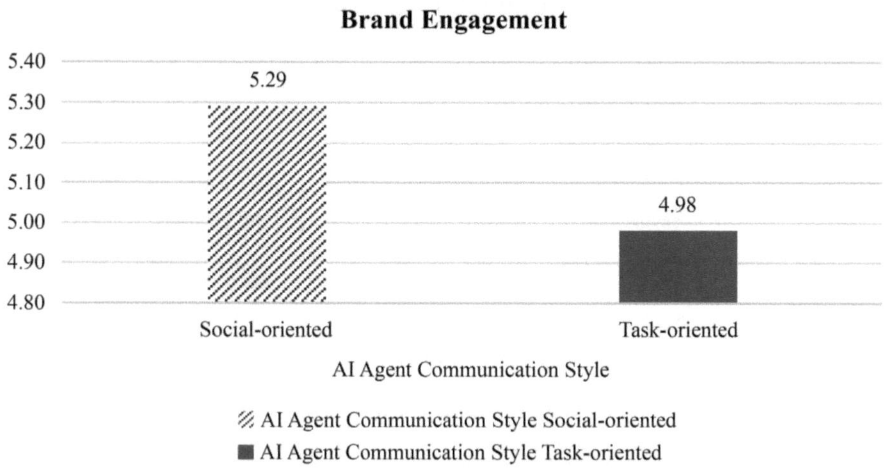

Fig. 6.3 Effect of AI communication style on brand engagement

(M task-oriented = 5.20, M social-oriented = 4.65, $t = 5.39$, $p < 0.001$). Conversely, in the social-oriented condition, participants rated the social-oriented style significantly higher (M task-oriented = 4.52, M social-oriented = 5.63, $t = -8.112$, $p < 0.001$). These findings confirm that the manipulation of intelligent customer service communication styles was successful.

Reliability and validity analysis. The brand engagement scale was adapted from prior research (Hari et al., 2022). Its Cronbach α coefficient reached 0.85, which was greater than the benchmark value of 0.7. The KMO index was 0.795 and the P value was less than 0.001, which was significant. The trust measurement scale was adapted from the measurement items of Chi's research (Chi et al., 2021). Its Cronbach α coefficient reached 0.797, which was greater than the benchmark value of 0.7. The KMO index was 0.779 and the P value was less than 0.001, which was significant.

Main effect hypothesis testing. A single-factor ANOVA was used for analysis, where task-oriented communication was encoded as "1" and social-oriented communication as "0". The results showed that the communication style of intelligent customer service had a significant impact on the brand engagement of customers ($p < 0.05$). Meanwhile, the social-oriented communication style was more capable of enhancing brand engagement compared to the task-oriented style (M task-oriented = 4.99, SD = 1.034; M social orientation = 5.36, SD = 0.8782), and the statistical results were shown in Fig. 6.4. The results provide additional support for Hypothesis 4.

Hypothesis testing of mediating effects. Next, to explore the mediating role of trust, the researcher adopted PROCESS Model 4 (Hayes, 2013) for mediating analysis, using 5000 self-service samples and setting a 95% confidence interval. The results are presented in Table 6.7. The results showed that trust played a mediating role in the

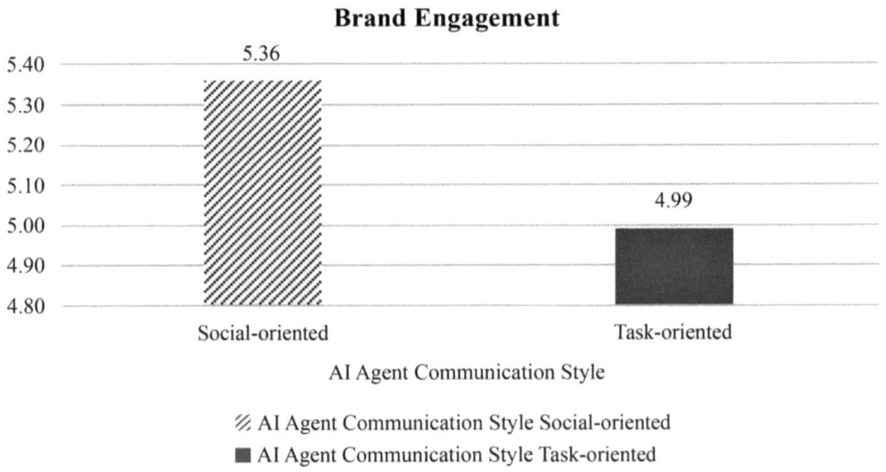

Fig. 6.4 Effect of AI communication style on brand engagement

Table 6.7 The mediating effect of trust on the relationship between AI communication style and brand engagement

			95% CI	
	Effect	Boot S.E.	LL	UL
Total effect	– 0.27	0.11	– 0.49	– 0.05
Direct effect	– 0.15	0.10	– 0.34	0.05
Indirect effect	– 0.12	0.06	– 0.24	– 0.03

Boot S.E.: Bootstrapping standard error (Boot S.E.), 95% CI: 95% confidence interval, LL: lower limit, UL: upper limit

relationship between the communication style of AI agents and brand engagement. The detailed explanation was as follows: Communication style can significantly predict trust ($\beta = -0.33$, $SE = 0.44$, $p < 0.001$), and brand engagement ($\beta = 3.37$, $SE = 0.09$, $p < 0.001$). Although the direct impact of communication style on brand engagement was not significant ($\beta = -0.15$, $SE = 0.10$, CI [−0.34,0.05]), its indirect effect was statistically significant ($\beta = -0.12$, $SE = 0.06$, CI [−0.24,−0.03]). In conclusion, the results confirmed the mediating role of trust in the relationship between communication style and brand engagement, and indicated that social orientation was more effective in enhancing trust compared to task-oriented orientation. The higher the trust, the higher the brand engagement of users, supporting Hypothesis 5.

6.2.3 Survey Regarding AI Communication Style

Reliability and validity analysis. The reliability and validity tests on the research items were conducted. The measurement scales for socially-oriented and task-oriented styles were adapted from Keeling (Keeling et al., 2010) with the socially-oriented group achieving a Cronbach's α coefficient of 0.939, KMO index of 0.767 ($p < 0.001$), and the task-oriented group achieving a Cronbach's α coefficient of 0.738, KMO index of 0.688 ($p < 0.001$), all demonstrating good reliability and validity.

Hypothesis testing of the moderating effects. Using Process Model 1 with 5000 bootstrap samples and 95% confidence intervals, the researcher examined age's moderating effect in the main relationship. The results revealed a significant interaction between age and social-oriented style, while the age and task-oriented style interaction was nonsignificant. Specifically, for younger consumers, social-oriented communication style significantly enhanced brand engagement ($B = 0.16$, $p < 0.001$), whereas this effect became nonsignificant among older consumers. These findings demonstrated that age moderates the relationship between social-oriented communication style and brand engagement, with social-oriented communication being particularly effective in boosting engagement among younger users, providing support for Hypothesis 6.

6.3 Data Assessment and Hypothesis Tests for AI Humanity

6.3.1 Experiment 1 Regarding AI Humanity

Manipulation checks. First, the level of AI humanity was coded (high humility = 1, low humility = 0). According to the results of an independent sample t-test, participants in the high humility condition reported a higher perceived AI assistant humility than those in the low humility condition (MHigh Humility = 5.533, MLow Humility = 3.669; $t = 9.904$, $p < 0.05$). The manipulation of AI assistant humility was successful. To assess the realism of the scenarios, study also adopted two items from (Liao, 2007), the mean score of the two checks was 6.312 out of 7 ($\sigma = 0.553$), an average similar to that found in prior studies (Yang & Yang, 2023).

Hypothesis testing. ANOVA was conducted to test the direct effect predicted by Hypothesis 7. The results show that there is a significant difference in user continuance intention due to high humility and low humility ($F = 37.23$, $p < 0.05$). And Fig. 6.5 presents a clearer picture of the significant difference between different levels of AI assistant humility (high vs. low) on user continuance intention. The results provide support for Hypothesis 7 that AI assistant humanity has a positive effect on user continuous intention in the context of service failure.

6.3.2 Experiment 2 Regarding AI Humanity

Manipulation checks. First, the level of AI humanity was coded (high humility = 1, low humility = 0). According to the results of an independent sample t-test, participants in the high humility condition reported a higher perceived AI

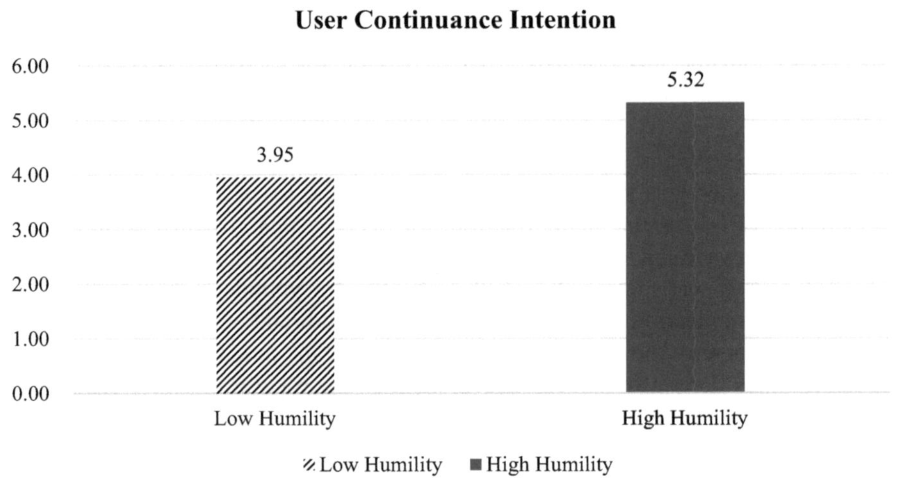

Fig. 6.5 The effects of AI humanity on user continuance intention

assistant humility than those in the low humility condition (MHigh Humility = 5.947, MLow Humility = 4.733; $t = 8.060$, $p < 0.05$). The manipulation of AI assistant humility was successful. To assess the realism of the scenarios, study also adopted two items from (Liao, 2007), the mean score of the two checks was 5.284 out of 7 ($\sigma = 1.275$).

Hypothesis testing. The ANOVA results show that there is a significant difference in user continuance intention due to high humility and low humility ($F = 65.386$, $p < 0.05$). And Fig. 6.6 presents a clearer picture of the significant difference between different levels of AI assistant humility (high vs. low) on user continuance intention. Further, this study utilized PROCESS Model 4 with 5000 repetitive samples and 95% confidence intervals in order to conduct the test of mediating effect, while gender, age, education, income and frequency of communication with AI assistants were used as control variables, and the results of the data are shown in Table 6.8. It indicated that the indirect effect was significant

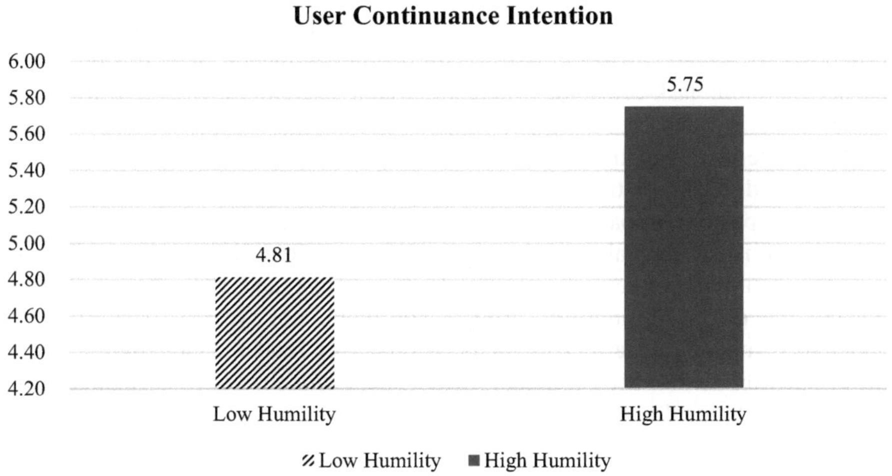

Fig. 6.6 Impact of AI assistant humility on user continuance intention

Table 6.8 The mediating effect of AI acceptance

		Effect	BootSE	BootLLCI	BootULCI
AI assistant humility - > AI acceptance - > user continuance intention	Total effect	0.89	0.19	0.51	1.27
	Direct effect	– 0.07	0.11	– 0.29	0.16
	Indirect effect	0.96	0.17	0.65	1.30

Boot S.E.: Bootstrapping standard error (Boot S.E.), 95% CI: 95% confidence interval, LL: lower limit, UL: upper limit

($\beta = 0.96$, BootSE = 0.17, 95%CI [0.65, 1.30]) that can support Hypothesis 8 that AI acceptance mediates the effects of AI assistant humanity on user continuous intention in service failure contexts.

6.3.3 Survey Regarding AI Humanity

This study utilized PROCESS Model 1 with 5000 repetitive samples and 95% confidence intervals in order to conduct the test of moderating effect. The interaction between AI assistant humility and frequency of communication with AI assistants was not statistically significant ($b = -0.163$, $p > 0.05$), indicating that the moderation effect is not supported. Therefore, Hypothesis 9 that "frequency of communication with AI assistants moderates the relationship between AI assistant humility and user continuance intention. Specifically, the positive effect of AI assistant humility on continuance intention is stronger for customers with high frequency of communication with AI assistants than for those with low frequency" is not supported. The hypothesis that high-frequency communication strengthens the positive effect of AI assistant humility on continuance intention may not be supported for several reasons. Users with a high frequency of interaction often engage in more task-oriented, efficiency-driven exchanges where instrumental value, reliability, and speed are prioritized over nuanced social cues like humility. In these repetitive, functional interactions, expressions of humility could be perceived as redundant, distracting, or even as a sign of uncertainty, thereby diminishing their positive impact. Conversely, for low-frequency users, who may have fewer established mental models of the AI, an initial interaction marked by humility could be more impactful in building trust and reducing skepticism, making the effect of humility stronger for them, not weaker. Therefore, the anticipated moderating effect might be reversed or rendered non-significant, as the primary drivers for high-frequency users likely shift toward performance utility rather than relational considerations.

6.4 Data Assessment and Hypothesis Tests for AI Humor

6.4.1 Experiment 1 Regarding GAI Humor

Manipulation check. Manipulation check was conducted to evaluate the effectiveness of the GAI humor scenario design. Participants completed a single-item multiple-choice question assessing GAI humor perception (i.e., whether this social media GAI was humorous, amusing, laugh-inducing, or boring (reverse coded); 1 = Strongly Disagree, 7 = Strongly Agree). Independent samples t-tests revealed that users of the high-humor GAI rated it as more humorous than the low-humor GAI ($M\_{high\text{-}humor} = 5.24$, $SD = 1.55$; $M\_{low\text{-}humor} = 3.62$, $SD = 1.52$), with highly significant differences between the two experimental groups ($p < 0.05$, $t = 7.43$, $F = 0.22$). Thus, the manipulation of GAI humor type was successful.

To investigate the correlation and degree of association among variables, a correlation analysis was conducted on GAI humor type (GAI high-level humor = 1, GAI low-level humor = 0), perceived warmth, and user satisfaction. The data reveal a significant positive correlation between GAI humor and both perceived warmth ($r = 0.67$, $p < 0.01$) and user satisfaction ($r = 0.78$, $p < 0.01$). This preliminary finding suggests that, compared to low-level GAI humor, high-level GAI humor elicits higher levels of perceived warmth and user satisfaction. The correlation analysis provides initial support for the relationships among the variables in this study. Next, the impact of GAI humor on user satisfaction was examined. A one-way ANOVA was conducted. Statistical results are presented in Table 6.9. Findings indicate that user satisfaction with social media platforms employing high-level GAI humor significantly exceeded engagement driven by low-level GAI humor ($M\_high\text{-}humor = 4.99$, $SD = 1.69$; $M\_low\text{-}humor = 4.45$, $SD = 0.77$); $p < 0.05$, $F(1198) = 4.80$). The results provide support for Hypothesis 10 that GAI humor is positively related to user satisfaction on social media.

Mediating effect of perceived warmth. The mediation effect of perceived warmth was examined using the PROCESS macro. Following Model 4 from Hayes (2013)'s SPSS macro, 5000 resampled iterations were conducted with a 95% confidence interval. Eight variables—GAI usage frequency, GAI usage duration, gender, age, education level, occupation, income, and scenario realism—were included as control variables in the model. Results are presented in Table 6.10.

Table 6.9 The impact of GAI humor on user satisfaction

		Descriptive statistics			ANOVA	
Variable	Group	Sample size	Mean	Standard deviation	F	p
User satisfaction	high-humor GAI	99	4.99	1.69	4.80	0.03
	low-humor GAI	99	4.45	0.77		
	Total	198	4.72	1.75		

$p < 0.05^{*}$, $p < 0.01^{**}$, $p < 0.001^{***}$

Table 6.10 The mediating effect of perceived warmth

		Boot	95% CI	
	Effect	S.E.	LL	UL
Total effect	0.78	0.05	0.69	0.87
Direct effect	0.47	0.15	0.36	0.57
Indirect effect	0.31	0.06	0.21	0.43

Boot S.E.: Bootstrapping standard error (Boot S.E.); 95% CI: 95% confidence interval; LL: lower limit; UL: upper limit

Statistical results indicate that GAI humor significantly predicted users' perceived warmth of GAI ($\beta = 0.59$, $SE = 0.04$, $p < 0.001$), and perceived warmth significantly predicted user satisfaction ($\beta = 0.56$, $SE = 0.07$, $p < 0.001$). Furthermore, the indirect effect of the model was significant ($\beta = 0.31$, $SE = 0.06$, 95% CI [0.21, 0.43] excluding 0), and the direct effect was significant ($\beta = 0.47$, $SE = 0.15$, 95% CI [0.36, 0.57]). Therefore, it can be concluded that perceived warmth plays a primary mediating role in the effect of GAI humor on user satisfaction, confirming Hypothesis 11 that perceived warmth mediates the impact of GAI humor on user satisfaction.

6.4.2 Survey Regarding GAI Humor

To investigate the correlations and their strengths among variables, a correlation analysis was conducted on GAI humor (GAI high-level humor = 1, GAI low-level humor = 0), sense of humor, perceived warmth, user satisfaction, usage frequency, and usage duration. Results indicate that GAI humor positively correlates with user satisfaction ($r = 0.36$, $p < 0.01$).

Next, regression analysis was employed to examine the moderating effect, controlling for usage frequency, usage duration, and demographic variables. The moderating role of sense of humor on user satisfaction was investigated. The results are presented in Table 6.11. The interaction term ($B = -0.17$, $p < 0.01$) significantly predicted user satisfaction. The results provide support for Hypothesis 12 that sense of humor moderates the impact of GAI humor on user satisfaction. Specifically, as the sense of humor decreases, GAI humor has a stronger positive impact on user satisfaction.

Table 6.11 Regression results for moderating effects of sense of humor

Variable	Model 1	Model 2	Model 3
GAI humor		0.24***	0.22***
Sense of humor		0.02	0.03**
GAI Humor*Sense of humor			– 0.17**
Frequency	0.29***	0.19**	– 0.03**
Duration	0.10	– 0.04	– 0.03
Age	0.16*	– 0.03*	– 0.06*
Education	– 0.05	– 0.07	0.09
Occupation	– 0.03	0.10	1.21
Gender	– 0.05	0.25	0.99
Income	0.13	0.06	– 1.36

Note N = 200; *p < 0.05, **p < 0.01, ***p < 0.001

References

Ahn, J., Kim, J., & Sung, Y. (2021). AI-powered recommendations: The roles of perceived similarity and psychological distance on persuasion. *International Journal of Advertising, 40*(8), 1366–1384.

Chi, O. H., Jia, S., Li, Y., & Gursoy, D. (2021). Developing a formative scale to measure consumers' trust toward interaction with artificially intelligent (AI) social robots in service delivery. *Computers in Human Behavior, 118*, 106700.

Hari, H., Iyer, R., & Sampat, B. (2022). Customer brand engagement through chatbots on bank websites—Examining the antecedents and consequences. *International Journal of Human–Computer Interaction, 38*(13), 1212–1227.

Hayes, A. (2013). Introduction to mediation, moderation, and conditional process analysis. *Journal of Educational Measurement, 51*(3), 335–337.

Keeling, K., McGoldrick, P., & Beatty, S. (2010). Avatars as salespeople: Communication style, trust, and intentions. *Journal of Business Research, 63*(8), 793–800.

Li, M., & Wang, R. (2023). Chatbots in e-commerce: The effect of chatbot language style on customers' continuance usage intention and attitude toward brand. *Journal of Retailing and Consumer Services, 71*, 103209.

Liao, H. (2007). Do it right this time: The role of employee service recovery performance in customer-perceived justice and customer loyalty after service failures. *Journal of Applied Psychology, 92*(2), 475–489.

Spears, N., & Singh, S. N. (2004). Measuring attitude toward the brand and purchase intentions. *Journal of Current Issues & Research in Advertising, 26*(2), 53–66.

Yang, F., & Yang, M. M. (2023). Examining motivation of IT vendors to share knowledge with clients. *International Journal of Information Management, 71*, 102646.

Discussion and Conclusion 7

This chapter presents the theoretical and managerial implications of the empirical findings on user-AI interactions and outlines directions for future research. Drawing on the results from experiments and surveys across key themes including AI versus human recommendations, AI communication styles, AI humility, and GAI humor, theoretical and practical implications are discussed. The next sections will present these implications and prospective avenues to advance service marketing and human-AI interaction research.

7.1 Theoretical Implications

The study regarding recommendation types offer some salient theoretical implications. Prior research has primarily examined contextual and product-related moderators of AI versus human recommendation effectiveness. For instance, consumers favor AI in embarrassing situations but prefer human agents when warmth or ethics are emphasized (Holthöwer & Van Doorn, 2023; Yang et al., 2024). AI is more useful for utilitarian products, whereas human recommendations are better for hedonic ones (Longoni & Cian, 2022; Wien & Peluso, 2021). However, these studies largely overlook how the intrinsic characteristics of the recommenders themselves shape consumer responses. To address this gap, the present study explores how AI and human recommendations differ in their impact on purchase intention. Moreover, while prior study has acknowledged the role of affective factors in shaping consumer purchase intentions and has begun to examine the impact of perceived warmth in AI interaction settings (Chen et al., 2022; Lee & Li, 2023; Li et al., 2023), the existing literature primarily focuses on the attributes of AI agents or contextual variables. There remains a lack of systematic comparison between AI and human recommenders in eliciting consumer perceptions of warmth and the consequent behavioral response. Therefore, this study identifies warmth as a key mediating mechanism,

F. Yang, *AI and Consumer Interaction in Business*, Management for Professionals,
https://doi.org/10.1007/978-981-95-9430-6_7

explaining how recommender types (AI vs. human) influence consumers' purchase intention via perceived warmth. Moreover, the boundary condition of product attitude is further explored. Drawing on Fishbein and Ajzen's (2011) multi-attribute attitude model, product attitude is conceptualized as an individual's overall evaluation of a product, which significantly predicts purchase intentions (Mitchell & Olson, 1981; Saleem et al., 2015). Previous research has primarily focused on how various product characteristics—such as utilitarian versus hedonic value—influence product attitudes and subsequently drive consumption behavior (Antonetti & Maklan, 2015; Batra & Ahtola, 1991; Wei et al., 2024). Empirical evidence shows that framing strategies, product type, and pricing perceptions can shape emotional responses and willingness to pay, thereby influencing product attitudes and purchase behaviors (Ayadi & Lapeyre, 2016; Wei et al., 2024). However, despite its recognized importance, product attitude has rarely been examined in conjunction with the characteristics of the recommender. This study theorizes and tests the interaction between product attitude and recommender type, revealing that when consumers have a negative view of a product, they are more persuaded by human recommenders than by AI agents. Conversely, when product attitude is positive, the effect of recommender type becomes negligible. These findings suggest that in low-attitude contexts, emotional and social cues such as warmth play a more critical role, enhancing the effectiveness of human recommendation, thus extending the theoretical scope of product attitude research.

The study regarding AI communication styles makes several key theoretical contributions to the literature on human-AI interaction in service contexts. First, it moves beyond a general focus on the positive effects of social-oriented communication (Verhagen et al., 2014) by introducing a critical comparative lens by examining the impact of social-oriented style vs. task-oriented style. Second, the research deepens the explanatory logic for why social-oriented styles are effective. It posits and empirically supports trust as the central psychological mediator, theorizing that a social-oriented style fosters brand engagement by strengthening the consistency of users' social cognition within the interaction, thereby enhancing perceived reliability and reducing psychological distance. Third, and most significantly, the study introduces and validates age as a vital theoretical boundary condition. The finding that younger consumers exhibit a stronger positive response to social-oriented AI communication provides a crucial refinement to existing models. It establishes that the psychological efficacy of communication style is contingent upon key consumer demographics, thereby bridging theories of technology adoption with individual characteristics. Collectively, this dual-focus framework—which contrasts communication styles, specifies the mediating pathway through trust, and uncovers the moderating role of age—provides a more nuanced and contingent analytical model. This model not only explains the situational limitations of AI efficiency but also elucidates the underlying psychological mechanisms governing effective AI-user dynamics, thereby enriching the theoretical toolkit for future research in this domain.

The study AI humanity offers several key theoretical insights that advance both service marketing and human–AI interaction research. First, by embedding the concept of humility within the domain of AI-driven service recovery, this study extends the theoretical scope of humility beyond its traditional roots in interpersonal psychology (Chancellor & Lyubomirsky, 2013). While humility has been known to foster interpersonal trust and cooperation (Owens et al., 2013), this study shows that it also serves as a relational mechanism in digital service failures, where perceived warmth and transparency from AI assistants can meaningfully impact user behavior. In doing so, the findings complement growing research on AI anthropomorphism and social presence in technology-mediated contexts (Huang & Rust, 2021; Van Doorn et al., 2017). Second, by identifying AI acceptance as a mediator between AI humility and user continuance intention, this research contributes to a more nuanced understanding of how users internalize relational cues from AI assistants. Unlike traditional service recovery research that primarily emphasizes economic or compensatory efforts (Tax et al., 1998), this study demonstrates that users' affective responses and perceived relational compatibility with AI assistants play a pivotal role in driving post-failure behavioral intentions. Specifically, the results align with recent theoretical advancements suggesting that trust, perceived usefulness, and emotional alignment are central to forming acceptance of AI tools, especially in complex or ambiguous decision environments (Norzelan et al., 2024). By bridging service failure literature and technology acceptance theory, this work provides a richer explanatory framework for understanding customer retention in the age of intelligent service automation. These insights contribute to the broader literature on user heterogeneity in digital service contexts and offer practical guidance for adaptive AI system development.

The study regarding GAI humor provides several theoretical implications. First, this research conceptualizes GAI humor as a social trait, examines its impact on user satisfaction in social media contexts, and identifies perceived warmth as the mediating mechanism—thereby enriching research on GAI characteristics and user emotional responses. Previous studies have mostly focused on the impact of GAI's technical capabilities (such as information generation efficiency and accuracy) on user behavior (Xu et al., 2024), while there has been less discussion on anthropomorphic emotional traits of GAI such as humor. Based on the social response theory, this study confirms that GAI humor can enhance user satisfaction by activating users' perceived warmth (i.e., users' subjective perception of GAI's friendliness and caring traits), revealing the path through which GAI's emotional cues affect user attitudes, and supplementing research on the micro-mechanism in human-computer interaction. Meanwhile, addressing the research gap in GAI applications in social media scenarios, this study clarifies the effect of GAI humor in promoting user satisfaction through perceived warmth, providing new empirical evidence for research on user satisfaction in the context of generative artificial intelligence. Second, this study introduces users' sense of humor as a moderating variable, expanding the application of attribution theory (in the field of the impact of social and environmental stimuli on cognition) in the context of GAI interaction. Attribution theory emphasizes that individuals' attribution of internal traits and external stimuli affects cognition and behavior (Folkes, 1984). This study considers GAI humor as an external stimulus and sense of humor as users' internal trait, confirming their interaction effect: users with lower sense of humor are more likely to be positively influenced by GAI humor, as they rely more on external humorous cues to obtain emotional satisfaction. This finding refines the framework of "internal-external factors interacting to influence cognition" in attribution theory, reveals the boundary role of individual trait differences in GAI emotional interaction, and enriches the application scenarios of attribution theory in human-computer social interaction. Additionally, although previous studies have focused on the impact of users' cognitive components (such as perceived social influence and anthropomorphism) on behavior (Chi et al., 2023), few have involved the association between sense of humor and GAI humor. By exploring the interaction effect between the two, this study provides a new theoretical perspective for understanding the heterogeneous impact of GAI humor. Finally, this study integrates the social response theory and attribution theory, constructing a mediating model of "GAI humor—perceived warmth—user satisfaction" and a moderating model of sense of humor, thus promoting the integrated application of cross-theories in human-computer interaction research. The social response theory explains users' social responses to GAI humor (perceived warmth), while the attribution theory clarifies how individual sense of humor moderates the intensity of this response. Together, they reveal the multiple pathways through which GAI humor affects user satisfaction, providing implications for subsequent studies that combine multiple theories to analyze the emotional interaction effects of GAI.

7.2 Practical Implications

The study regarding recommendation types (AI vs. human) provides critical insights for businesses when optimizing recommendations in an increasingly AI-applied world. This research underscores that the strategic integration of human judgment remains a critical, value-creating component in the age of automation. While AI recommendations excel in processing vast datasets for efficiency and scalability, the findings affirm that human recommenders possess a distinct and often superior capacity to enhance consumer purchase intention. This advantage stems from the inherent social credibility, nuanced understanding of context, and ability to convey authentic empathy that human agents provide—qualities that build a deeper, more affective form of trust, particularly for products or services where emotional resonance, identity expression, or perceived risk is high. Consequently, a key implication for practice is that managers should not view human and AI recommendation systems as mutually exclusive but as complementary assets. Our findings also suggest perceived warmth is a significant mediator between recommender type and consumer response. Human recommenders, with expressive language use and emotional engagement, more effectively trigger warmth (Cheng et al., 2022). In contrast, AI agents often lack warmth and appear emotionally detached, which might be detrimental to affective engagement. To mitigate these issues, businesses should endow AI systems with more human-like features, such as empathetic language and responsive designs. These characteristics, for instance, friendly tone and adaptive feedback, could help users connect better with AI agents (Ahn et al., 2021; Ma et al., 2025). The findings also suggest that product attitude moderates the main effect of recommender type on purchase intention (Babin & Babin, 2001; Lee & Lee, 2009; Wei et al., 2024). When consumers have favorable product attitude, the effect of recommender type attenuates. Thus, for businesses, it is necessary to design personalized and contextual recommendation strategies.

The study regarding AI communication style yields direct and actionable implications for practitioners designing and deploying AI-driven consumer interactions. Foremost, it provides clear guidance for strategic style selection: managers should actively prioritize social-oriented communication (e.g., using greetings, empathetic language, and social cues) over a purely task-focused style in customer-facing AI, as the latter can actively damage the trust that is foundational to brand engagement. For service recovery or sensitive interactions, this recommendation is critical. Furthermore, the findings offer a blueprint for personalization at scale. Recognizing that younger consumers are significantly more responsive to social-oriented AI, brands can implement age-adaptive systems—for instance, by enabling more conversational and socially-rich interactions on platforms predominantly used by younger demographics while employing a more balanced, efficiency-focused tone for general or older audiences. Finally, the research challenges the prevalent "efficiency-at-all-costs" mindset in AI implementation. It argues that the strategic objective should shift from mere transactional completion to fostering relational trust. Therefore, investment should be directed not only into algorithmic accuracy but also into the sophisticated design of AI personalities and dialogue that build social-cognitive consistency, turning AI agents into credible brand ambassadors that enhance long-term customer relationship value.

This study regarding AI humanity provides several practical insights for organizations seeking to optimize the role of AI assistants in customer service settings, particularly in high-risk scenarios like service failure. One key implication is the strategic value of embedding humility within AI assistant behavior. Rather than focusing solely on speed or efficiency, firms should design AI interactions that reflect emotional intelligence including admitting mistakes, acknowledging user concerns, and demonstrating a willingness to improve. These behaviors serve as relational cues that help repair trust and promote forgiveness, ultimately increasing users' willingness to continue engaging with the service. Such relational design not only enhances post-failure experiences but also allows companies to differentiate their AI interfaces as socially intelligent, responsive, and user-centered. Another important implication is the role of user acceptance as a foundational mechanism driving continued use of AI services. While technical features such as functionality and ease of use are necessary, they are not sufficient for long-term adoption. Acceptance is shaped by both cognitive evaluations and emotional responses, particularly in service contexts that require relational sensitivity. Firms should therefore invest in strategies that strengthen users' acceptance of AI assistants. This could include transparent onboarding, interactive feedback loops, and AI behaviors that demonstrate responsiveness and adaptability. Communicating that the AI is learning-oriented and open to feedback can foster a sense of partnership between the user and the assistant, building trust and enhancing service retention.

The study on GAI humor provides concrete guidance for the development of social media platforms. First, social media platforms should simultaneously emphasize both the functional roles of GAI and the emotional value it can deliver. Given that 64% of users' time on social media is spent on entertainment (Grover & Kar, 2020), platforms should leverage this by endowing GAI with humorous traits—such as adopting human-like humor styles and incorporating emojis (Liu et al., 2023)—to enhance users' perceived anthropomorphism during interactions. Humorous responses from GAI can strengthen emotional connections, thereby boosting user satisfaction and platform engagement, ultimately driving greater benefits for the platform. Second, social media service providers need to optimize GAI's expressions to enhance perceived anthropomorphism. This can be achieved through algorithmic improvements, such as refining humor delivery or increasing the use of emojis (Liu et al., 2023), to create more human-like emotional value. Recognizing that over half of social media users prioritize the platform for entertainment and socialization (Grover & Kar, 2020), integrating elements that foster perceived anthropomorphism across interaction touchpoints (e.g., conversational tone, response timing) will effectively elevate user satisfaction. Finally, this study highlights the need for tailored GAI humor strategies based on users' sense of humor. Given that the positive impact of GAI humor on user satisfaction is stronger for users with lower sense of humor, platforms should segment their user base: For users with lower sense of humor, GAI should employ more explicit humorous cues (e.g., straightforward jokes, playful emojis) to compensate for their reduced internal humor processing; for those with higher sense of humor, more subtle or context-aware humor can maintain engagement without overwhelming them. Additionally, platforms can cultivate users' receptivity to humor through targeted content (e.g., humorous posts, interactive challenges), thereby amplifying the effectiveness of GAI humor across broader user groups. Since improving user satisfaction remains a significant challenge (Shams et al., 2024), these strategies offer actionable pathways to enhance platform performance and user loyalty.

7.3 Limitations and Future Research Directions

While the research offers valuable insights, its acknowledged limitations simultaneously establish a vital agenda for subsequent scholarly inquiry. Specifically, data for all studies were collected from Chinese consumers, offering rich insights into the behaviors of individuals in a collectivist, high-context culture (Lee, 2014; Rawal et al., 2024). However, this cultural specificity limits the generalizability of our findings to broader populations. Therefore, future research could extend the current theoretical exploration into different cultural contexts (Yin et al., 2019). For instance, compared to Western samples, conducting a comparative study between samples from East Asian countries could explore how different cultural orientations (individualism vs. collectivism) moderate the effect of recommender type on the warmth perception and its downstream effect on purchase intention (Jakubanecs et al., 2023). It would help enrich the robustness of the model and further extend the social perception theory in digital recommendation environment.

The study on recommendation type (AI vs. human recommendation) has several limitations that provide future research opportunities. First, this study used a static and text-based chatbot scenario to control the type of recommender and conduct the experiment. Although this controlled experiment design is helpful for the causal inference, it may not cover all aspects of real recommendation scenarios in real-world application. That is, recommendation agents (especially AI agents) may have multimodal features, including voice, images, avatars, or dynamic conversation, and human recommenders may also appear in different types, such as experts, influencers, or emotional friends (Cheng et al., 2022; Singh et al., 2022). Future studies could extend this design to encompass more diverse recommendation scenarios—for instance, adopting more naturalistic designs involving audio-based AI agents, virtual influencers, or interactive avatars, to further explore whether there is still the same effect of warmth perception when using other modalities. In addition, future research should use more interactive experimental paradigms to reflect the reciprocal relationship between consumers and recommenders, and further explore how consumers construct social perceptions in a dynamic interaction with recommenders. Second, this study focuses on the mediating effect of warmth in the relationship between recommender type and purchase intention. The current results show that consumers are more likely to generate strong warmth perceptions in the case of human recommenders, and these perceptions positively affect consumers' willingness to purchase. However, according to the stereotype content model, social perception has two fundamental dimensions of warmth and competence. In addition to warmth, future research may further develop a dual-mediation model and explore whether there is still the same effect of competence when consumers perceive AI recommenders, which may further complement or offset the effect of warmth (Fiske, 2018; Fiske et al., 2002). In addition, other social perception dimensions, such as trust, morality, and affinity may also further extend the mediating model.

While this study regarding AI communication styles elucidates the cognitive pathways through which AI communication styles influence brand engagement and clarifies the moderating role of age, it is subject to several limitations that outline avenues for future work. First, methodological constraints present a key boundary condition. Although the use of scenario-based experiments and surveys effectively controlled for extraneous variables, the simulated nature of these interactions may not fully capture the complexity of consumer behavior in real-world, longitudinal engagements. To address this, subsequent research could implement longitudinal field experiments, incorporating techniques such as eye-tracking or physiological measures to capture cognitive and emotional fluctuations during dynamic, naturalistic interactions. Such an approach would enable more precise predictions of sustained consumer-brand engagement. Second, the study's contextual scope is constrained. The investigation was confined to e-commerce settings, excluding high-stakes or high-involvement domains such as healthcare, finance, or personalized education. This limitation suggests a critical direction for future inquiry: expanding the research scope to different risk-perception scenarios—comparing, for example, AI-mediated medical consultations with routine product browsing.

This expansion would help validate and potentially refine the proposed framework by examining how communication style efficacy varies across domain-specific contexts where trust and perceived risk are fundamentally different.

While this study regarding AI humanity establishes the significant role of AI anthropomorphic qualities (e.g., humility) in fostering user continuance intention through the mediating pathway of AI acceptance, its conclusions are necessarily bounded by methodological and theoretical scope. Primarily, the reliance on scenario-based experiments, while effective for establishing causal relationships, may limit the ecological validity of these findings when generalized to long-term, real-world human-AI interactions. The mediating construct of AI acceptance, as operationalized here, captures a critical initial adoption mindset but may not fully represent the evolving, multi-faceted nature of user trust and reliance over time. Furthermore, while user's AI use frequency was found to not be a significant boundary condition, the exploration of other potentially consequential user traits—such as digital literacy, cultural orientation, or specific cognitive styles—remains an open avenue. To build upon this foundation, future research should pursue longitudinal designs or field studies to validate the durability of the proposed mediation model. It should also expand the theoretical framework by testing alternative or additional moderators (e.g., prior experience with technology failure, privacy concerns) and mediators (e.g., perceived enjoyment, affective commitment) across diverse service domains and cultural settings, thereby constructing a more comprehensive model of how AI humanity translates into sustained user engagement.

Although this study regarding GAI humor empirically explores the core mechanism of "GAI humor influencing user satisfaction through perceived warmth" and verifies the moderating effect of individual humor sensitivity, limitations exist due to research design and objective constraints. First, the singularity of the research setting may limit the external validity of the conclusions. The study focused on social media platforms (using Sina Weibo's GAI comment bot as a typical scenario) for experiments and questionnaire surveys, whereas GAI humor applications span diverse domains such as e-commerce customer service, intelligent assistants, and educational interactions. User expectations regarding GAI functionality (e.g., social media prioritizes entertainment and e-commerce emphasizes efficiency) and emotional needs vary significantly across contexts. This may result in differing intensities and pathways of GAI humor's impact on perceived warmth and user satisfaction, limiting the direct generalizability of these findings to other settings. Second, the manipulation and measurement of GAI humor exhibit simplistic tendencies. Experiments primarily manipulated "GAI humor" based on textual content (e.g., humorous reply scripts), failing to adequately account for humor type variations (e.g., situational humor, pun-based humor, self-deprecating humor) and presentation formats (e.g., text + emojis, voice-based humor). Furthermore, the questionnaire's measurement of GAI humor perception relied primarily on a single dimension ("humor intensity"), failing to capture key sub-dimensions like "humor appropriateness" (the match between GAI humor and the user's content theme). This simplification may overlook the differential impact of different humor characteristics on perceived warmth, leading to less precise interpretations of core variable relationships.

Furthermore, self-reporting bias in questionnaire methods may compromise data accuracy. This study relies on self-administered questionnaires to measure core variables such as "perceived warmth" and "user satisfaction." While controlling for variables (e.g., excluding extreme responses) mitigates some biases, it cannot entirely eliminate "social desirability bias" (e.g., users tending to report more positive satisfaction ratings) and "recall bias" (e.g., users struggling to accurately recall their actual perceived warmth during GAI interactions).

To address these limitations in the study of GAI humor, future research could deepen the theoretical framework linking GAI humor and user behavior through the following directions. First, future research is recommended to expand research scenarios and conduct cross-scenario comparative studies. Subsequent studies could select scenarios like e-commerce customer service (e.g., GAI humor alleviating service failure anxiety) or intelligent education (e.g., GAI humor enhancing learning interest). Through multiple experimental groups, they could compare how GAI humor influences perceptions of warmth and user satisfaction across different contexts. This would help identify matching patterns between "scenario characteristics – GAI humor design – user responses," providing targeted guidance for GAI emotional design across various fields. Second, refine the manipulation and measurement dimensions of GAI humor. On one hand, experimental designs should incorporate multi-factor manipulations like "humor type × presentation format" to analyze the interactive effects of different combinations on perceived warmth. On the other hand, future research is encouraged to draw on from established humor research scales to develop a GAI humor perception scale tailored for GAI contexts. This scale should incorporate sub-dimensions such as "humor intensity," "appropriateness," and "amusement value" to enhance the validity and precision of variable measurement. Third, future research can reduce bias by integrating mixed methods (experimental design + longitudinal tracking + physiological measurement). Future research may employ an "experimental design (manipulating GAI humor) + longitudinal tracking (multiple questionnaire surveys)" to reveal dynamic causal relationships among variables. Concurrently, future research can introduce physiological measurement tools (e.g., eye tracking, skin conductance response) to objectively validate perceived warmth and user satisfaction levels through physiological indicators (e.g., pupil dilation reflecting interest, skin conductance activity reflecting emotional arousal), thereby mitigating self-report bias. Finally, future research is encouraged to explore the long-term effects and practical applications of GAI humor. Future research could conduct long-term tracking experiments (e.g., having users engage with GAI humor features for 4-8 weeks) to analyze trends in users' perceived warmth and satisfaction levels (e.g., whether "aesthetic fatigue" occurs). Concurrently, practice-oriented research can be conducted in collaboration with enterprises. For instance, designing "humor strategy toolkits" for GAI across different scenarios (e.g., situational humor for social media or soothing humor for e-commerce customer service) and empirically testing their commercial impact (e.g., user retention rates or increase in recommendation intent) to achieve mutual enrichment between theory and practice.

7.4 Chapter Summary

This chapter synthesizes the key findings from the empirical investigations into user-AI interactions, offering theoretical, managerial, and forward-looking insights. Theoretically, this study advances existing literature by elucidating how AI and human recommendations differentially impact purchase intentions (mediated by perceived warmth and moderated by product attitude), comparing the effectiveness of these two types of recommenders, highlighting the role of social-oriented communication styles in fostering brand engagement, demonstrating how AI humility enhances continuance intentions via user acceptance, and revealing the positive effects of GAI humor on user satisfaction through perceived warmth. These contributions enrich service marketing, human-AI interaction, emphasizing relational cues in digital environments.

From a managerial perspective, this study yields several actionable strategies for optimizing AI-enabled services. Practitioners can enhance consumer engagement by strategically deploying human recommenders for low-involvement products and designing social-oriented AI interfaces for youth demographics. To improve service recovery and customer retention, AI agents should be programmed with high-humility communication traits. Furthermore, tailoring generative AI (GAI) humor to align with individual user preferences can significantly increase satisfaction on social platforms. Collectively, these implications provide a framework for practitioners to design AI systems that achieve greater emotional resonance and operational efficiency.

The generalizability of the findings is constrained by sample homogeneity and the specificity of the experimental scenarios. Subsequent research should expand these findings across diverse cultural contexts and refine the methodological design through longitudinal or dynamic interaction approaches. In conclusion, this investigation substantiates the critical need for a strategic equilibrium between artificial intelligence's technical capabilities and its anthropomorphic design elements. The findings demonstrate that optimal AI-user engagement is not achieved through technological supremacy alone but through a careful calibration of functional efficiency and simulated human-like qualities—such as social orientation, humility, and humor. By providing a framework for this nuanced balance, the research paves the way for the development of more empathetic, trustworthy, and effective AI-mediated interactions. This advancement holds significant promise for transforming user experience paradigms in the domain of digital marketing.

References

Ahn, J., Kim, J., & Sung, Y. (2021). AI-powered recommendations: The roles of perceived similarity and psychological distance on persuasion. *International Journal of Advertising, 40*(8), 1366–1384.

Antonetti, P., & Maklan, S. (2015). How categorisation shapes the attitude–behaviour gap in responsible consumption. *International Journal of Market Research, 57*(1), 51–72.

Ayadi, N., & Lapeyre, A. (2016). Consumer purchase intentions for green products: Mediating role of WTP and moderating effects of framing. *Journal of Marketing Communications*, *22*(4), 367–384.

Babin, B. J., & Babin, L. (2001). Seeking something different? A model of schema typicality, consumer affect, purchase intentions and perceived shopping value. *Journal of Business Research*, *54*(2), 89–96.

Batra, R., & Ahtola, O. T. (1991). Measuring the hedonic and utilitarian sources of consumer attitudes. *Marketing Letters*, *2*(2), 159–170.

Chancellor, J., & Lyubomirsky, S. (2013). Humble beginnings: Current trends, state perspectives, and hallmarks of humility. *Social and Personality Psychology Compass*, *7*(11), 819–833.

Chen, H., Chan Olmsted, S., Kim, J., & Mayor Sanabria, I. (2022). Consumers' perception on artificial intelligence applications in marketing communication. *Qualitative Market Research: An International Journal*, *25*(1), 125–142.

Cheng, X., Zhang, X., Cohen, J., & Mou, J. (2022). Human vs. AI: Understanding the impact of anthropomorphism on consumer response to chatbots from the perspective of trust and relationship norms. *Information Processing and Management*, *59*(3), 102940.

Chi, O. H., Chi, C. G., Gursoy, D., & Nunkoo, R. (2023). Customers' acceptance of artificially intelligent service robots: The influence of trust and culture. *International Journal of Information Management*, *70*, 102623.

Fishbein, M., & Ajzen, I. (2011). *Predicting and changing behavior: The reasoned action approach*. Psychology Press.

Fiske, S. T. (2018). Stereotype content: Warmth and competence endure. *Current Directions in Psychological Science*, *27*(2), 67–73.

Fiske, S. T., Cuddy, A. J., Glick, P., & Xu, J. (2002). A model of (often mixed) stereotype content: Competence and warmth respectively follow from perceived status and competition. *Journal of Personality and Social Psychology*, *82*(6), 878–902.

Folkes, V. S. (1984). Consumer reactions to product failure: An attributional approach. *Journal of Consumer Research*, *10*(4), 398–409.

Grover, P., & Kar, A. K. (2020). User engagement for mobile payment service providers—Introducing the social media engagement model. *Journal of Retailing and Consumer Services*, *53*, 101718.

Holthöwer, J., & Van Doorn, J. (2023). Robots do not judge: Service robots can alleviate embarrassment in service encounters. *Journal of the Academy of Marketing Science*, *51*(4), 767–784.

Huang, M. H., & Rust, R. T. (2021). A strategic framework for artificial intelligence in marketing. *Journal of the Academy of Marketing Science*, *49*, 30–50.

Jakubanecs, A., Supphellen, M., Helgeson, J. G., Haugen, H. M., & Sivertstøl, N. (2023). The impact of cultural variability on brand stereotype, emotion and purchase intention. *Journal of Consumer Marketing*, *40*(1), 112–123.

Lee, J. A. (2014). Adapting Triandis's model of subjective culture and social behavior relations to consumer behavior. *Cultural Psychology*, *9*(2), 117–126.

Lee, J. K., & Lee, W. N. (2009). Country-of-origin effects on consumer product evaluation and purchase intention: The role of objective versus subjective knowledge. *Journal of International Consumer Marketing*, *21*(2), 137–151.

Lee, K. W., & Li, C. Y. (2023). It is not merely a chat: Transforming chatbot affordances into dual identification and loyalty. *Journal of Retailing and Consumer Services*, *74*, 103447.

Li, B., Yao, R., & Nan, Y. (2023). How do friendship artificial intelligence chatbots (FAIC) benefit the continuance using intention and customer engagement? *Journal of Consumer Behaviour*, *22*(6), 1376–1398.

Liu, D., Lv, Y., & Huang, W. (2023). How do consumers react to chatbots' humorous emojis in service failures. *Technology in Society*, *73*, 102244.

Longoni, C., & Cian, L. (2022). Artificial intelligence in utilitarian vs. hedonic contexts: The "word-of-machine" effect. *Journal of Marketing*, *86*(1), 91–108.

Ma, N., Khynevych, R., Hao, Y., & Wang, Y. (2025). Effect of anthropomorphism and perceived intelligence in chatbot avatars of visual design on user experience: Accounting for perceived empathy and trust. *Frontiers in Computer Science*, *7*, 1531976.

Mitchell, A. A., & Olson, J. C. (1981). Are product attribute beliefs the only mediator of advertising effects on brand attitude? *Journal of Marketing Research*, *18*(3), 318–332.

Norzelan, N. A., Mohamed, I. S., & Mohamad, M. (2024). Technology acceptance of artificial intelligence (AI) among heads of finance and accounting units in the shared service industry. *Technological Forecasting and Social Change*, *198*, 123022.

Owens, B. P., Johnson, M. D., & Mitchell, T. R. (2013). Expressed humility in organizations: Implications for performance, teams, and leadership. *Organization Science*, *24*(5), 1517–1538.

Rawal, M., Saavedra Torres, J. L., Bagherzadeh, R., Rani, S., & Melancon, J. (2024). The role of individualism, collectivism, and promotional reward type on consumer response to amplified word-of-mouth strategies. *Journal of Consumer Marketing*, *41*(3), 298–313.

Saleem, A., Ghafar, A., Ibrahim, M., Yousuf, M., & Ahmed, N. (2015). Product perceived quality and purchase intention with consumer satisfaction. *Global Journal of Management and Business Research: E Marketing*, *15*(1), 21–28.

Shams, G., Kim, K. K., & Kim, K. (2024). Enhancing service recovery satisfaction with chatbots: The role of humor and informal language. *International Journal of Hospitality Management*, *120*, 103782.

Singh, G. V., Firdaus, M., Ekbal, A., & Bhattacharyya, P. (2022). Emoint-trans: A multimodal transformer for identifying emotions and intents in social conversations. *IEEE/ACM Transactions on Audio, Speech, and Language Processing*, *31*, 290–300.

Tax, S. S., Brown, S. W., & Chandrashekaran, M. (1998). Customer evaluations of service complaint experiences: Implications for relationship marketing. *Journal of Marketing*, *62*(2), 60–76.

Van Doorn, J., Mende, M., Noble, S. M., Hulland, J., Ostrom, A. L., Grewal, D., & Petersen, J. A. (2017). Domo arigato Mr. Roboto: Emergence of automated social presence in organizational frontlines and customers' service experiences. *Journal of Service Research*, *20*(1), 43–58.

Verhagen, T., Van Nes, J., Feldberg, F., & Van Dolen, W. (2014). Virtual customer service agents: Using social presence and personalization to shape online service encounters. *Journal of Computer-Mediated Communication*, *19*(3), 529–545.

Wei, Q., Bao, A., Lv, D., Liu, S., Chen, S., Chi, Y., & Zuo, J. (2024). The influence of message frame and product type on green consumer purchase decisions: An ERPs study. *Scientific Reports*, *14*(1), 23232.

Wien, A. H., & Peluso, A. M. (2021). Influence of human versus AI recommenders: The roles of product type and cognitive processes. *Journal of Business Research*, *137*, 13–27.

Xu, M., Du, H., Niyato, D., Kang, J., Xiong, Z., Mao, S., Han, Z., Jamalipour, A., Kim, D. I., Shen, X., Leung, V. C. M., & Poor, H. V. (2024). Unleashing the power of edge-cloud generative AI in mobile networks: A survey of AIGC services. *IEEE Communications Surveys and Tutorials*, *26*(2), 1127–1170.

Yang, Y., Zheng, J., Yu, Y., Qiu, Y., & Wang, L. (2024). The role of recommendation sources and attribute framing in online product recommendations. *Journal of Business Research*, *174*, 114498.

Yin, X., Wang, H., Xia, Q., & Gu, Q. (2019). How social interaction affects purchase intention in social commerce: A cultural perspective. *Sustainability*, *11*(8), 2423.

MIX
Papier aus verantwortungsvollen Quellen
Paper from responsible sources
FSC® C105338

If you have any concerns about our products,
you can contact us on
ProductSafety@springernature.com

In case Publisher is established outside the EU,
the EU authorized representative is:
Springer Nature Customer Service Center GmbH
Europaplatz 3, 69115 Heidelberg, Germany

Printed by Libri Plureos GmbH
in Hamburg, Germany